D1121709

WITHDRAWN
UTSA LIBRARIES

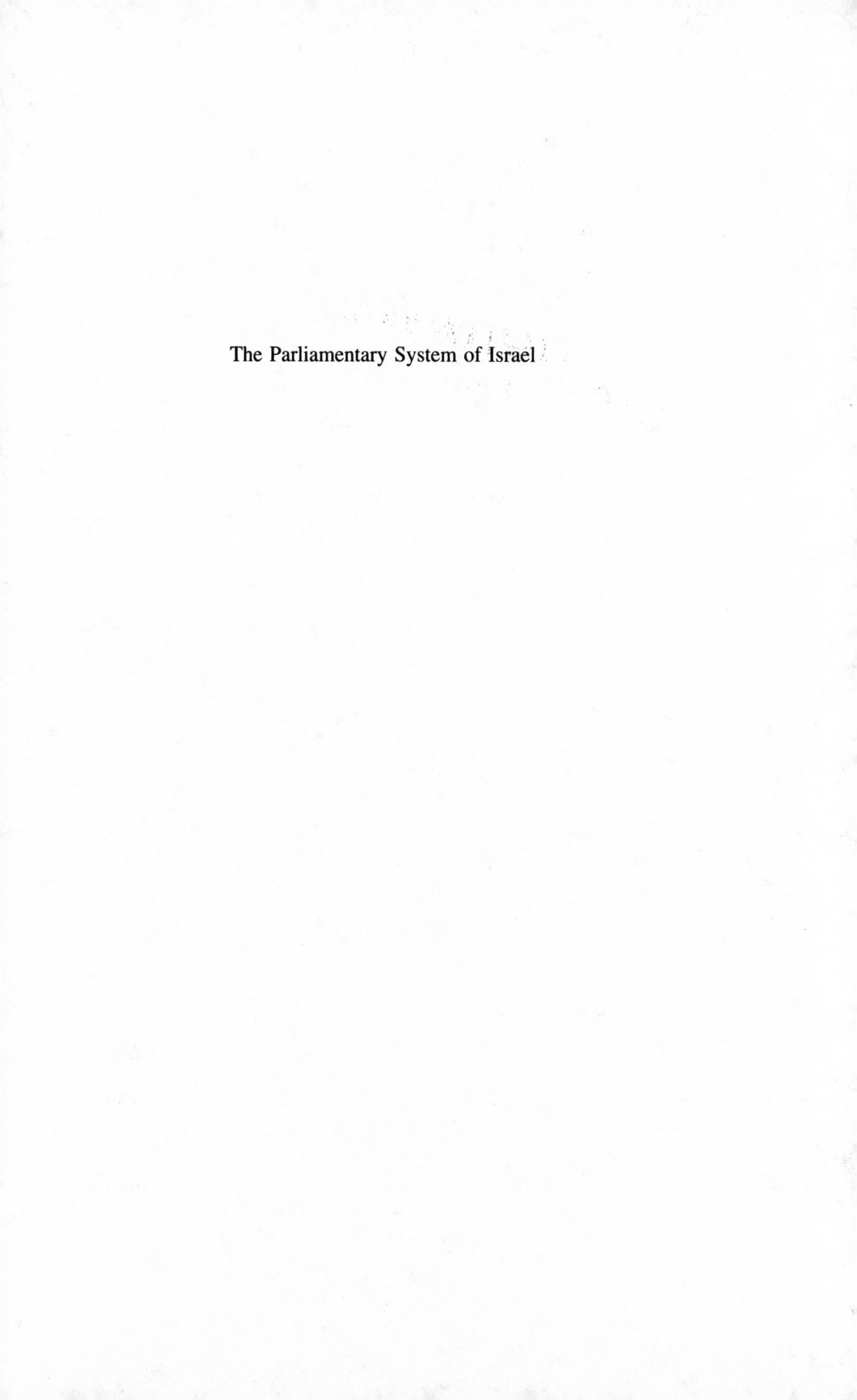

The Parliamentary System of Israel

The Parliamentary System of Israel

SAMUEL SAGER

With a Foreword by ABBA EBAN

SYRACUSE UNIVERSITY PRESS

1985

LIBRARY
The University of Texas
At San Antonio

Copyright © 1985 by Syracuse University Press
Syracuse, New York 13210

All Rights Reserved

First Edition

Library of Congress Cataloging in Publication Data

Sager, Samuel.
The parliamentary system of Israel.

Bibliography: p.
Includes index.
1. Israel. Knesset. 2. Israel—Politics and government. I. Title.
JQ1825.P35S24 1985 328.5694 85-12631
ISBN 0-8156-2335-6

The paper used in this publication meets the minimum requirements of American National Standard for Information Sciences—Permanence of Paper for Printed Library Materials, ANSI Z39.48-1984. ∞

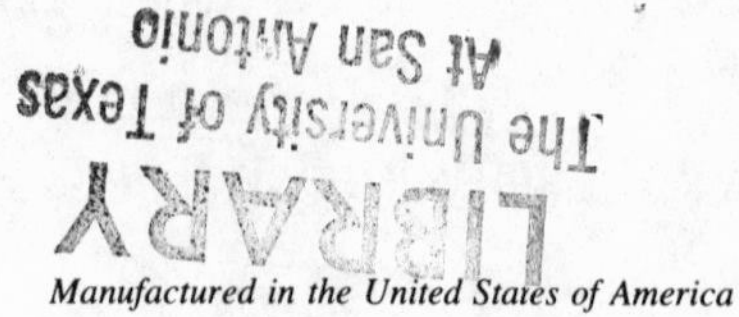

Manufactured in the United States of America

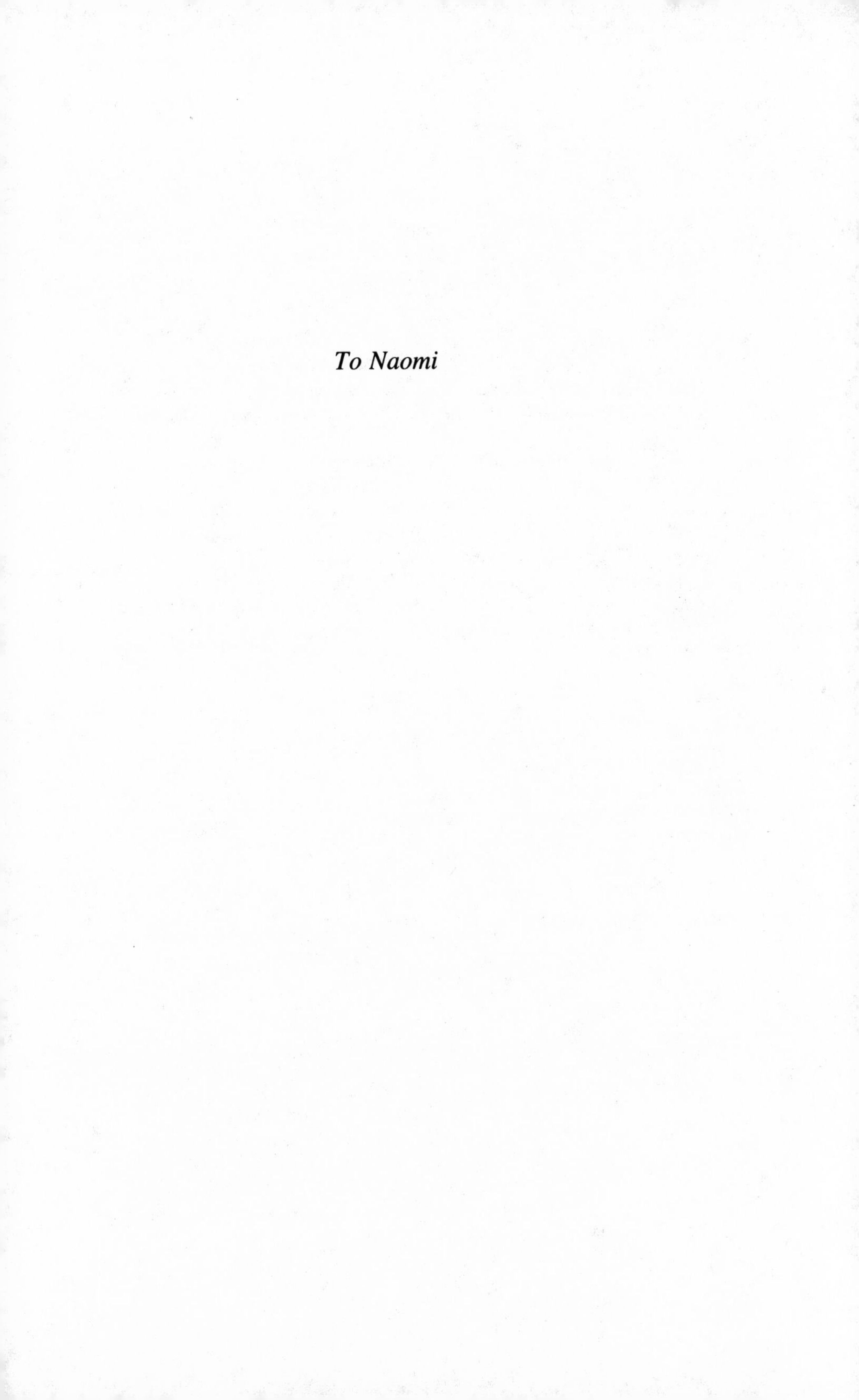

To Naomi

SAMUEL SAGER received degrees from McGill and Carleton universities. His parliamentary experience began in Ottawa at the Canadian House of Commons, where he set up the Hansard Index and Reference Branch, serving as its Chief from 1955 to 1961.

He has been on the staff of Israel's Knesset for twenty-three years. Before assuming his present position as Secretary of the Constitution, Law and Justice Committee of the Knesset, he served at different periods as Secretary of the Knesset's committees on Education Reform, Health Insurance, and Basic Laws, as well as Editor of the Knesset Record Index.

His writings have appeared in *Canadian Public Administration, The Parliamentarian, Parliamentary Affairs, Middle Eastern Studies,* and *American Journal of Comparative Law*.

Contents

Figure

Tables

Appendix Tables

Foreword

GOVERNMENTS DERIVE THEIR JUST POWERS from the consent of the governed." This phrase in Thomas Jefferson's draft of the American Declaration of Independence epitomizes the democratic ideal in its briefest form. In the Middle East, Israel is the only nation in which this principle applies. Executive power is restrained by popular will, and that will is expressed in the Knesset.

The Israeli parliament came to birth amidst the havoc and peril of war. There was little time or mood for a prolonged constitutional debate. Yet the experience of nearly four decades confers much credit on the founders of our parliamentary system. Israel's parliament has functioned in full momentum in peace and in war, in victory and in adversity, in economic crisis and in relative prosperity. A parliament conceived by a community of 600,000 has operated efficiently for a population of 4.3 million with a markedly different composition. There has been no serious appeal against the idea that the parliamentary principle is an inseparable part of the Israeli experience. All who cherish that principle across the world should draw encouragement from Israel's performance in this field.

Samuel Sager has produced a scholarly analysis of the way in which the Israeli Knesset works. His writing is lucid and his objectivity is beyond challenge. I strongly recommend this work to students and readers who understand the importance and moral power of parliamentary institutions.

Jerusalem
Spring 1985

ABBA EBAN

Preface

THE LEGISLATURES of many of the nations born since the end of World War II were quick to disappear. Israel's Knesset is a more robust newcomer. With its nascent period well past, it is approaching four decades of existence, during which time it has evolved procedures suited to its needs while weathering economic crises and wars. On any reckoning, it may be said to have passed its initiation rite in 1977, with the orderly transfer of office that took place when, for the first time, one Government was replaced by another of largely different political complexion.

The object of this book is to present a comprehensive account of Israel's parliamentary system, giving equal attention to its historical development and to the composition, structure, and functioning of the Knesset, as well as to Knesset-Government relations, which lie at the heart of the system. I have attempted to provide pertinent examples throughout with the purpose of illuminating the subject matter. Though generalizations follow inescapably from the facts recorded, my chief purpose has been objective description. If, nevertheless, I seem to reveal a bias in favor of such things as constituency elections or a quorum rule, these, after all, have long been cross-party issues.

The ephemeral nature of some of the new parliaments may perhaps be ascribed to facsimile transplantation of an institution from an entirely different setting. Some have claimed to see also in the more hardy Knesset the stamp of the "Westminster model." The first chapter of this book all but lays to rest that notion. Though popularly, as in the *Jerusalem Post,* the chairman of the Knesset is styled "speaker," let no one expect to see him with robe, wig, and mace, or in pageant of procession. But the differences between Knesset and Commons reach more deeply. While there have been British influences on Knesset procedure—a recent example being oral questions, introduced in 1983—Israel's parliamentary system, in its broader aspects, is to be traced back rather to continental European and republican traditions, transmuted through experience with native parliamentary frameworks, albeit rudimentary in character, that spanned the half-century preceding the birth of the state.

It is significant that constitutional reforms that have been proposed and are being widely debated in Israel, such as electoral reform or a presidential system, have as their main purpose the strengthening of the executive arm of a Government ever beset by coalition problems. In the search for such remedies, the Knesset's position has been only secondarily in question. On the other hand, blemishes peculiar to the Knesset that come to the public's attention, whether concerning attendance in the chamber or indecorous verbal clashes in debate, incense every class of citizens because they are never indifferent about anything concerning their lively central forum, whose proceedings have been brought by television into every livingroom. Israelis display a near possessive instinct toward their representatives in Jerusalem, never sparing the rod of criticism. They are likely to lampoon most those parliamentarians whose names are household words. So intertwined, however, are Israel's parliament and Government that at the end of the day even a Knesset secure in the citizens' affection must suffer the adverse results of a destabilized executive; coalition vagaries touch both. I trust that the present study contributes to a better understanding of this problem.

Source material for this book was plentiful though scattered. While the two most helpful sources were the Knesset Record and the daily press, I made use also of every relevant and publicly available document that came to my knowledge. Pre-state material was kindly made available to me by the Central Zionist Archives in Jerusalem, while the Israel State Archives obligingly offered me access to its early files. Other parliamentary and government publications, and secondary sources, which I had to consult, but are not in my possession, were to be found in the Knesset Library, whose staff has always been the most helpful of colleagues.

I am much indebted to Samuel Jacobson, with whom the many conversations I had on Knesset procedure, before he assumed the onerous duties of secretary-general, made me aware of the great extent to which the written rules are inevitably modified by the "oral law" of parliamentary practice.

Without the steadfast encouragement and helpfulness of my wife, Naomi, and her typing and checking of the manuscript, I could hardly have seen this project through. To my daughter, Miriam, I am indebted for the many ways in which she was helpful.

My thanks for their friendly assistance are also due to Ms. Cecile Panzer and to Ms. Norma Schneider.

The first three chapters of the book are revisions of my articles in *Parliamentary Affairs* (Winter 1971/72), *Middle Eastern Studies* (January 1978), and the *American Journal of Comparative Law* (Winter 1976). To the editors of those journals I am grateful for permission to make this use of the earlier publications.

Let me add that the unique experience of serving on the staffs of two quite different parliaments—nearly a quarter century with the Knesset, and before that, six years with the Canadian House of Commons—furnished me with an invaluable perspective for putting this work together.

Jerusalem
Spring 1985

SAMUEL SAGER

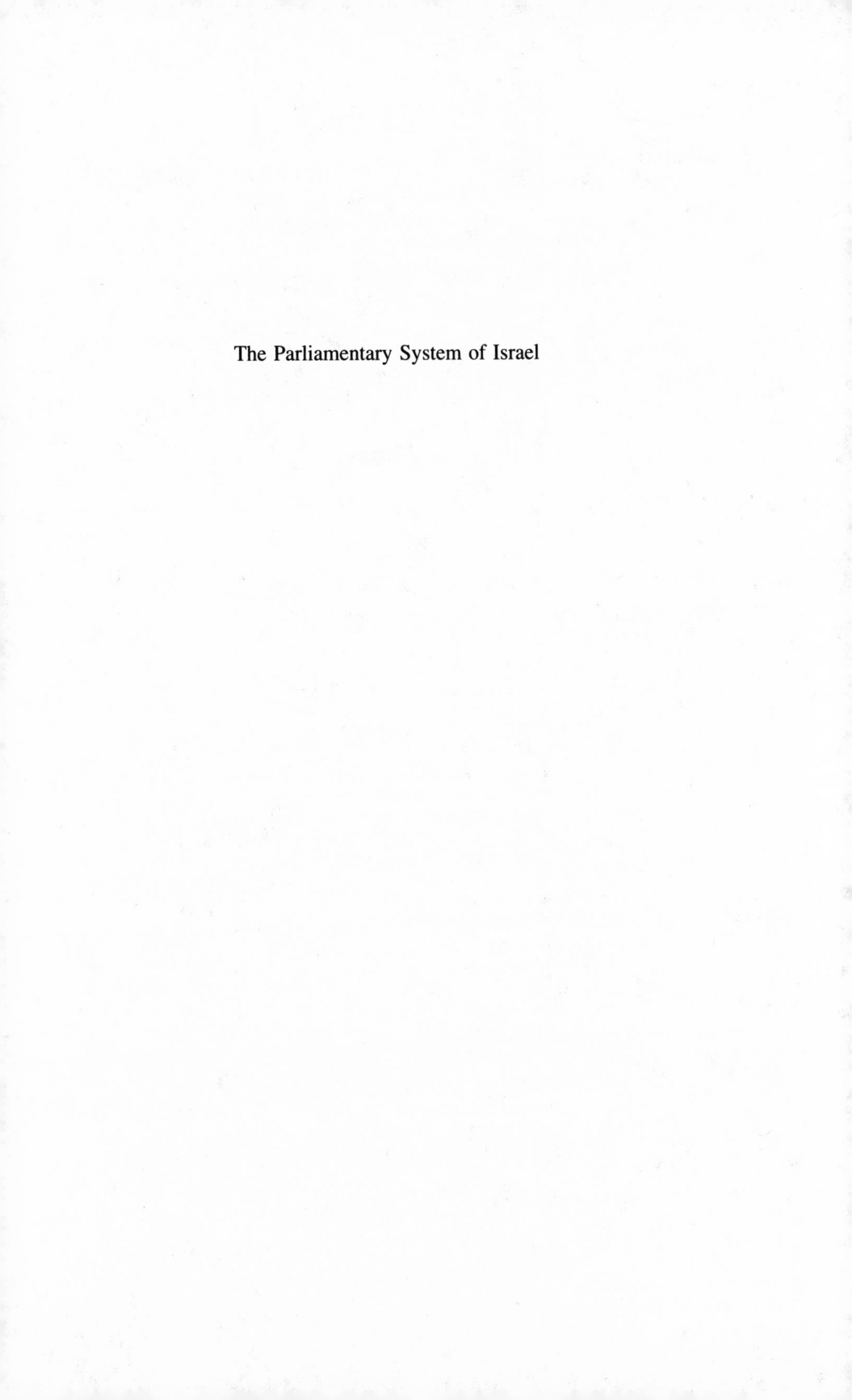

The Parliamentary System of Israel

1

Pre-State Influences

THE RESUSCITATION OF ANCIENT JEWISH SYMBOLS in Israel's public life did not skip over her parliament. Meaning "assembly" in Hebrew, the word *Knesset* was adopted as the name of Israel's legislature in recall of its distant precursor, the *Knesset Gedola* (Great Assembly) or *Ecclesia,* which was the supreme legislative authority under Ezra and Nehemia in the fourth and fifth centuries B.C. The Knesset's membership of 120 is also reminiscent of that body. However, with respect to composition, procedure, and function, the Knesset has drawn from sources much closer to our time.

The Knesset is the direct descendant of the Provisional State Council *(Moetzet Hamedina Hazmanit),* which served as the legislature of the new state during its first nine months, from May 1948 to February 1949. That link leads further back to two pre-state quasi-parliamentary bodies whose influence on the Knesset, although not as direct, was no less significant—the Congress of the Zionist Organization and the Elected Assembly of Palestine's Jewish Community. The half-century which preceded the birth of the state witnessed the establishment and growth of a political Zionist movement, the replacement in Palestine of Turkish rule by a British Mandate after the first world war, and the development there again of a sizable Jewish community with a considerable measure of autonomy. While the Ottoman and mandatory rulers of Palestine both left their mark on Israel's legal system, neither had any notable influence on the development of her parliamentary institutions. Britain's legacy to the Knesset was not negligible but came from London and not through the mandatory administration. Direct experience for future Israeli parliamentarians was provided by the above-mentioned Zionist and Community bodies; Israel's provisional organs of government, her major political parties, her system of elections and coalition government, and much of the Knesset's procedure can also be traced to these bodies and to the organizations of which they were a part.

THE ZIONIST CONGRESS AND GENERAL COUNCIL

When Theodor Herzl[1] convened the First Zionist Congress at Basle, in 1897, he created a forum which has endured to this day. Congresses still meet at fixed intervals in Jerusalem since the World Zionist Organization has set for itself the task of assisting in the consolidation of Israel. While their influence as a parliamentary platform diminished with the emergence of a full-fledged legislature in the new state, the twenty-two Congresses which preceded the inception of Israel's parliamentary life bequeathed to it a substantial legacy. The pre-state Congresses met first annually and later biennially in one or another Central or West European city. The First Congress formulated the Zionist Program which had as its aim the creation for the Jewish people of a home in Palestine secured by public law. To carry out the program, that Congress established the World Zionist Organization. In the face of intolerance and repeated anti-Semitic outbursts in czarist Russia and in other parts of Europe, the Organization grew rapidly, with membership and the right to vote for delegates to subsequent Congresses based on adherence to the "Basle Program," as it came to be known, and the annual payment of one shilling or its equivalent as dues. Wherever Jewish communities were to be found, local Zionist societies sprang up and were organized into territorial federations each of which was coextensive, as a rule, with the boundaries of one or a number of national states. A further spur to Zionist activity was provided by the Balfour Declaration of 1917 in which Britain expressed her sympathy with Zionist aspirations and support for the establishment of a Jewish national home in Palestine, a declaration which was of real significance since British forces entered Jerusalem almost simultaneously and by 1918 had taken all of Palestine from the Turks.

The Zionist Organization won international legal status in the Palestine Mandate which was conferred upon Great Britain in 1920 by the Peace Conference at San Remo and ratified by the League of Nations in 1922. The mandate designated the Zionist Organization as the "Jewish Agency . . . for the purpose of advising and co-operating with the Administration in matters affecting the establishment of the Jewish National Home" (Article 4). During the years from 1929 to 1939 the Jewish Agency included also non-Zionists whose aid was enlisted in the development of the national home. After the outbreak of the second world war the Zionist Organization again carried out alone all political and economic tasks as the Jewish Agency for Palestine.

The Zionist Congress in its composition, functions, and procedures possessed most of the attributes of a parliament. It consisted of a few hundred delegates whose mandates were valid from the beginning of the Congress to which they were elected until the convening of the next one. The system of election was proportional, with each territorial federation returning delegates according to the size of its membership. In consequence of the growth of the body of voters, the number of members necessary for election of a delegate was raised in 1921 from 200 to 2,500, and in 1946 to 8,000.[2] Proportional representation assumed new and increased significance when political parties within the movement formed worldwide ''separate unions'' which established ''territorial branches'' apart from the federations and put up their own lists of candidates for election to Congresses. Each of the separate unions was entitled to make use of any vote remainders in the various territories for the election of representatives from its central world list.

Although a Congress rarely sat for longer than a fortnight and never assembled more than once, it was the major forum of debate and the highest decision-making authority of the worldwide Zionist Organization. Each Congress elected a small cabinet-like Executive to carry out its decisions and to direct the affairs of the Organization, after first debating the report of the outgoing Executive and fixing the program of work and the budget for the next administrative period. A clear separation of powers was effected when the Eighth Congress (The Hague, 1907) resolved that the presiding officer at future Congresses could not be either the president of the Organization or a member of its Executive. In fact the presidium of the Congress was a collegiate body. At first it consisted of a president and three vice-presidents. As it became desirable to provide representation on the presidium for the increasing number of party Groups on a proportionate basis, that body grew in size and a maximum of eight vice-presidents was fixed.

The Standing Orders of the Congress, amended from time to time, were initially the work of Herzl, who presided over the first six Congresses. The parliamentary procedure most familiar to him was that of France under the Third Republic, where he had been a political correspondent for an Austrian daily at the Palais Bourbon in the early 1890s. It is worthy of note in this connection that debates in the Congress took place on subjects more or less generally couched, in the manner of the French and other European legislatures, where no question is proposed until the speeches are all made, unlike the British procedure by which the debate is held on one precise question, formally stated as a motion. The Congress system of conducting debate provided a model for the Elected Assembly of the Palestine Jewish Community and for the Knesset. Until 1965, the Knesset Rules of Procedure contained provisions for the disposal of resolutions following a general debate which were virtually identical to those laid down in the Congress Standing Orders.[3] Also the practice of allocating debating time to Knesset Groups according to their respective size is derived from Congress usage. From crucial debates in Israel's Provisional State Council it is clear that the Zionist experience was consciously held up as an example in the shaping of parliamentary institutions.[4]

The Congress made most of its substantive decisions by means of a system of Commissions. The plenum would vote on a resolution after it had been first examined for its material contents by the competent Commission and finally formulated by a six-man Committee on Resolutions so as to insure its agreement with other proposed resolutions and with the Organization's constitution. Each of the Commissions mirrored the plenum in its political composition. Its members were appointed by a Nominations Committee on the proposals of the Groups, with each Group entitled to one representative on a Commission for every ten delegates at the Congress. The Congress came to have nine Commissions according to subject-matter: Organization and Information; Political Affairs; Settlement; Finance and Budget; Immigration; Culture and Education in Palestine and in the Diaspora; Position of Jewry in the Diaspora; Labor Questions; Health and Social Welfare. In a fortnight crowded with sittings morning, noon, and night, the Congress had also to allow for an interval in which the Commissions could prepare their report to the plenum.

The Nominations Committee and the Standing Committee which prepared the elections of the Executive, of the Congress Court, of the Court of Honor, and of the Congress attorney were both all-party committees, performing between them the tasks assigned by the Knesset today to its all-party Organizing Committee. The Congress Court was a small panel of lawyer delegates for deciding on the validity of elections to Congress as well as for settling organizational disputes. The Court of Honor dealt with disputes between individuals. The attorney represented the Organization in the proceedings of these Courts. The idea of instituting a Court of Honor like that of the Congress was entertained by the Knesset early on, as is evident from the resolutions of its House Committee on 9 August 1949, and 30 June 1953; however, the matter was let drop.

Because of the far-flung character of the Zionist Organization and the difficulty of convening a Congress more than once or for an extended period, each Congress elected a General Council from among its delegates by proportional representation of party Groups to act as a legislative body until the meeting of the next Congress. The smaller membership of the General Council, which varied from fifteen at the First Congress to seventy-seven at the Twenty-Second Congress, made it possible to convene that body for urgent special meetings. It was required to meet at least twice a year and was empowered to receive reports from the Zionist Executive, to approve the Organization's budget in non-Congress years, and to make changes in the Organization's constitution. It could also dismiss the Executive in special cases and make other important decisions. It fixed the place and time of the new Congress, although the Executive prepared the agenda. To ensure good attendance at the Congress despite the great distances involved, deputy delegates were elected simultaneously with the delegates. If a delegate could not attend the Congress, a deputy delegate from his party was to act for him. The same device was adopted for the General Council; the Congress elected to that body deputy members equal in number to the members and distributed in the same proportion among the Groups. A quorum was required in the General Council; in 1929, when the Council's membership was fifty, the quorum was eighteen.[5]

The later Congresses were an important training ground for future members of the Knesset. On the one hand the Zionist Organization developed subsidiary institutions and enterprises with budgets and large economic investments which were subjected to parliamentary forms of control by the Congress. On the other hand, as the Jewish community of Palestine grew its delegations played an increasing role at the Congresses—often out of proportion to its size. While Zionist politics were perhaps in the realm of theory to Jews in other countries, in Palestine they exercised a direct influence on the social and economic life of the Community. Consequently, most Palestinian Jews joined the ranks of some Zionist party. Moreover, in general recognition of the greater importance which Zionist policies had for Jews who already lived in the national home, proportional representation in the Congress was weighted so that a Palestinian Zionist had in effect a double vote.[6] In the election of a new Executive by the Congress, the proposals of the delegates from Palestine were expressly entitled to prior consideration.[7] A Palestine Executive Office of the World Organization was constituted in 1921 when the maximum membership of the Zionist Executive was enlarged from seven to fifteen. While the Central Office was maintained in London to keep in contact with the British Colonial Office, it was provided that members of the Executive in Jerusalem must be resident in Palestine. By the Nineteenth Congress (Lucerne, 1935) the majority of the Executive elected were from Palestine. That Congress also replaced German with Hebrew in the official stenographic record.

In the mid-1930s political developments affecting the Jewish national home entered a phase which demanded more frequent meetings of an authoritative Zionist deliberative body than could be managed by the General Council, whose members lived scattered all the world over. To meet this exigency the General Council set up the Inner Zionist Council, consisting, in effect, of the former's thirty or so Palestinian members. Although the Inner Council never received formal recognition in the constitution of the Zionist Organization, it assumed, in time, virtually all the functions of the General Council. Consequently, during the second world war, when no Congress was convened, the effective legislative organ of the Zionist Organization was centered entirely in Palestine.

The growth of political parties in Zionism, and the endeavors of each party to assert its particular standpoint, had much to do with the development of the Congress into a genuine parliamentary forum. Unlike the territorial federations of the Zionist Organization, which were dedicated generally to the restoration of the Jewish national home, the separate unions were each based on a distinguishing political or religious principle. The labor and religious Zionist parties had their beginnings in the early years of the Organization. The nondoctrinaire federations, while they did not organize a separate political union, formed a General Zionist Group at the Congress. At the Twelfth Congress (Carlsbad, 1921) the delegates were divided clearly for the first time into their main groupings, with 306 General Zionists in the center of the hall, 97 Religious Zionists *(Mizrahi)* facing the right of the president, and 38 Labor delegates on his left.[8] The Labor Zionists represented three separate parties, one Marxian *(Poalei Zion),* another socialist but non-Marxian (*Zeirei Zion),* and the third a nationalist labor party that eschewed all class struggle in its program *(Hapoel Hazair).*

The above seating arrangement was observed at all subsequent Congresses, although from 1923 on there were additions to the ''wings,'' as the parties on either side of the center were called. By 1925, with the appearance on the right wing of the Revisionists, who stood for a maximalist Zionist policy vis-à-vis the mandatory power, all the major elements of the Zionist political spectrum had emerged. In the course of the 1920s the General Zionists, too, cohered into a political party although its members held widely divergent views; in 1931 they formed two groups designated General Zionists ''A'' and ''B,'' with the ''A'' group more labor oriented and milder in its Zionist policy. The factionalism which was to become so rife in Zionist and Israeli politics was already apparent at the 1921 Congress. To stem the proliferation of parties, that Congress altered the constitution of the Zionist Organization by increasing the number of members required to form a separate union from three thousand to twenty thousand.

The Zionist Organization was in fact an incubator for Israel's major political parties. That influence can hardly be overestimated when one bears in mind the central role of the parties in the country's life. Some thirty years ago it was noted that the parties in Israel occupy a place more prominent and exercise an influence more pervasive than in any other country, with the sole exception of some one-party states; and it was estimated that one-third to one-quarter of all Jewish voters held membership in a political party.[9] In the interval partisanship and dogmatism have indeed abated, as the joining of forces of the labor parties and the "right-of-center" parties (the heirs of the Revisionists and the General Zionists) shows; however, the original groups still maintain their separate identities within both larger political formations, which have to govern themselves, in practice, like federations of parties. The coalition cabinets that have always governed Israel are part of the same Zionist legacy. As soon as the party system in the Zionist Organization became clearly developed, coalition Executives were elected—with rare exceptions. This practice was not always due to the absence of a majority party; in the 1921 Congress, mentioned above, a coalition Executive was elected although the General Zionists had an undisputed majority. The Zionist predilection for coalitions lay rather in the voluntary character of the Organization, which made representation of all parties on its governing bodies both desirable and necessary, and was bound up with the notion that a broad coalition gave the Organization's governing bodies greater legitimacy as representatives of the entire Jewish people.

In the State of Israel no single party enjoyed an absolute majority in the Knesset, making every Government dependent on coalition partners—until January 1969, when the labor parties together formed a new Alignment giving them 63 of the 120 Knesset seats. The National Unity Government in office then, formed at the outbreak of the Six Days War of 1967 and resting on 90 percent of the house membership, was not affected by that merger. What should occasion surprise, however, is that the Alignment did not do everything to consolidate its unprecedented majority in the following election campaign which came later that year. By all logic the Alignment should have said clearly to the electorate: "Give us just a few more votes or, at least, send us back in the same strength, and we will show you for the first time the advantages of a Government untrammelled by coalition deals." But such clear note was not sounded; instead, the Alignment preferred a vaguer approach and appealed generally to the nation's confidence in a seasoned leadership.[10] In the event, the Alignment lost its small majority in the election of October 1969, and was able to go back comfortably to its old partners of the outgoing Government (and ironically, after David Ben-Gurion had for years waged a campaign for an electoral reform that would produce a two-party system, it was his tiny State List Group that at this crucial turn deprived the fifty-six-man Alignment and its affiliated Arab lists of a majority in the Knesset). Though, arguably, emergency conditions at the time necessitated another National Unity Government in any event, there is no doubt, beyond those special circumstances, that the ingrained coalition habit with its roots in the Zionist movement made both parties and electorate recoil from the idea of government by one political party in Israel.[11] At the same time,

M. Duverger would find support here for his generalization that in multi-party regimes a party with a majority most often tries to govern with others in order to make them share the responsibilities of power; it remains dominated by the psychology of the regime, which is one of alliances.[12]

Zionist organizational features and party politics took root and developed in Palestine's Jewish community, before the advent of the State of Israel, to a degree that went beyond direct participation of the community's members in the activities of the Zionist Organization. Of course, the Zionist enterprise was the vital factor in the growth of the Jewish national home and in its preparation for statehood. But of more significance for the present account, was the adoption of Zionist models by Palestine Jewry in its internal political organization. The representative bodies of Israel's pre-state Jewish Community, however, were born and took shape during the years of the mandatory administration, and before examining them, it will be useful to look briefly at the government of Palestine and to consider at the same time the British influences on Israel's parliamentary system, which were a by-product of that British rule.

BRITISH INFLUENCES

Within the Ottoman Empire before the first world war Palestine did not exist as a distinct political entity or as one administrative unit. The north of Palestine then formed part of the Province *(Vilayet)* of Beirut, and its south constituted a separate District *(Sanjak)* of Jerusalem governed independently from Constantinople. Trans-Jordan formed part of the Province of Syria. There existed in every province an Administrative Council which consisted of senior Turkish government officials, the heads of the religious communities, and a few elected members. The Council was purely advisory, and the Turkish governor of the province, who wielded wide powers, was not bound by its decision. After the revolution of the "Young Turks" in 1908, an empire-wide Ottoman Parliament was created consisting of a Senate and a Chamber of Deputies, the latter elected by an electoral college on the basis of one deputy for every fifty thousand male subjects. The number of deputies elected from the territories which later formed mandated Palestine was six. However, the outbreak of the first world war cut short that democratic reform.

The Government which was established in Palestine by the British Mandatory in 1920, and which lasted until 1948, was of a Crown Colony type. A high commissioner assisted by a small Executive Council of officials was given the power to promulgate ordinances after consultation with a nominated Advisory Council composed of ten official and ten nonofficial members, the latter consisting of four Moslems, three Christians, and three Jews. In 1923 the nomination of nonofficial members to the Advisory Council was abandoned and that body remained a council of officials only. It was used rather for formal assent to legislation than for purposes of consultation or discussion. Two attempts were made under the mandate to set up a partly elected legislature in Palestine, both of which failed. The first attempt, made in 1922, fell through because the Arabs of Palestine refused to have anything to do with a scheme which involved the recognition of the Jewish national home. The second offer was made in 1936; it was opposed by Palestinian Jewry for fear of being consistently outvoted by the Arabs in vital matters such as the freedom of Jewish immigration. The second proposal was dropped after it was attacked in the British Parliament.

Although Britain did not succeed in establishing an elected legislature in Palestine, her own vigorous parliamentary life was observed by Palestine's Jews with more than casual interest during the thirty years of her rule in their country. When British government policy took a turn that put their national home in jeopardy, they saw to what extent the ventilation of opinion in both houses at Westminster had a tempering effect on the Colonial Office. Questions to the colonial secretary in the House of Commons on Palestine policy were of course a regular feature of question time. The emulation of British parliamentary practice, though generally applied with a difference, is discernible in some of the usage which has grown up in the Knesset. Although the presidium of the Knesset is collegial, the influence of the British speakership is apparent in the unchallenged preeminence of the Knesset chairman and in his recognition by the whole house as its impartial moderator of debate. The chairman's rulings carry weight as precedents although the Knesset Rules regard only the decisions of its House and Interpretations committees as binding. The first secretary of the Knesset, Moshe Rosetti, who served in that capacity for twenty years, was English-born and received the appointment, in part, because of his familiarity with British parliamentary life.

As in the House of Commons, a bill in the Knesset successively goes through stages of general debate, committee consideration, and floor discussion of amendments. But differences of terminology and procedure in the two parliaments are considerable at the committee stage since a permanent committee of the Knesset is a standing, select, and specialist committee all wrapped in one. Unlike the formal public debate in a Commons standing committee, the committee stage of a bill in the Knesset takes place *in camera,* in an informal manner, allowing for evidence from officials and other interested parties as well as the minister. The procedure of Committee of the Whole is unknown to the Knesset. As a "new" parliament the Knesset was spared the need of sweeping away archaic forms of procedure.

The question period in the Knesset, though it has been a tame thing compared to that of the House of Commons because of the restriction of supplementary questions, bears the unmistakable stamp of the latter's example. The limitations as to admissible questions laid down in the Knesset Rules, though fewer than those applied in the Commons in consequence of speaker's rulings, are notably similar. Two recent changes in the Knesset's questions procedure attest that the influence of English parliamentary procedure is still vital. First, a ruling in 1976 by the chair that a minister need not reply from the rostrum to an absent questioner, but may have it printed in the Knesset Record, has been followed since as a precedent. Second, in 1983 an oral question period was instituted experimentally; though not "private notice" questions as in the Commons, they are answered within the week and allow freer use of supplementary questions.

The more general influences of the British parliamentary system are not easy to distinguish. Collective Government responsibility in Israel has something British in its theory. As for Israel's uncodified constitution, which is sometimes ascribed to British influences, the position is not really the same in both countries since the First Knesset decided in 1950 that separate Basic Laws, to be adopted on specific subjects, would be ultimately consolidated into a single constitution. Eight Basic Laws have been passed, and while in the hierarchy of legal norms, they are generally no different from other statutes, some of them contain entrenched sections requiring an absolute majority of the house in order to be varied. The absence of such a majority thrice provided occasion for the annulment of legislation by the High Court of Justice: in 1969 and 1983, in regard to election financing of parties; and in 1981, respecting an amendment to the law on election propaganda. The legislation of the Knesset is thus not immune to the courts like that of the British Parliament. Nor are other proceedings in the Knesset altogether excluded from the area of judicial review as they are in England. When petitioned, in 1981, over the Knesset chairman's deferment of a sitting at which a no-confidence motion had under the Rules to be considered, the Court held that it had jurisdiction in the matter though it denied the petition.

In some of its most important features the unicameral Knesset, elected by pure proportional representation resulting in a multiparty system with coalition governments and with oppositions deeply divided, bears no resemblance at all to the "Mother of Parliaments." More apparent here, as in the Knesset's process of debate and specialized standing committees, are the traditions of the Zionist Congress, and those of the Elected Assembly of the pre-state Jewish community organization in Palestine which now remain to be described.

THE ELECTED ASSEMBLY AND NATIONAL COUNCIL OF PALESTINE JEWRY

For close to three decades preceding the establishment of the State of Israel, from 1920 to 1948, the majority of Palestinian Jews were organized as a distinct body politic, the Community of Israel *(Knesset Yisrael)*, possessing in certain matters the character of a state within a state. The readiness with which the Community set up its own governing bodies after the first world war reflected a measure of autonomy already existent. Although the Ottoman rulers had opposed separate nationalisms within the confines of their empire, the Jewish community there, like other minorities, enjoyed autonomous cultural-religious rights whose administration was vested by law in its religious heads.[13] The Turkish administration, which by its laxness left Palestine to stagnate, contributed also, paradoxically, in another way to the emergence of a self-reliant Jewish community. Taxes were light, but very few services were provided. As a result, the Jewish population often assumed governmental tasks and duties, such as the protection of life and property, the paving of roads and streets, and the administration of justice. However, the organization of Palestinian Jewry until the beginning of the century was confined to local communities. Under the Zionist impetus various attempts were made between 1900 and the outbreak of the first world war to form a general organization of Palestine's Jewish community based on some form of suffrage. It was, however, only with the Balfour Declaration and change of regime that the full possibilities of such an organization were generally recognized. While the country was still under a military administration, in the years 1917–20, the Community prepared the way for its first elected assembly by means of a number of provisional committees and conferences.

The central constituent bodies of the Community, not of a religious character, which were established in 1920, consisted of an Elected Assembly *(Asefat Hanivharim)* which was to meet at least once a year, a National Council *(Vaad Leumi)* appointed by the former from among its members to meet between sessions, and an Executive Committee selected in turn by the National Council from its membership to administer Community affairs through a number of departments, of which the major ones were social welfare, culture, health, education, and religious affairs. This constitution received mandatory confirmation in the Jewish Community Regulations of 1927 and their amendments.

The three-tier structure—Elected Assembly, National Council, and Executive Committee—resembled the Zionist Organization's Congress, General Council, and Executive described earlier. However, the important differences should be noted. While the Zionist General Council was elected by the Congress for geographic reasons and charged with important legislative functions, the National Council elected by the Assembly in Palestine was intended to be essentially an executive body. In fact, the National Council, which never numbered fewer than twenty-three members and sometimes exceeded forty, was too large a body to be an efficient executive committee. However, since the National Council met once a month or more often and took decisions which were binding on the Executive Committee who had been chosen by it from among its own members, it became the pivotal constituent body of the Community.

The position of the National Council was buttressed further by the Regulations of 1927 which, while they took no cognizance of the Executive Committee.[14] charged the former with the administration of the affairs of the Community. Among other things, the National Council was to prepare the election regulations, present an annual budget to the Elected Assembly and an annual report on the Community's activities to the high commissioner, convoke the Assembly as often as necessary but not less than once in twelve months, and maintain the Register of the Jewish Community which determined membership. While these functions were performed in fact by the Executive Committee, they were all carried out in the name of the National Council. The preeminence of the National Council in the Community was further reinforced by the practice borrowed from the Zionist bodies of appointing deputy members. While there were no immense distances within Palestine which might keep down the attendance of the regular members, the informality which prevailed at National Council meetings permitted also the simultaneous attendance of any number of deputy members. Although not permitted to vote, the supernumerary deputy members could speak. The National Council thus became a deliberative body which sometimes numbered more than half the parent Assembly.[15]

The Elected Assembly was nonetheless the central forum of the Community. The First Assembly, at its first session, in October 1920, proclaimed that it "had laid the foundations of the self-government of the Jewish people in Palestine" and declared itself to be the "supreme organ in conducting the communal and national affairs of the Jewish people in Palestine and its sole representative internally and externally."[16] The latter part of this declaration was in fact somewhat pretentious at the time since the mandatory, while prepared at the outset to confer on the Jewish community the status of an autonomous religious group such as it had experienced in the Turkish Empire, balked at the novel idea of granting self-government, even in a limited degree, to a section of the country's population. When the Community Regulations were at last approved by the Palestine Government, after seven years of negotiating, they were promulgated under the Religious Communities (Organization) Ordinance, adopted a year earlier, in 1926, in order to provide the accommodating legal framework. The Elected Assembly and its National Council were to be regarded somewhat as lay councils designed to assist in the administration of a religious community. (Of the Regulations' three operative parts, the first dealt entirely with the constitution of rabbinical bodies.) This sectarian constitutional garb did not prevent the Community from making the fullest use of its secular authority. But there were also other limitations. The Regulations provided only for nonobligatory membership in the Community while they laid down wide powers of control and supervision by the Government. The budgets and tax rates adopted by the Assembly, as well as its election regulations and rules of procedure, were to be submitted to the high commissioner for approval. The accounts of the National Council were to be examined by auditors similarly approved.

The voluntary character of membership in the Community enabled an individual to leave it by having his name struck from the Register of the Jewish Community. To take that step, however, he had to sign a declaration according to a set form and pay up any taxes he owed to the Community. Dissenting groups presented a graver problem. The ultraorthodox *Agudat Yisrael* opted out because any secular constitution for the Jewish people was anathema to them. It was not uncommon for a group which could not secure a desired revision of the election regulations to boycott elections to the Assembly. However, the majority of Palestinian Jews, deeply aware of their role as the nucleus of the projected national home, gave their support to the Community. The Palestine Government, cognizant of this loyalty, had recognized the Community's organs de facto long before it issued the Regulations of 1927. As early as 1921 the high commissioner had requested a regular weekly interview with the Executive Committee of the National Council to discuss current legislative and administrative matters.

Financial surveillance of the Community by the high commissioner was inevitable since its services, education in particular, were dependent to a large extent on government subventions. During the years in which the Elected Assembly lacked legal standing it had no statutory powers to levy rates, and the National Council and its Executive Committee had to function on a basis of insecure voluntary contributions. The taxing powers granted by the Regulations of 1927 could not be applied until 1931 for it was only then that the first legally recognized Elected Assembly met. The tax rates, set as a percentage of the house rents, and imposed by Local Communities *(Kehillot)* constituted under the Regulations, never produced enough revenue to meet expenditures. To finance its services, the Community received, in addition to its own revenues and government aid, regular and substantial assistance from the Zionist Organization. To carry out projects of an emergency character the National Council made use of a clause in the Regulations (Section 14) investing it with the authority to administer funds that might be turned over to it by Local Communities, individuals, and institutions. In this way resources were mobilized in the Community to combat unemployment, to consolidate newly founded settlements, and for other special purposes.

The four Elected Assemblies of the Community, elected at irregular intervals, were each quite different in size and composition and spanned a period during which the electorate increased more than tenfold, primarily through immigration. Table 1 indicates the extent of these changes in summary form.

Each list had one member elected to the First Assembly for every eighty votes it received. For the later Assemblies the number of mandates was fixed in advance before each election. The elections were carried out by a proportional party-list scheme by which the whole country was deemed to be one electoral area; only in one of the four elections—that to the Second Assembly—was the country divided into ten districts and each was allotted mandates according to the number of its registered electors. The system adopted for Assembly elections was approved by the Government of Palestine in 1930 as the Community's Election Regulation. It was adopted later, in its essentials, as the system of election to the Knesset.

As Table 1 shows, the number of party lists represented in each Assembly was phenomenally large for an electorate which ranged from some thirty thousand in 1920 to three hundred thousand in 1944. The mushrooming of political groups in the Community was due to three main factors—the extreme leniency of the election regulations, the influence of the Zionist multiparty pattern, and the heterogeneous character of the population. The condition for presenting a list was simple. Any group of fifty eligible voters, that is, persons of either sex above the age of twenty, whose names were

Table 1

The Pre-State Elected Assemblies

Year of Election	Jewish Population in Palestine	Registered Electors	Votes Cast	Assembly Membership	Lists Represented in Assembly
1920	67,000	28,765	22,200	314	20
1925	122,000	64,764	36,437	221	26
1931	174,610	89,659	50,436	71	12
1944	565,000	300,018	202,448	171	18

The population figures for 1931 and 1944 are from D. Gurevich and A. Gertz, eds., *Statistical Handbook of Jewish Palestine, 1947* (Jerusalem: Jewish Agency for Palestine, 1947), p. 37; those for 1920 and 1925 are estimates of Mr. M. Sicron of Israel's Central Bureau of Statistics. The figures on the Elected Assemblies are from M. Attias, ed. *Sefer Hateudot shel Havaad Haleumi Leknesset Yisrael b'Erez Yisrael* (Documents of the National Council of the Jewish Community of Palestine), 2d ed. (Jerusalem: Raphael Cohen, 1963), pp. XIII, XIX, XXXI–XXXII, XLVIII.

included in the Register of the Jewish Community, could submit a list of candidates. While the influx of immigration in relation to the Community's size was high throughout most of the mandatory period, the voters' residence requirement was only three months.

The groups who submitted lists fell into a number of categories. First in size and importance, and antedating for the most part the organization of the Community, were the Zionist parties in Palestine, each based on a particular politicosocial program for the rebuilding of the national home, and drawing its strength from identification with the ideals and aspirations of its parent political organization in the Zionist movement. Indeed, the parties had more adherents abroad than at home—mainly in Eastern Europe, where most of the world's Jews lived until the Nazi holocaust. Each of these parties sought the largest possible representation in the Elected Assembly as in the Zionist Congress. Together they outnumbered by a considerable margin all other groups in every Assembly but the First.[17] They consisted of four major camps—the Labor, Religious, General, and Revisionist Zionists—each made up of a number of rival groups who contested the elections to the Assembly with separate lists. The divisions between some of the groups within each camp rested often on doctrinal niceties which produced a succession of party splits, mergers, and changes of framework over the years. For all that, the several mainstream Zionist parties preserved their identities and remained to dominate Israel's political scene.

A different category of election lists was that based on community of origin and the most notable of which were the Sephardim and Yemenites. The Yemenites boycotted the official polling to the Second Assembly in 1925, claiming that they had been discriminated against by the Electoral Committee of Tel Aviv. Upon appealing to the Central Electoral Committee they were permitted to vote at special polls a month later and to send twenty delegates to the Assembly, which in fact secured them overrepresentation.[18] Later both the Sephardim and the Yemenites, on the ground that the members of their communities were less advanced politically than those of East and Central European origin, insisted that their fair representation be assured by allotment to their separate lists of a fixed number of Assembly seats in proportion to their total numbers on the Register of the Jewish community. For the sake of unity the National Council yielded to these demands and embodied them in the Election Regulations as transitory provisions. They were applied only in the elections to the Third Assembly in 1931 and produced some unintended results. Since the number of assemblymen from the Sephardim and Yemenite lists was preestablished as eighteen out of the total membership of seventy-one, the members of these two communities could with impunity vote for other lists or absent themselves from the polls. In consequence, a marked discrimination in reverse was created. While every one of the other fifty-three assemblymen were elected by an average of 794 votes, it took only 412 votes to elect an assemblyman from the Sephardim and Yemenite lists.[19]

The occasion for a communal list was sometimes provided by a sudden large flow of immigration from one country. Such was the case of the Polish immigrants list in 1925, and of the *Aliyah Hadashah* (New Immigration) in 1944, made up largely of German-speaking refugees from Central Europe. Communal lists continued to appear at election time also after statehood but, in the process of integration, lost their appeal to the voter. The only exception was the above-mentioned German refugee group which survived by transcending its ''landsmannschaft'' framework and merging with other like-minded groups to form the small but influential middle-of-the-road Progressive party.

In a third class belonged a varying number of lists representing groups whose interests were narrowly occupational or local, like the artisans, who submitted a list in every one but the last of the four elections, the office clerks, who contested the election to the First Assembly only, and the Safed and Bnei Brak lists, who were represented only in the Second. One such group, the independent farmers, was influential beyond its numerical strength, particularly in the older settlements. Denied a fixed allocation of seats such as was provided for the communal groups, it boycotted the election to the Third Assembly. Since the tax rates voted by the Assembly were imposed by the Local Community committees, the cooperation of the farmers was important, and to mollify them a provision was adopted in 1938 for seating thirty additional representatives in the Assembly to be elected by the larger local and regional councils. These representatives could participate in the Assembly's deliberations but could not vote on the budget or tax rates as their status was not confirmed by the Regulations. That arrangement was not continued in the Fourth Assembly, after the farmers had again stayed away from the election. Generally, the special interest groups were quite small and loosely organized. Together with the General Zionists, whose numbers and homogeneity in Palestine were not nearly as marked as they were abroad, the representatives of these diverse groups formed a weak center at the Assemblies. They were flanked by a dominant Labor Zionist bloc on the left and a right consisting of the religious and communal factions—and in the Second and Third Assemblies—also of the Revisionsts. While the special interest groups did not survive the birth of the state as separate electoral forces at the national level, they continued to exercise influence through existing political parties.

A separate women's list, the Jewish Women Equal Rights Association, returned representatives to the first three Assemblies. In the Fourth Assembly three women's lists secured representation two of which were women's movements within existing political groups. Separate women's lists were a phenomenon provoked by a drawn out controversy over female suffrage which had threatened the disruption of the Community early in its history. In the 1920 elections to the First Assembly special polls were set up for Orthodox males who excluded their womenfolk from the voting, and where each vote was given double weight. Nevertheless the Orthodox party withdrew from the First Assembly because it could not secure the elimination of the clause granting women full suffrage from the proposed new election regulations. The Religious Zionists were for a long time of the opinion that women should be permitted to vote but not to stand for election; however, in embarrassment at the intransigence of the ultraorthodox elements in the community, they were won over to the acceptance of full election rights for women.

The Regulations of 1927 required the election of a new Assembly every three years, and according to an amendment of 1937, every four years. These conditions were never met. The first two Assemblies were elected before the Regulations were issued. By the time the Third Assembly, the first legally recognized, reached the close of its term in 1934 the problem of updating the Register of the Jewish Community, which served as the voters list under the Election Regulation, had assumed formidable dimensions with the rapidly growing immigration induced by the Nazi persecution. For the forthcoming elections the National Council requested the right to prepare a new Register from the Government of Palestine; these negotiations entailed some delay. In the meanwhile Palestine entered a turbulent period which compelled the Community to put aside the election time after time. In 1936 the country was shaken by Arab riots over the Jewish national home. The riots were followed by a period of political uncertainty marked by Royal Commission investigations and the London Conference with Jews and Arabs of 1939. Then came the second world war in which the Community mobilized all its energies behind the anti-Nazi cause. The long deferment of elections left the Third Assembly in office for thirteen years. That Assembly, elected in 1931, and the National Council which it appointed in 1934, retained their authority to impose taxes and to administer the Community through a validation ordinance passed by the Government in 1936. Only when victory for the Allies was in sight in 1944 were elections held to the Fourth Assembly.

The Elected Assembly had three statutory duties—to elect a National Council each year, to vote the National Council a budget after considering the estimates presented by the outgoing Council, and to set the tax rates. The budget debates provided assemblymen with an opportunity to express their views on all questions of Community importance. However, the short term of the National Council and its correspondence with the budget year—except during the decade 1934–44, as mentioned above—were not calculated to give stability to the Community, as it meant that each National Council had to operate on a budget fixed by its predecessor. This shortcoming was mitigated by the fact that the political composition both of the National Council and of the Executive Committee remained unchanged during the life of an Assembly, and by the disposition of the Groups in the Assembly to choose the same persons, sometimes in rotation, for those two bodies. The National Council was representative of all but the tiniest Groups on a proportional basis; the Executive Committee was only slightly less representative of the political rainbow. Broad coalitions were essential here, as on the Zionist bodies, for the preservation of unity in an organization in which membership was optional.

No Assembly ever finally adopted binding rules of procedure. The First Assembly accepted provisional rules and turned over the task of their final drafting to its Standing Committee. Under the Regulations (Section 16) the Assembly was to submit its rules to the high commissioner for approval. Consequently, the Third Assembly adopted a set of rules and referred them to the National Council who were to revise them before their submission for official endorsement. The National Council did not carry out this step. The Fourth Assembly appointed a special committee to draw up its standing orders. That committee's recommendations, like the earlier draft, were referred by the Assembly to the National Council for final decision. That referral, made in mid-1947, after Britain had already turned over the Palestine question to the United Nations, was forgotten and never acted upon. The Assembly's recourse, with regard to its own standing orders, to the National Council was not required by the Community Regulations and must seem an odd proceeding if one conceives of those two bodies as legislature and executive.

The procedure of the Assembly, as much as the organizational features mentioned earlier, was inspired by the Zionist Congress since the latter was the parliamentary model with which many of the Community leaders were directly acquainted as Congress delegates. The collegial and politically representative presidium, the compression of deliberations into a few days with an interval for the committees to hammer out resolutions for a final marathon sitting which lasted late into the night—familiar institutions at Congresses—became part of the Assembly's working. The committee system of the Assembly was less elaborate than that of the Congress. The Assembly's Standing Committee, which had combined duties of a steering, rules, and nominations committee, was its most important one. The agenda of the Assembly, prepared by the National Council, required the approval of the Standing Committee before the opening of a new session: the Committee's chairman brought the agenda to the session for final approval. In the beginning the Assembly elected its presidium anew each session. Later on it was left to the Standing Committee to approve any personnel change in the presidium and to bring it to the notice of the new session. In its nomination to committees, the Standing Committee adhered to the Assembly balance of parties and accepted the recommendation of each group as a matter of course.

At each session of the Assembly general debates were held on addresses made by the chairman of the Executive Committee and a number of its members who headed administrative departments. These addresses came, formally, as supplements to a tabled report of the National Council which reviewed all departmental activities. The number of departments increased over the years so that only a few of the major ones could be considered in one session, which seldom lasted beyond a fourth day. By the end of 1944 there existed Departments of Political Affairs, Finance, Organization of the Local Communities and Rabbinate, Health, Social Work, Education, Culture, Sport and Physical Training, Press and Information, Municipal Affairs, and Veterans Affairs—eleven in all. A Law Department to scrutinize mandatory legislation came into being in 1947. In the years 1936–44, during which no new Assembly was elected and the same National Council remained in office, the procedure of the Assembly was most rudimentary. Sessions then lasted generally not more than a day, although they were held more often than once a year. That period was one of unceasing tumult in the life of the national home. While Arab hostility and British restrictions increased, the storm clouds over Europe broke and brought the near total destruction during the second world war of a large and vital segment of Jewry and resulted in a desperate stream of refugees to the country's shores. In these circumstances the Assembly served primarily, as the central tribune of the Community, to demonstrate Palestine Jewry's dismay, defiance, grief, and solidarity, leaving the close supervision of the Community's administration and services to the National Council.

As a parliamentary platform the Elected Assembly did not attract the same interest as the Zionist Congress, even within Palestine. This difference is accounted for to some extent by the protracted negotiations of the Community for recognition, the long deferment of elections to the Fourth Assembly, and the fact that the assiduous National Council tended to overshadow the Assembly as the Community's representative body. A more basic cause of the lesser reputation of the Assembly was the role of the Community as junior partner in the rather singular alliance which existed between it and the Zionist Organization. Both of these organizations aimed to rebuild the Jewish national home. However, the world Zionist movement was much larger in membership and had at its disposal greater financial resources. Recognized in the Palestine Mandate as the Jewish Agency to be consulted in matters affecting the national home, the Zionist Organization was responsible for immigration, settlement, agricultural and urban development, and external affairs—that is, relations with the mandatory and with the League of Nations. The Community was confined to matters more purely local in character.

The division of functions between the two organizations was not always clearly drawn. To cite but a few instances, the Community's National Council sent memoranda to the Mandates Commission of the League of Nations and called protest strikes over the halt of immigration; on the other hand, purely local matters like health and education, which were to be within the Community's jurisdiction under the Regulations of 1927, were in the hands of the Zionist Organization until 1931 and 1933 respectively. The relations between the two organizations preoccupied every one of the Elected Assemblies and was the cause of occasional friction. Nevertheless, a resolution adopted by the First Assembly in 1920, accepting the authority of the Zionist Organization over the Community in all matters concerning the national home, was usually adhered to until the establishment of the state. The concerted effort of the two organizations was necessary for the success of each, and close cooperation between the constituent bodies of both at all levels was the general rule. The two Executives met frequently and joint committees for special matters were sometimes appointed. The National Council was entitled to send two delegates to the Zionist General Council. A member of the Zionist Executive addressed every session of the Elected Assembly; his address would be debated by the Assembly in the same manner as one delivered by a member of its own Executive Committee. Few political steps were taken by Community bodies without previous consultation with the Political Department of the Zionist Executive.

The most important links between the Community and Zionist bodies were the Zionist political parties, each guided by the same ideology in both organizations. It was common for a party to be represented to a large extent by the same persons both in the Assembly and in the Congress. Of the seventy-two-man Palestinian delegation to the Twenty-Second Congress (Basle, 1946), the last to be convened before the birth of the State of Israel, at least thirty were also members of the coeval (Fourth) Assembly which had been elected in 1944. A comparison of lists also provides a quantitative indication of the extent to which both of these quasi parliaments served as a source of experience for future members of the Knesset. Of the above-mentioned delegation, at least thirty-eight members—more than half—sat later in the Knesset, twenty-one of them with a background of experience in the Assembly as well as in the Congress. Of the 171 members of the Fourth Assembly, at least 55 were elected later to the Knesset. Further, the men who entered the Knesset as veterans of the pre-state representative bodies were leading figures in the newly created parliament. Not a few of the younger among them continued their active political life into Israel's third decade. In the Seventh Knesset, elected in October 1969, there were twelve members—a full 10 percent of the house—who had attended the 1946 Zionist Congress as delegates, while there were eleven who had sat in the Fourth Elected Assembly.[20]

The close connection between Congress, Assembly, and Knesset was capped in the person of Yosef Sprinzak, who served as a member of the presidium of the Elected Assembly from its inception in 1920, with a few interruptions, and as a vice-president of the Twelfth Zionist Congress (Carlsbad, 1921) and later of every Congress from 1935 until the birth of the state; he became chairman of the Provisional State Council of Israel and was later elected the first Knesset chairman, in which capacity he served for more than ten years, until his death in 1959.

If the representative bodies of the Community were somewhat eclipsed by those of the Zionist Organization, they gained much from the latter's tutelage, not the least advantages of which were regular financial assistance and timely intercession by the Zionist Executive at the Colonial Office in London for the sake of furthering the Community's self-government. It was clearly in the Zionist interest that Palestine Jewry should secure the widest measure of autonomy. The financial, political, and moral support of the Zionist movement encouraged the Community to extend in every possible way the limited scope of activity afforded it under the Regulations. In the absence of an elected legislature, or any semblance of responsible government for the whole population of Palestine, most of the country's Jews considered the Elected Assembly and the National Council with its Executive Committee, together with the Palestine Zionist Executive, as truly representing the sovereign authority of their national home; they regarded the decisions of these bodies as binding while they complied only reluctantly, at times, with the regulations of the mandatory government.

In the unsettled period which followed the decision of the United Nations Assembly of 29 November 1947, to partition Palestine, the Community and Zionist bodies continued their close collaboration in laying the foundations of the projected Jewish state, and acted together to prepare its provisional legislative and executive authorities. The last Elected Assembly dissolved itself on 12 February 1949, at a session called for that purpose. This was a purely formal and symbolic step on the eve of the first meeting of Israel's Constituent Assembly, for the central Community organization had virtually ceased to function nine months earlier when it had turned over its administrative machinery to the new state. As early as March 1948, the National Council's Executive Committee together with the then members of the Palestine Zionist Executive had entered the People's Council *(Moetzet Ha'am),* which was to become Israel's Provisional State Council with the declaration of independence on 14 May 1948.

2

The Provisional State Council and Government

FROM COMMUNITY TO STATE

THE SELF-ADMINISTRATION achieved by the Jews of Palestine served them well in the unsettled period which followed the United Nations Assembly decision of 29 November 1947 to partition the country. Arab opposition to the scheme and the consequent refusal of Britain to facilitate its implementation did not deter the Community and Zionist bodies, working in close collaboration, from laying the foundations of the projected Jewish state. When David Ben-Gurion read out the Declaration of the Establishment of the State of Israel in the Hall of the Tel-Aviv Museum on 14 May 1948, he spoke as the chairman of the People's Council *(Moetzet Ha'am),* composed for the most part of the membership of the Palestine Zionist Executive (better known by then as the Jewish Agency Executive) and of the Executive Committee of the Community's National Council. Made to coincide with the termination of the mandate, the declaration provided for the transformation of the thirty-seven man People's Council into the Provisional State Council *(Moetzet Hamedina Hazmanit),* which was to serve as the country's provisional legislature for the first nine months of independence. The executive arm of the People's Council, the People's Administration *(Minhelet Ha'am),* consisting of thirteen members, became the Provisional Government by the same instrument.

The form and composition of the Provisional Council and Provisional Government were the result, to some extent, of contingency. The United

Nations resolution on partition required the establishment in the new state, before 1 April 1948, of only one body, a "Provisional Council of Government," to act both as administrative and legislative authority until a Constituent Assembly, democratically elected, should choose a Provisional Government. In conformity with that resolution the National Council of the Community provided at its meeting on 1 March for the setting up of the Provisional Council of Government to be composed of the Zionist and Community executives, with the authority to co-opt additional members from groups not represented on either of those two bodies.

A few weeks later, when asking for the due appointment of the Provisional Council of Government by the United Nations Palestine Commission, charged with implementing the partition scheme, the Zionist and Community authorities supplied a list of twenty-five names for the membership. The Commission having been in effect prevented by the mandatory from carrying out its assignment, even to the point of being refused entry into Palestine until two weeks before the date set for the termination of the mandate, did not comply with the request of the Jewish representative bodies. Moreover, the Palestine Government had warned against any attempt to set up institutions of the Jewish state while the mandate was still in force. Then, on 19 March, the United States proposed a trusteeship for Palestine which would have the effect of deferring partition indefinitely.

The Jews of Palestine were determined, however, to prevent the partition resolution from becoming a dead letter. In view of the uncertain situation, and the danger of chaos that would result from a political and legal vacuum with Britain's departure, they telescoped the procedure laid down in the United Nations resolution by providing for the simultaneous creation of the Council of Government and Provisional Government—in effect distinct legislative and executive bodies—of the projected state. This step was taken by the Zionist General Council, meeting in Tel-Aviv on 12 April, when it confirmed the March resolution of the National Council and decided also to form a more restricted executive group from among the members of the projected Council of Government.

While the sense of urgency in face of the backtracking which had taken place since the adoption of the partition resolution, and which threatened the entire scheme, was the most important consideration in the speedy elaboration of the provisional arms of government, internal factors were also at work. Since virtually all of Palestine Jewry, in its full political diversity, rallied at this time to the idea of a Jewish state, there resulted an inflation of the projected Council of Government. To that body's membership, comprising initially the Community and Zionist executives, who alone numbered respectively fourteen and nine members, there were added on a proportional basis representatives of political groups who had until then followed a separatist course—the Revisionist party, *Agudat Yisrael,* the Communist party, and others.

The proposed Council of Government would now total thirty-seven members, a size not intended and one too cumbersome to constitute a practical administration. Consequently, the appointment at once of the smaller executive body was also a practical necessity. The membership of thirteen fixed for it was not, however, without some elements of design. It bore some correspondence to the thirteen proposed ministries into which had been grouped the many departments of the mandatory, Community, and Zionist administrations by the Joint Planning committee *(Va'adat Hamatzav)* of the Community and Zionist executives, set up six months earlier, while the United Nations were debating partition.

But to avoid clashing with the Palestine Government in its April resolutions, the Zionist Council brought the two bodies into existence nameless and referred to them as "The Thirty-Seven" and "The Thirteen." For the same reason the word "government" was also avoided in the names given them at the first meeting of the smaller body, on 18 April—People's Council and People's Administration, respectively. In fact the "Provisional Council of Government" was not to be called by that name although it was so designated in the draft declaration of the establishment of the state as late as 10 May, just four days before the assumption of statehood.[1] In the end, as provided in the final draft of the declaration, the People's Council became the Provisional State Council, that name being chosen to avoid semantic confusion between "Provisional Council of Government" and "Provisional Government."

The People's Council existed for a month before being transformed, with national independence, into the Provisional State Council. But it could not hold sittings as planned. One-third of its members, those who lived in Jerusalem, were effectively cut off from Tel-Aviv, where the meetings were called, since many of the roads away from the coastal areas were by that time under the control of Arab irregulars set on defeating any attempts to create a Jewish state. Nor did the Jerusalem members get to the meeting at which independence was declared. However, the smaller People's Administration, soon to become the Provisional Government, managed to meet frequently in the weeks which preceded the termination of the mandate.

THE ORGANIZATION AND PROCEDURE OF THE COUNCIL

As Israel's first legislature, the Provisional State Council bridged the gap between the mandate, under which both legislative and executive powers were vested in the office of the high commissioner, and the elected Constituent Assembly *(Asefa Mechonenet),* which opened nine months after the state was declared, on 14 February 1949. The Council's organization and work were colored in particular by a number of factors: its avowed provisional character, the state of war emergency which prevailed in the first months of the new nation, the adoption by the Council of practices followed in the pre-state quasi parliaments, and the problematic character of the Council's relation to the Provisional Government when neither body was popularly elected or regularly constituted.

In keeping with its provisional functions, the Council sought to confine its legislative activity to an essential minimum. In order to prevent the occurrence of a hiatus, it provided in its first enactment for the continuance in force virtually of the whole corpus of mandatory law as well as of the regulations and orders that had been issued by the Jewish Agency for Palestine and by the Community's National Council from the date of the United Nations partition resolution. Nevertheless, in meeting emergent demands of the new state, the Council, during its short life of forty weekly sittings, passed ninety-eight ordinances, including important organic laws, fiscal measures, and amendments to mandatory ordinances. All of this legislation was initiated by the Provisional Government though some of the groundwork for it had been done in the pre-state period by a Law Board *(Moatza Mishpatit)* set up by the Joint Planning Committee. Like a mandatory enactment, a legislative act of the Council was termed "ordinance" *(pkuda)* so as to reserve the name "law" *(hok)* for the enactments of the parliament to be elected.

In addition to its legislation, the Council held some twenty major debates, most of them on the political and security situation. The agenda was fixed by the Provisional Government. Most sittings of the Council opened with a question period for which up to half an hour was allowed. A question had to be submitted to a member of the Provisional Government at least forty-eight hours in advance of the sitting at which it was to be answered, and was then read out by a clerk together with the answer.

Since it was not until late in February 1949 that Egypt signed an armistice agreement with Israel—but the first warring neighbor to do so—the Council in fact conducted all of its business while the country was in a state of war. The isolation of the Jerusalem members from the Council's seat in Tel-Aviv continued for weeks after the declaration of the state. This situation was relieved by a system of substitute members according to party affiliation, which could be applied when a member was certified absent due to the state of emergency. However, the speedy adoption of the amending ordinance making such provision, at the Council's third meeting and without debate, suggests that while the blockade of Jerusalem was the ostensible reason for the measure, its chief inspiration was the ready example of the Zionist and Community organizations where deputy delegates had been an accepted practice for decades. Also the absence of a Council member from the country on public business was allowed as a reason for appointing a substitute. Pursuant to the ordinance, the appointment of a substitute to the Council was valid only for the sitting in which it was made, and the proceedings show that a number of substitutes were appointed at the opening of nearly every sitting until the day of the Council's dissolution, well after Jerusalem's link with the coast had been renewed.

Council members did not receive salaries, but any expenses incurred by a member in connection with his attendance at Council sittings were defrayed by the state treasury.

To its committees the Council appointed substitutes from without its membership at the same time as it appointed the regular committee members, and in some cases even before the latter were named.[2] But a more fundamental feature of the Council committee system that can be traced to prestate practices was the dual consideration of draft ordinances. A draft would be examined both by the appropriate subject matter committee and by the Legislation Committee, a procedure identical to that followed at Zionist Congresses before taking resolutions (and described in Chapter 1). In the Council this procedure led to a frequent and sometimes discordant overlapping of functions since the Legislation Committee generally went beyond the consideration of the formal side of the draft and made changes also in the material contents. In the absence of any disposition in the Council's rules with regard to this point, charges that the Legislation Committee was arrogating authority to itself were rejected by its assertive chairman, Nahum Nir, and any differences between it and a subject matter committee, if not settled by their joint meeting, had to be resolved by the Council plenum. However, many draft ordinances went through only the Legislation Committee because that committee began functioning as early as July 1948, while three of the seven subject matter committees—Interior, Immigration, and Public Welfare—did not have their members appointed until September.

The Council's subject matter committees were set up according to areas of ministerial responsibility, and as together they embraced the whole range of the Provisional Government's administration, the scope of a committee might include more than one ministry. Thus, for example, the Finance and Economics Committee was concerned with five ministries: Finance; Trade and Industry; Agriculture; Transport; Labor and Reconstruction. Broadly, the duty of each committee was to advise the minister and to examine his draft legislation, while curiously, the specific scope of the committee's activity and powers was left by the Council to the joint determination of the committee and the ministry concerned.[3] The Legislation Committee, although it examined all draft ordinances, served also as a subject matter committee advising the minister of justice. The membership of these committees ranged from seven to eight, the five largest party groups being represented on every committee, while the seven smaller ones, mostly one-man, fared less well in this respect. Each committee elected its chairman after an understanding had been reached among the party groups.

The distribution of chairmanships between Groups was more random in the Council than it was to be later in the Knesset, where the chairmanships of the "key" Committees—Selection, House, Finance, Foreign Affairs and Security—all went to the largest group, *Mapai,* and subsequently to the Israel Labor party. In the Council not one of these chairmanships went to *Mapai.* One chairmanship, that of the Public Welfare Committee, went to a member of the Revisionist group which was not represented in the Provisional Government. The practice of choosing committee chairmen also from the opposition was continued in the Knesset.

The Selection Committee, appointed by the Council at one of its earliest sittings, had the task of distributing the committee places among the party Groups. That committee also prepared the election of the Council presidium and of the Supreme Court. The Council elected, besides, a number of other special committees for the discharge of particular tasks. The most important of these was the Election Committee, which drew up the system of elections to the Constituent Assembly. A Constitution Committee was charged with the duty of assembling and sifting constitutional proposals and preparing a draft constitution to serve as material for the Constituent Assembly.

In the summary procedures followed by the Council, which enabled it to pass an ordinance upon one plenary debate, and often within one sitting, the role of the committees in the legislative process was a primary one. After approval by the Provisional Government a draft ordinance was submitted to the subject matter committee as well as to the committee on legislation if the relevant subject matter committee was already set up and functioning. The committees might amend the draft, and it was this revised version that came before the Council for debate.

Debating procedure was not prescribed in detail by the Council rules, whose provisions were few and sketchy, but was the product of improvisation and the natural resort to familiar Zionist and Community practices. Not surprisingly, the *Protocol* of the Council is replete with records of procedural tangles. Considering too that the Council's entire existence was confined to a period of nine months, generalization about its procedure might be a doubtful exercise. However, in the free-for-all participation which often ensued in unprecedented situations, the Council was fortunate in the agility with which Chairman Sprinzak used "feedback" to steer proceedings to their destination. The legislative process in particular settled down from the beginning to a fairly regular procedure.

The one continuous plenary debate on a draft ordinance in fact comprised three stages. In the first stage the minister concerned introduced the measure and was followed occasionally by one of the two committees' chairmen with additional comment. The draft was then read out, in the first few months by the minister, and later by a clerk; the reading was more than a mere formality since not infrequently the Council members who were on neither the subject matter nor legislative committees would not have seen the draft ordinance until just before the plenary debate.

In the second stage the Council took up amendments that had been defeated in either committee and whose movers had reserved the right to bring them up again in the plenum. Such amendments could oppose the principle of the draft ordinance. There might also be comments or questions; but a member could comment only if he had requested that right in committee. Replies to movers of amendments and to other speakers would be made by the committee chairman and sometimes by the minister. If the Government differed with a committee, the Council resolved the question by a vote, as it did for each amendment. The final stage of the process was the vote on the draft ordinance as a whole. In a few instances there followed a statement explaining the stand of a particular party Group on the vote. Some of the more important measures, however, took more than one Council sitting, and a number of ordinances were sent back to committee for further study and review. On the other hand, not a few noncontroversial ordinances were passed without any explanation or discussion.

COUNCIL-GOVERNMENT RELATIONS

Division between coalition and opposition, which was to come with the formation of the first parliamentary cabinet in March 1949, could be described as inchoate in the Provisional State Council. Party strife was not absent in the Council, and on a few occasions it flared up sharply, as it did after the defense forces shelled a munitions vessel of the erstwhile underground organization, *Irgun Zevai Leumi,* and when the import of nonkosher meat was challenged by the religious parties. But since Israel was waging her war of independence, it was a time of maximum national unity and minimum party conflict. The groups who had entered the provisional legislature, deeply opposed as they were ideologically, were all in essential agreement on major policies affecting the state; and all larger party Groups in the Council, but the three-man Revisionist group, were represented in the Provisional Government, which included even the members of two one-man Groups. And, concomitantly, Group discipline was not rigid; important measures like the

Budget and the Income Tax Ordinance, for example, found the General Zionist vote divided. Also in its procedure the Council reduced the weight of the party Group relative to that of the individual member. A provision for the allocation of speaking time according to Group strength, like that which had existed at the Zionist Congress and at the Community Assembly, was deleted by the Council from its draft rules.

Nor did the Provisional Government always present a united front. Differences and misunderstandings between its ministers were frequently aired in open debate before the Council. There were instances also of disclosure by ministers to the Council of the stand taken by their colleagues on specific matters at cabinet meetings.[4] Questions seeking clarification from a minister piloting a draft ordinance through the Council were put, as a matter of course, by cabinet colleagues as much as by private members.

Although in reply to a question by a Council member, Ben-Gurion claimed that there was collective responsibility in the Provisional Government,[5] twelve years later he stated the opposite in the Knesset.[6] The weight of evidence bears out Ben-Gurion's later assertion. Although the Government took decisions that were binding on all of its members, these were not binding on the members of their respective party Groups in the Council. Some distinctive marks of collective responsibility were absent from Government-Council relations: when two ministers resigned from the Government over the shelling of the *Irgun* ship *Altalena,* the Council learned of the step in the course of a speech by a member from the resigned ministers' party Group;[7] and this announcement was not required either. When the two men rejoined the Government shortly afterward, the Council was not informed of the event at all. On another occasion the Council chairman accepted and put to the vote a motion of no-confidence in one minister.[8]

There was in fact no constitutional basis for the Government's collective responsibility to the Provisional State Council. The Council had not confirmed the Government in office and could not remove it by a vote of no-confidence; both bodies had been appointed by the Zionist Council at the same time, and there were anomalies in the differentiation between them. As we have seen, the Council, composed in fact of the Executives of the pre-state institutions, had initially been intended to serve as the administrative authority of the new state. As for the distribution of legislative powers between Council and Government, this had remained still undetermined as late as two days before the termination of the mandate.[9] The declaration of the state was not explicit on this point, and the Council assumed the primary legislative power by a proclamation issued after the declaration.

The Council's draft rules of procedure provided that the prime minister was to preside over it in the absence of its president, whose position was purely honorary. (At its opening meeting the Council had elected Dr. Haim

Weizmann "president of the Council" from outside its membership, in recognition of his lifelong Zionist labors.) A late draft of the state's first organic law had contained also a disposition that the Council's vice-chairmen were to be members of the Provisional Government.[10] Although in the end the Council decided to elect only non-ministers as its presiding officers, it did so only after two months of existence. Until 15 July 1948, when the Council elected its chairman and three vice-chairmen from the four largest party Groups, its meetings were chaired by Prime Minister Ben-Gurion. In accordance with the Council rules the Government secretariat served also as that of the Council. The Council appointed its own secretary only at the end of October and did not amend the rules accordingly until the following January.

The first Council committee, appointed ad hoc to consider the drafts of the state's primary organic law and the Council rules, was chaired by the minister of justice. The rules had also been drafted by him.

The problematic character of a common origin and somewhat blurred distinction produced a continuing state of tension between Council and Government that was more marked, on the whole, than any confrontation between coalition and opposition. Opposition of Council and Government showed up almost from the beginning, when the two bodies still existed as the People's Council and Administration, in the month preceding statehood. In a letter that Ben-Gurion addressed to his colleagues of the People's Administration on 19 April 1948, after that body had held its first meeting, he urged them to proceed with the organization of essential services without waiting for the meeting of the People's Council;[11] and indeed, in the month that preceded the termination of the mandate the People's Administration met upward of a dozen times, issued orders and proclamations to the Jewish Community, and took momentous decisions that steered the state-in-the-making to its destination, while the People's Council, in the same period, heard just one brief review of the security and political situation from Ben-Gurion but held no debate on it—or on any other subject—and took no decision, its Jerusalem members absent.

The only business transacted by the People's Council was the consideration and issue, within a few hours of each other, of the declaration of the state and of the proclamation that followed, on 14 May 1948. Although complaints over the inactivity of the People's Council were voiced chiefly by the parties not represented in the Provisional Government, concern over the situation was general.[12]

After independence the Provisional State Council met weekly for the discharge of its legislative and other duties; and an explicit disposition in the Law and Administration Ordinance—the Council's first organic enactment—provided that the Provisional Government was to act in accordance with the policy laid down by the Council and to carry out its decisions. Consequently, the two-thirds of the Council who were not members of the Government sought to be included as far as possible in decision-making processes and to assert the Council's right at every opportunity, while the Government, for its part, was intent on the most expeditious and summary conduct of affairs that would enable it to meet the exigencies of war.

Resentment was voiced often by Council members over the lateness with which copies of draft ordinances were supplied to them in advance of debate. To expedite one of its interim budgets the Government proposed a simple resolution in the Council although a statutory provision required that the budget be passed as an ordinance. Only when a Council member objected to this procedure did the Government concede the point.[13] To all appearances the Provisional Government expected the Council to consider and pass the Law and Administration Ordinance, providing for a rudimentary constitution, in one sitting, although no Council committee had considered it previously. The Council resisted this pressure, and as it had not yet constituted its committees, it set one up ad hoc (as referred to above) to study the measure.

Objection came from all quarters of the Council also to the section on Emergency Regulations in that ordinance, under which the Government would be empowered at its discretion to authorize a minister to make regulations in the interest of national defense, or for the maintenance of essential services that might have the effect of altering or suspending any law. The ad hoc committee restored the Council's paramountcy by providing, among other amendments to the ordinance, that the grounds for an Emergency Regulation could be only a state of emergency declared by the Council, and that when the Council proclaimed that the state of emergency had ceased to exist it would determine the dates of repeal of any existing Regulations. With the forces of at least four enemy nations on Israel's soil, the Council proclaimed a state of emergency almost immediately after passing the ordinance on 19 May 1948. Since the Law and Administration Ordinance laid down that any emergency regulation should lapse unless extended by the Council within three months, such renewals became a regular feature of Council legislation (as they did later of Knesset legislation) and account for fifteen of the Council's ninety-eight ordinances. But here too arose an element of discord between Council and Government; at one point Council Chairman Sprinzak found it necessary to rebuke the Government for rushing extending ordinances through the Council under the threat of imminent expiry dates.[14]

The departmental character of the Council's subject matter committees, as described earlier, enabled them to focus their supervisory activity on ministries to a degree not always welcome to the Provisional Government. Only after a solid cross-party stand was a Foreign Affairs Committee of the Council set up, despite opposition from the Provisional Government, and Prime Minister Ben-Gurion's curious argument that "the Government was itself the most efficient foreign affairs committee."[15] The same position was taken by the Government on a security affairs committee, and the Council was persuaded to make do with a reorganized form of the Security Committee of the pre-state Community, including both Council members and former committee members from without the Council.

No doubt, the relative numbers of the Council and the Government, as well as their common appointment by the Zionist and Community bodies, was a factor in the never quite resolved relationship between the two bodies. As one Council member baldly said. "We are only thirty-eight (including President Weizmann). The whole difference between Council and Government is that between thirty-seven and thirteen."[16]

THE COUNCIL'S LEGACY

Set against its forerunners, the Zionist Congress and the Elected Assembly of the Palestine Jewish Community, the appointed Council was a regression in parliamentary terms, its members being drawn largely from the Executives of the pre-state organizations. For although the Zionist Congress and Elected Assembly represented voluntary organizations, they were elected bodies; further, the Congress elected its Executive while the Assembly did so at least indirectly (see Chapter 1). Yet the criteria of statehood and range of action are no less important for assessing the Council's record. Notwithstanding its constitutional singularity and short history, the Provisional State Council handed down a significant ballast to Israel's elected parliament. Much of the Council's legislation, including parts of the Law and Administration Ordinance, still remains on the statute book. The simple proportional representation laid down in the Election to the Constituent Assembly Ordinance has remained essentially the same despite the enactment of many changes in the election law and a continual agitation, including parliamentary moves, to introduce some form of regional elections.

While the Provisional State Council came on to an improvised stage and began activity with its status and functions rather unclearly defined, it provided for an orderly transfer of authority to its successor in the Transition to the Constituent Assembly Ordinance. That measure also provided that the Council rules of procedure prevail initially in the Constituent Assembly, and the Rules Committee of the Constituent Assembly confirmed the provision. Some of the Council's eighteen rules served through the Third Knesset, up to 1959.

The unwritten practice in the Council's question period of having both question and answer read by a clerk without the minister's presence being required was continued in the Knesset until November 1950. To this day the Knesset leaves to its Finance Committee the entire consideration and vote of the defense budget as was done by the Council: the Knesset has modified the proceeding only by providing that its Foreign and Security Affairs Committee sit jointly with the Finance Committee for that purpose. The Council's parliamentary experience was also passed on through its members, of whom more than two-thirds were elected to the Constituent Assembly; quite a number of the Council's substitute members were similarly elected. Most members of the Provisional Government entered the first regularly constituted parliamentary government, where the distribution of portfolios remained largely the same.

However, the relative freedom of a member to differ with his party colleagues and with the Government went out with the Council. Group discipline became the rule in the Knesset, although effective coalition cohesion was only haltingly secured.

The elections to the Constituent Assembly were held on 25 January 1949. The Council met for the last time on 10 February and ceased to exist with the convocation of the Constituent Assembly on 14 February. The Provisional Government, however, continued in office until the first parliamentary Government was approved, on 10 March.

3

In Quest of a Constitution

EARLY DEVELOPMENTS

ALTHOUGH THERE WERE EARLY INDICATIONS, before and immediately after statehood, that Israel would promptly adopt a complete written constitution, her constitutional development has followed a halting and uncertain course marked by intermittent and seemingly endless debate both in the Knesset and among the interested public. After nearly four decades of independence a written constitution remains yet to be accomplished. The United Nations resolution of November 1947 on the partition of Palestine stipulated the drafting of democratic constitutions both by the Jewish and Arab states. Even before the United Nations Committee on Palestine Question submitted its report recommending partition, the Jewish Community's National Council had appointed a Committee on Constitutional Questions. That committee drew up a number of memoranda on the main constitutional problems which would arise upon the setting up of the state. Immediately after the partition resolution was adopted, the Jewish Agency for Palestine assigned the task of preparing a draft constitution to one of its legal officers, Dr. Leo Kohn.

The declaration of the state too envisaged a constitution in conformity with the United Nations resolution. Accordingly, the Provisional State Council appointed a Constitution Committee to consider and consolidate material for a draft constitution. After using the Kohn draft as the basis for its discussions, the Committee published its proceedings in a series of booklets to guide the Constituent Assembly.[1]

As provided by the United Nations resolution and the declaration of the state, though almost four months after the time limit of 1 October 1948 which they both specified, a Constituent Assembly was elected on 25 January 1949. The declaration of the state assigned to the Constituent Assembly no other task than the adoption of a constitution. The provisional legislative function was to be carried out by the Provisional State Council as provided by a proclamation issued by that body immediately after the declaration of the state. The Provisional Council should then have coexisted with the Constituent Assembly. But on the eve of the election of the Constituent Assembly, the Provisional Council provided for its own dissolution and for the Assembly's assumption of its powers. Thus the constitution-making body was also to serve as legislature and parliament until it provided otherwise. However, with respect to the constituent function, although the majorities of the Council's Constitution and Legislation committees were in favor of providing explicitly that the Constituent Assembly adopt a constitution and that its term of office be restricted to a limit of two years, a motion by the Provisional Government and a minority of committee members to delete both of these stipulations was carried.[2] Here then was the first definite shift from the generally held view that a formal and expeditiously adopted constitution was necessary. This Council debate also adumbrated coming constitutional developments. While it was still believed that the Constituent Assembly would adopt a written constitution, there were broad hints that this might consist of separate laws. Prime Minister Ben-Gurion intimated that the Constituent Assembly might change its name and remarked significantly that it would itself determine its order of business.

In the event, the body elected in the state's first democratic ballot met as the "Constituent Assembly" for only four sittings, between 14 and 16 February 1949. In those three days the Constituent Assembly, among other things, passed the Transition Law, providing in very broad outline for Israel's legislature, presidency and Government. Although the measure was termed "Transition Constitution" *(Hukat Ma'avar)* on first reading, and referred to in the press as a "small constitution," the minister who introduced it made clear that its essential purpose was to make the transition from the provisional to a regular government possible. Further, its first section provided that Israel's legislature be named the Knesset and the Constituent Assembly the First Knesset. The renaming, following as it did upon the defeat of an amendment that would have obliged the Assembly to enact a constitution and to terminate its office thereupon, was tantamount to a deletion of the last remaining statutory reference to a constitution.

A curious result of the retreat from the commitment to a constitution was the failure to fix a limit to the term of office of the Knesset in the Transition Law. Apparently it was acknowledged, even after the omission of any explicit reference to the adoption of a constitution, that the fixing of a term for the First Knesset would imply a time limit for that task, which it had after all been elected to accomplish. When this neglect was cited later by the advocates of a constitution as strengthening their case, Ben-Gurion was prompted to declare that a new election would be held four years after the first one whether a constitution was adopted or not. In fact, because of the resignation of the Government in 1951, elections were held that year, so that the First Knesset lasted only two and a half years. However, before that occurred, a term of four years for future Knessets was fixed by law.

DEBATE IN THE FIRST KNESSET

The question of a constitution came up again when the Knesset was setting up its permanent committees for the first time. When it was proposed that as one of the nine permanent committees a Constitution, Law, and Justice Committee be established to consider, besides a constitution, all ordinary legislation of a technical legal character that would not fall within the area of competence of any of the other committees, some parliamentary Groups objected and moved that a separate committee be set up for the task of preparing a constitution. Their spokesmen charged the Government—now regularly constituted and confirmed by the Knesset—with seeking to drop the whole idea of a constitution, and noted that the first draft of the Government's recommendation for a committee system had not provided for the function of constitution-making at all. It was recalled that even the Provisional State Council, which had no constituent powers, had appointed a separate committee to prepare material for a constitution. The Knesset, however, approved the proposal for one Constitution, Law, and Justice Committee (briefly the ''Law Committee'') as it did later every term despite repeated proposals for a separate committee on the constitution; and as time was to show, that committee, which became one of the Knesset's busiest, could not deal at all expeditiously with constitutional matters. Even when a special subcommittee on Basic Laws was appointed, as was done in most Knessets, little was gained, as the parent committee would go over much the same ground on receiving a report from the subcommittee.

In November 1949 Prime Minister Ben-Gurion told the Knesset that he did not believe a constitution to be a pressing need at a time when the nation was bent on doubling its population in four years. He expressed the opinion that it was rather ''basic laws'' without special status that were needed, hinting on this occasion too at the direction that would be taken. The disposition of the Government to oppose the adoption of a formal constitution—even more clearly marked than that of its predecessor in the provisional period—led to a positive cabinet decision toward the end of 1949 favoring postponement of a constitution. The decision was taken while the Knesset's Law Committee was still considering the question. Although the Government's intervention on the question of a constitution was criticized even by members of the coalition, the Committee invited Ben-Gurion to appear and state the Government's position. In the end the Committee could not agree on any constitutional proposals and placed the whole problem before the house after circulating the protocols of its debates to all members of the Knesset and to the press. This inconclusive report resulted in a full-dress debate in the Knesset that ended with a compromise resolution adopted on 13 June 1950: "The First Knesset charges the Constitution, Law and Justice Committee with the duty of preparing a draft constitution for the State. The Constitution shall be composed of individual chapters in such a manner that each shall constitute a basic law in itself. Each chapter shall be brought before the Knesset as the Committee completes its work, and all chapters together will form the State Constitution."[3] The debate leading up to the resolution was of marathon proportions by Knesset standards. It took up seven sittings and drew forty speakers from all Groups. No time limit was fixed for speeches. Although the debate was not held on a party basis a clear alignment emerged: the great majority of the largest labor party, *Mapai,* and the Religious Front, opposed an early codified constitution while all other Groups and a few *Mapai* members were as strongly for adopting one. Since the arguments presented by both sides in this debate embraced virtually the whole gamut of opinion on the subject and resulted in the decision that still provides the procedural guideline for Israel's constitution makers, they deserve some attention.

The advocates of a written constitution asserted the need for the protection of civil rights and for setting limits to the powers of a simple parliamentary majority and of the Government. They declared that the failure to adopt a constitution would disappoint the people's expectations in view of the provisions of the United Nations Resolution, the declaration of the state, the promises held out by the work of the Provisional Council's Constitution Committee, and the election of a Constituent Assembly. They denied that the absence of a constitution in England could serve as an example since the legal system there was the product of centuries of tradition and many volumes of common law judgments. In particular they emphasized the educational value of a constitution and the cohesive social force it could provide in a country of immigrants with no firmly established political tradition.

The reasons advanced in opposition to a written constitution, or for seeking its postponement, were more various. It was contended that, as in the United States in the 1920s and early 1930s, a rigid constitution might be interpreted by a reactionary high court; that a minority would be able to prevent change or bar emergency laws essential for the state's security. But these arguments were scarcely applicable to a flexible constitution as proposed by some members, and in any case it was admitted that all constitutions have emergency provisions. There were pleas that dynamism would not be served by a rigid framework and that special legislation to meet concrete problems was a more urgent need at a time when many thousands of immigrants were still in transit camps. Some speakers insisted that the state was not yet fully established, that 7 percent of the Jewish people had no right to adopt a constitution for the nation, and that, moreover, the inspiration and experience for the writing of a constitution were lacking. The examples of the United States, where it took from 1776 to 1791 to produce the Constitution, and of the Soviet Union, where it took thirteen years, were adduced. It was also asserted that in a free country, where all that is not forbidden by law is permitted, it was not necessary to declare the freedoms, and that at all events the state already had a constitution in the Transition and other organic laws. The weakness of some of these temporizing arguments was that they in fact lent greater force to the plea for an immediate start on the preparation of a constitution.

With a note of sarcasm one member drew attention to a circular argument used by the opponents of a constitution: "When the subject was debated in the Provisional State Council we were referred to the First Knesset, which would have sovereign power, and today, when we come to the Knesset, we are told that the Provisional State Council already decided not to write a constitution."[4]

The most impassioned argument against a constitution was that of the Religious Front speakers: that as a Jewish nation Israel had a constitution in the Torah or Mosaic law, and that no secular document could take its place. This objection was perhaps the most influential factor underlying the shift of position on a constitution that had occurred since the early days of the state. Religious opposition in fact extended also to a flexible constitution in the mistrust of any preamble making declaratory statements as to the nature of the state. Also many speakers from the socialist *Mapai* Group alluded to the ideological strife that would attend the drafting of a constitution; although some had in mind economic ideology as well, it was apparent that they were much more concerned about the sensibilities of their chief coalition partner, the Religious Front, than about those of the Marxian opposition, *Mapam* (United Workers Party), who admitted to small hopes of securing recognition of their doctrines in a state constitution, although they argued for one strongly.

But the *Mapai* speakers not only sought to preserve the coalition. Beyond the welter of arguments which were raised against a constitution was the natural interest of the dominant party in the coalition of preserving for itself the largest measure of unhampered freedom to govern. Conversely, most smaller and opposition Groups sought to put limitations on the powers of the

Government and of the parliamentary majority. In this connection it should be noted that the achievement of a simple majority presents little difficulty in the unicameral Knesset, which is one of the very few parliaments without quorum requirements. Force was lent to this argument with the enactment of the Basic Law on the Knesset in 1958, whose Section 24 provided that "The Knesset shall hold debates and pass decisions whatever the number of members present." In reading through some twenty constitutions of parliamentary democracies the author found that only in two other parliaments, those of Sweden and Finland, is no quorum required. However, the constitutions of those two countries are silent on the subject (so that they at least leave it open to parliament to provide for a quorum by legislation or by its own rules of procedure). No example was found of a preemptive clause like the aforesaid Section 24. Moreover, since Section 25 of the Basic Law goes on to say "the Knesset shall pass its decisions by a majority of those participating in the voting," a tiny minority of the Knesset, in the absence of delaying powers by a Second Chamber or veto authority by the president of the state, may have the final say in all but a few entrenched matters to be discussed below.

More recently it has been further argued that because of the different strata comprising Israel's legal system—Ottoman and mandatory law, the English common law and doctrines of equity, the personal status laws of the various religious communities and, of course, original Israeli laws—the Knesset lacks guidelines to legislative acts to determine if they comport to fundamental norms.[5]

BASIC LAWS

The debate did not in fact end with the resolution of 1950 but narrowed down to the issue of constitutional rigidity, with Ben-Gurion and his followers interpreting the resolution as a decision for a completely flexible constitution permitting no privileged laws. Indeed the resolution said nothing about the scope of the Basic Laws and contained no definite provision for their codification. It did not state at all whether, when, and how the separate Basic Laws or ultimate code were to be placed above ordinary legislation. Although its wording indicated the intention of completing the task in the First Knesset, it fixed no time limit for the adoption of the Basic Laws. In fact, it was not until well into the Third Knesset, nearly eight years after the resolution was passed, that the first Basic Law, that on the Knesset (1958), was enacted. It took a further stretch of twenty-six years for the passage of seven more Basic Laws: Israel Lands (1960), the President of the State (1964), the

Government (1968), the State Economy (1975), the Army (1976), Jerusalem, Capital of Israel (1980), and the Judiciary (1984). With the normative status of these laws as constitutional chapters unclear, the 1950 resolution, though framed as a compromise, was in effect a successful dilatory move.

The subject matters of the eight Basic Laws, as evident also from their titles, are distinctly organic in character. But since the resolution of 1950 did not define the term "Basic Law," many considered it to apply to all laws of fundamental constitutional content passed by the Knesset, like, for example, the Law of the Return (1950), which provides that every Jew has the right to immigrate to Israel, or the Nationality Law (1952). And since Basic Laws in the formal sense of the resolution were slow in coming, the distinction between these and other laws basic in the material sense was easily blurred. At one point Knesset Chairman Kadish Luz cited twenty-two "laws of a constitutional nature" in addition to the two formal Basic Laws then on the statute books and asserted that the task laid down in the 1950 resolution had already been largely accomplished.[6] As more Basic Laws were passed and drafts of others presented, while each new Government promised in its Policy Fundamentals to hasten their enactment and each Knesset had a subcommittee appointed for the preparation of Basic Laws, differentiation between Basic and other laws became an accepted fact.

However, except for their titles, which designate them Basic Laws and omit the year of enactment, there is little that sets these eight statutes unmistakably apart as constitutional norms. Five of them begin with a short declarative section; and only four, those on the Knesset, the State economy, the Army, and the Judiciary, are also couched in general statements that expressly leave details to ordinary legislation in the manner of a constitutional law.

All eight Basic Laws and amendments to them were enacted by the ordinary legislative procedure; one of the amendments was not even passed as an amendment to a Basic Law but simply as a section within an ordinary statute.[7] Although these Laws and amendments were as a rule prepared for their second reading by the Knesset's Law Committee, only the first Law was initiated in the spirit of the 1950 resolution by that Committee: six were sponsored by the Government and one by a member of the Knesset. A Government-sponsored amendment to the Basic Law on the State Economy, to enable it to delay the 1984 budget presentation, was not even referred to the Law Committee: the house sent it instead to the Finance Committee.

The most significant feature of the Basic Laws is the entrenched clauses which a number of them contain. The Basic Law on the Knesset has sections providing that the electoral system may be altered only by an absolute majority of the Knesset, and that the Law is to remain unaffected by Emergency Regulations unless a two-thirds majority decide otherwise. The Basic

Law on the Government has a similar provision concerning Emergency Regulations but stipulates an absolute majority for its alteration. A section in the Judiciary Law makes it unconditionally immune from such Regulations.

A significant turn in the state's constitutional development resulted from the existence of the extra-ordinary majority clause for the electoral system. The Election Financing Law of 1969, held to be repugnant to that clause in that it created an inequality between political parties, was annulled (in *Bergman* v. *Minister of Finance*)[8] by the Israel Supreme Court, sitting as the High Court of Justice, because the measure had not been passed with an absolute majority of the Knesset. Opponents of a rigid constitution had argued for long years that the Knesset could not bind itself and that the judiciary could not properly have a role in constitutional matters. The right of the courts respecting Basic Laws was recognized, however, by the Knesset itself when it amended the Election Financing Law, later in 1969, to conform to the requirements of equality established by the High Court decision, while also making sure of an absolute-majority vote.

Following the 1969 judgment in the Bergman case, election legislation was twice again invalidated on the very same ground, after being enacted without the required majority of sixty-one. In 1981 an amendment to the election propaganda law, which cut the television time allotted to new parties and increased the time given to large parties, was found by the High Court of Justice to contravene the equality provision in the entrenched election clause and was therefore annulled; the Knesset responded on that occasion with an amendment less disadvantageous to small parties and adopted with an absolute majority. Similarly, when a 1982 amendment to the Political Parties Financing Law retrospectively increased the ceiling on party spending, thus favoring the parties that had overspent in the 1981 election campaign, the Court quashed the retroactivity clause and required those parties to pay the statutory penalty amounting to 15 percent of their state funding.

In recognition, as it were, of the facts created by the Bergman decision, two drafts for Basic Laws published by the Justice Department in 1971—one on the Courts and the other on the legislative process—included dispositions that purported to define Basic Laws and to provide for the review of other laws in their light by the Israel Supreme Court sitting as the Constitutional Court. A Basic Law was defined simply as one passed by an absolute majority of the Knesset. By the same token it would be subject to alteration or repeal by an ordinary law, provided that law too was adopted by such a majority. Judicial review would be confined, first, to an examination of whether a statute contradicts a Basic Law, and then, if it does, whether it was enacted by the proper majority.

While the 1971 draft law on the Courts made no progress, a fresh bill for such a Basic Law, introduced by a later Government, was enacted as the Basic Law on the Judiciary in 1984, after the legislative process had spanned two terms. The draft law on the legislative process was tabled in the Knesset only in 1975, and brought forward by the minister of justice after some months, after being urged that the Subcommittee on Basic Laws was without employment;[9] but it did not reach the committee stage. In 1978 Justice Minister S. Tamir tabled a new draft law on legislation which he described as an improvement on the earlier draft; for the alteration of any provision of a Basic Law it would require a two-thirds majority of the Knesset and a declaration to the effect that the law is being adopted notwithstanding the provisions of the Basic Law. Though the bill did not proceed then beyond the minister's opening speech, its formulation continued to be a subject of debate as the rigidity of the constitution will rest essentially on its provisions.

Although the Government has taken the initiative in the enactment of most Basic Laws, and ministers of justice of whatever party affiliation have consistently promised to expedite outstanding bills for Basic Laws with a view to achieving a constitution, their conduct in this regard, as in the above instance, seemed at times forced. The bill for the Basic Law on the State Economy, though ready in 1971, was tabled by the Government only two years later, in the last session of the Seventh Knesset, and then as if only to forestall a similar bill tabled a month earlier by an opposition member.[10] The bill was not reported back to the house from the committee before the Knesset completed its term; and only in the following Knesset, in 1975, was it passed into law. The Basic Law on the Army, also enacted in 1975, clearly came in response to contingency: Justice Minister Zadok in introducing the bill admitted that it was primarily an answer to the need emphasized by the Agranat Commission on the Yom Kippur War, of clearly defining relations between the civil and military authorities. However, one can hardly charge any Government with procrastination in the enactment of Basic Laws since the Knesset resolution of 1950 did not place responsibility on the executive for initiating or expediting such legislation.

Of the many Basic Laws proposed by members, the only one enacted (not counting amendments), that on Jerusalem, was due to the initiative of an opposition member. The bill was supported by a majority mainly for reasons of sentiment, and in reaction to a growing campaign by the PLO (Palestine Liberation Organization) and the United Nations to make Jerusalem subject to negotiation.

The most drawn out course has been that of the proposed Basic Law on civil rights. As far back as 1955 or 1956 the attorney general told the Law Committee of the Knesset that he had ready a draft for the civil rights chapter of the constitution.[11] Between 1960 and 1964 the Knesset was told by two successive ministers of justice at least on three occasions of the bill's preparation.[12] Yet, as if nothing had come before, J. S. Shapira, a third minister of Justice—in another Government but of the same coalition—told the house in 1966 that the Government had turned to the Law Committee and asked it to prepare such a bill.[13] Two years later the Chairman of the Subcommittee on Basic Laws that had been set up in the course of the same Knesset said that the Subcommittee was considering a civil rights bill on its own initiative.[14]

The Subcommittee, under a different chairman, considered the bill further for more than three years before completing its preparation in October 1972. It was then referred back to the Law Committee, which went over it in detail and approved it only in July 1973, just a week before the final adjournment of the Seventh Knesset. The draft Basic Law on Human and Civil Rights was gazetted on 12 August, well after the last regular sitting of the house. Despite attempts by opposition groups to secure its first reading at a special session, the bill made no further headway in the Seventh Knesset; it was given first reading in the Eighth in August 1974. In December 1979, more than five years later, and halfway through the Ninth Knesset, the Law Committee requested that the Continuity Law (see Chapter 10) be applied to the bill. But the bill went no further.

The tortuous progress of the human rights measure was not accidental; it points up Israel's keen awareness that she is a nation under siege by most Arab countries, and helps to explain the arguments repeatedly advanced in the 1950 debate, that she must have the legal means to protect herself swiftly against extremist and subversive elements. Hence also the repeated reference to a civil rights bill as a particularly "difficult and delicate" matter.[15] The problem was frankly stated in 1973 by Knesset Member H. J. Zadok, who later became minister of justice:

> I admit to some hesitation about the propriety of the present time, which is one of emergency for us, surrounded as we are by enemies from without and defending ourselves against saboteur acts from within, for enacting a law on civil liberties. I am troubled by the thought that in these circumstances we may fail to strike a reasonable balance and will tend to lean the scale in favour of increased governmental authority, to the detriment of the individual's basic rights.[16]

It is significant therefore that while the above civil rights bill contained a repugnance clause, it was excluded from applying to existing laws; only legislation enacted after the Basic Law and found to contradict one of its provisions would have been invalid. This distinction, which might well have produced confusion in Israel's legal system, can be explained only as an attempt to leave intact the various defense regulations and emergency provisions dating largely from the time of the mandatory regime, that had been found necessary for the nation's security but that would have been at variance with the dispositions of the proposed Basic Law on civil rights.[17] Significantly too, unlike the Basic Laws on the Knesset and on the Government, the proposed law did not contain an entrenched clause preventing its alteration by Emergency Regulations without a special majority.

A further impediment to comprehensive civil rights legislation should not be overlooked. The apprehensions of the religious parties about a written constitution, noted earlier, were given specific expression in relation to the civil rights bill. In particular, Section 14 of the proposed law, that "Every person is entitled to the freedom of divine worship," struck a note that could not but threaten encroachment on the favored position of Orthodoxy in the state. The spokesman for the Religious Torah Front called that section the most "shocking."[18]

The thorny problem of civil liberties in Israel notwithstanding, legislators have continued to press for a bill of rights. The Tenth Knesset saw another serious attempt when, in 1983, first reading was given to a draft Basic Law on Human Rights which had been struck off the agenda in 1964; originally the initiative of H. Klinghoffer, it was reintroduced, with small exaggeration a generation later, by his former student, A. Rubinstein. In committee, more than a year of intensive work on the proposal—in which use was made of the earlier versions and other constitutions, and specialists and material witnesses were heard—produced a draft that sought to meet objections which had stymied previous efforts. But the bill still awaited passage into law.

In generalizing about Israel's constitutional development it is pertinent to note that the very concept of Basic Laws as constitutional acts has been questioned with the argument that such acts can derive only from a trust relationship between the electorate and the particular men whom they have elected for the avowed purpose of writing a constitution. However, the prevailing view is that since the First Knesset, undeniably a constituent assembly, transferred its powers by statute to all succeeding Knessets,[19] the constituent power has remained legally unbroken. At the same time no one has ever challenged the effective reaffirmation by every Knesset of the "individual chapters" resolution of 1950 as the procedure for writing a constitution. And as the process inches forward its realization appears to be within sight. With the adoption of the Basic Law on the Judiciary in 1984, Justice Minister M. Nissim expressed confidence that within the following two years the Knesset could pass the three additional Laws necessary for the constitution's completion—those on human rights, state control, and legislation—and held out the prospect of early codification by compression of the eleven Laws together into some one hundred sections.

4

Elections and Parties

THE PARTY-LIST SYSTEM

THE KNESSET IS ELECTED by a proportional party-list system in which the entire country forms one constituency. The requirement of "general, country-wide, direct, equal, secret and proportional" elections, which had formed part of the Election Law from the outset, was reenacted in 1958 as Section 4 of the Basic Law on the Knesset, with the further provision that the section shall not be altered save by an absolute majority of the Knesset. The entrenchment by a special majority clause was tacked on through the initiative of members primarily concerned with preserving the system of proportional representation.

In its essentials the electoral system dates back to 1918, three decades before the establishment of the state, when it was adopted at Jaffa as the Election Regulations for Palestine Jewry's first Elected Assembly. However, the party-list system in Knesset elections is less flexible in two ways than was that of the pre-state Assemblies. First, though proportional party representation in the Assembly was calculated on a countrywide basis (except in the 1925 election, to the Second Assembly, which was according to districts), lists of candidates were initially submitted locally, and elected members were technically representatives of local communities. Second, in the pre-state polling the voter had the right to erase names from the list for which he ballotted. A candidate whose name was deleted on half the ballot papers cast for his party would drop to the bottom of its list. On the other hand, in elections to the Knesset each party or electoral bloc presents one countrywide list of candidates that cannot be altered in any way by the voter; the ballot contains only the Hebrew letter or letters which are the election symbol of the party or bloc. The voter's right to erase names might have become a feature also of the state's electoral system since the Election Ordinance proposed by the Provisional Government contained such a disposition; but it was deleted by the State Council.

The system of election prescribed by ordinance of the Provisional State Council in 1948 has remained essentially the same over the years, subsequent enactment of new or amending election laws notwithstanding. In the provisions for the administration of elections by an all-party Central Elections Committee chaired by a Supreme Court judge, with a parallel system of District and Polling committees, there is little difference between the 1948 ordinance and the consolidated election law of 1969. Politically composed committees for the conduct of voting at the polling-station level, where one or two state-employed and trained clerical workers could do the job more efficiently, have been repeatedly criticized. But the only result was the provision, in 1973, for secretaries of polling committees in an advisory capacity. In 1981, the politicization of the polling committees was carried even a step further by an amendment transferring from the regional elections committee to the parties the right to appoint the representatives of the parties on the polling committees; representatives of at least three party lists, or candidates lists, as the law neutrally terms them, were still required on every polling committee.

The 1948 ordinance required the endorsement of a candidates list by 250 signatures. The Second Knesset Election Law, 1951, raised the number of signatures needed for a list to 750 but exempted parties represented in the outgoing Knesset from this requirement. The number of required signatures for a new list was raised further from time to time and stood at twenty-five hundred in 1984. The deposit of a sum of money with the Elections Committee by a new list, to be forfeited in part to the Treasury if it failed to be confirmed by the Committee and forfeited entirely if it failed to have a single candidate elected, was first required in 1961; it amounted in 1984, after a number of increases to take account of devaluation, to IS 500,000 (equivalent to 2,800 US$). A stipulation introduced by an amendment in 1951 that a list must receive at least 1 percent of the vote in order to share in the distribution of Knesset seats, has remained unchanged. However, as Table 2 shows, none of these restrictions had any long-term effect in reducing either the number of Groups in the Knesset or of "fly-by-night" lists.

The fortunes of small parties, and less fatefully of the larger, have varied according to the method used for allotting Knesset seats which remain after the initial distribution following elections. There are always a number of such seats since in the first round of distribution mandates are awarded to each list according to the whole number obtained by dividing its vote by the

Table 2

Success Rates of Candidates' Lists in Elections to the Knesset

Election	Candidates Lists	Lists Failing to Secure One Seat	Parliamentary Groups in the Knesset*
1949	21	9	12
1951	17	2	15
1955	18	6	12
1959	24	12	12
1961	14	3	11
1965	17	4	13
1969	21	11	10
1973	21	11	10
1977	22	9	13
1981	31	21	10
1984	26	11	15

*As at the opening of each Knesset. In the course of most terms one or more splits or mergers altered the figure.

quota per seat. The quota is determined by dividing the total vote (minus votes cast for lists which have not crossed the 1 percent qualifying threshold) by 120. In the 1977 election six seats remained to be allocated after the initial distribution, and in the 1981 election seven seats. The law with regard to allotting remaining seats has zigzagged between two methods: one, of awarding additional seats to the lists with the largest remainders of votes; the other, of awarding each additional seat to the list with the highest average vote per seat. The award of seats, according to largest remainder, which was practiced in the pre-state period and through the years 1951–69, offers the same chance of securing an additional seat to all lists; indeed, in the pre-state period even a list that failed to gain a single seat in the Elected Assembly in the initial distribution, might secure one of the additional seats by that method. On the other hand, the highest-average formula, which was applied in the 1949 election and again from 1973, is advantageous to the larger parties while it is more rigorously proportional. It should be noted that the Second Knesset Election Law, 1951, which first required 750 signatures and the 1 percent minimum vote, both restrictive to new and small groups, in effect redressed the balance by replacing the highest-average with the largest-remainder formula for additional seats; once a list passed the raised barrier, even if it obtained just one seat, it had a like chance with all other lists of securing another with its surplus.

When in 1973, after the largest-remainder method had been applied in six elections, a member's bill reverting to the highest-average formula came before the Knesset, it was vigorously supported by the two largest parliamentary Groups, the Labor Alignment and *Gahal*. Although respectively of the coalition and opposition, the two Groups united on a measure which could benefit them equally, with a member from each as its cosponsor. (Hence the bill's label, ''Bader-Ofer Formula,'' though it was in fact only a slight modification of the D'Hondt system.) But the first and second reading debates turned into all-night sittings as the smaller Groups used every procedural maneuver they could summon up to obstruct the bill's passage, without success. In character with this large-versus-small-party hassle, the National Religious party (NRP), which was the third largest party and faced no threat from the highest-average formula, seemed to be of two minds; though its spokesman attacked the bill, more than half the Group's members were absent from the roll-call votes on the first and third readings, while on second reading none of its members brought amendments as did all the smaller Groups. Vindicating the position taken by each side in the above debate, the subsequent election in December 1973, brought an additional seat to both the Alignment and *Likud* (*Gahal,* combined with smaller allies), while the earlier method, of largest remainders, would have awarded these seats to *Moked* and to the Independent Liberals, both small parties. NRP would have fared alike by either method.[1]

The law has remained unchanged with respect to prearranged combination of votes. Any two parties which have made a prior agreement, registered with the Central Elections Committee, to pool their votes for the purpose of sharing in the distribution of the mandates, can combine them so that the list whose separate remainder was the larger may get an additional seat. For example, such arrangement in the 1981 election between *Shinui* and the Civil Rights and Peace Movement secured a second mandate for *Shinui* after each list had earned only one in the initial distribution.

The electoral system has been criticized on three main grounds: that in encouraging multipartism and coalition rule it impedes truly responsible government; that it facilitates undemocratic choice of candidates; and that it separates between electors and representatives. The last two strictures are clearly interrelated. We shall consider each in turn.

While proportional representation makes for a regime of many parties, the State of Israel was in fact founded on a multiparty system (as shown in Chapters 1 and 2), the method of election serving merely to reinforce the preexisting structure. One can fairly say that Israel's proportional electoral system was chosen to suit the existing political patterns. Her first and appointed legislature, the Provisional State Council, representing the political spectrum of Palestine Jewry—and that incompletely—had eleven political

Groups (with two religious Groups formed by four parties). A national election held nine months after independence, in January 1949, altered the political landscape but little. Its main result was to correct distortions of Group strength due to the smallness of the Provisional State Council and to the disproportionately high representation in it of the General and Religious Zionists, whose relatively stronger position in the World Zionist Organization was reflected in its Palestinian governing bodies; and these bodies had taken the leading part in creating the provisional legislature (see Chapter 2). The changes effected by that first election are shown in Table 3.

It cannot be denied, however, that if the electoral system has not produced multipartism, it has helped preserve it. And while the coalition necessary to maintain a government has usually shown a remarkable capacity to survive, the price has often been concessions to some partners beyond what is justified by their popularity at the polls. As a consequence of coalition

Table 3

Changes of Political Composition from the Provisional State Council to the First Knesset

	Provisional State Council		First Knesset	
Party Group*	Percentage	Members	Percentage	Members
Mapai	27.0	10	35.7	46
General Zionists	16.2	6	5.2	7
Mizrahi and *Hapoel Hamizrahi*†	13.5	5		
Agudat Yisrael and			12.2	16
Poalei Agudat Yisrael†	8.1	3		
Mapam	13.5	5	14.7	19
Revisionists, *Herut*‡	8.1	3	11.5	14
Aliyah Hadashah Progressives §	2.7	1	4.1	5
WIZO	2.7	1	1.2	1
Sephardi Association	2.7	1	3.5	4
Yemenite Association	2.7	1	1.0	1
Communist party	2.7	1	3.5	4
Others			2.9	3
Total		37		120

*For explanation of Group names, see Glossary.

†The four parties formed one United Religious Front in the First Knesset.

‡The Revisionists were represented in the Provisional Council. *Herut*, which largely absorbed that body, was represented in the First and later Knessets.

§*Aliyah Hadashah*, represented separately in the Provisional Council, joined with dissident General Zionists to form the Progressive party in the First Knesset.

agreements, the charge is frequently made that there is only a weak correspondence between ballotting results and the kind of Government which takes office (see also Chapter 12).

The elimination of tiny political groups and the inducement of mergers have been the chief motives behind repeated proposals to raise the one-percent minimum of votes required by a candidates list since 1951 for sharing in the distribution of Knesset seats. The simple and direct way in which such a step would have effect and the prospect it offers of forestalling more fundamental electoral reforms have won it advocates time and time again. In 1953, the two largest parties at the time, *Mapai* and the General Zionists, considered setting the minimum percentage of votes at 10 percent. The smaller parties vigorously opposed the idea. In 1954, the Progressive party refused to enter the coalition Government until the latter abandoned the idea of raising the minimum percentage. In 1981, although the Government was committed to the introduction of district elections, so that the need for any minimum-vote clause would be eliminated, a member's bill was introduced that would set a 2½ percent threshold. The bill was defeated by a vote of forty-four to thirty-seven. The substantial support for the bill, and the fact that its chief sponsors were coalition leaders, indicated perhaps a wishful pessimism about prospects for the more radical reform. Labor then opposed the bill because it would have eliminated the small Arab lists formed on a regional and personal basis, who traditionally supported labor, as well as two tiny Groups to whom Labor was obligated for cooperative voting against the Government.[2] In the event, Labor reserved a safe slot for an Arab candidate on its own list in 1981 and continued to do so in subsequent elections. Labor's partner in the Alignment, *Mapam,* had always included Arabs among its candidates.

The method by which most political parties nominate candidates for election to the Knesset has been subject to criticism no less than the multi-party system. Except for the short-lived Democratic Party for Change (DMC), whose rank-and-file membership determined the candidates list in the 1977 election, political parties have generally employed centralized and oligarchic methods for putting together their lists. The most usual practice has been for the leadership of the party to turn over the preparation of the list to a small nominations committee which reports to the party's Central Committee; the last body may, perhaps, by secret vote effect changes in the personnel and in the list order which after all determines the real chances of each candidate. A somewhat more democratic method which has gained favor has been to leave the choice of a proportion of the candidates to the party's regions or sectors; but then too, the final order on the list has been fixed by the nominations and Central committees. In 1981, the five-member nominations committee appointed by Labor party Chairman Shimon Peres was itself overruled by two powerful branch chiefs.[3] *Herut* and the Liberals have in recent elections both entrusted the choice of head of the list and the entire task of naming the candidates and arranging their order to their Central Committees numbering, respectively, 1,000 and 240 members.

However, even the least democratic nomination methods have not been wholly arbitrary. A nominations committee whose aim is to draw the largest number of voters must attempt to produce a candidates list representative in some degree of the party's natural constituencies whether of region, faction, community of origin, or other nature. For example, in the elections to the 1973–77 Knesset, the Labor party took into consideration seven constituencies for its safe places on the joint Labor Alignment list: Tel Aviv, Haifa, Jerusalem, cooperative settlements, affiliated collectives (kibbutzim), the north of the country, and the south. The National Religious party divided its list among its four organized factions in that election. To take a small party as an example, in the 1973 election the Independent Liberals allocated the five "realistic" places on their list to three urban leaders, one kibbutz member and one representative of the Eastern communities. A party will usually seek to include on its list also women, representatives of young-members divisions and of influential occupational and economic sectors, and so on. A candidate who can represent more than one of the party's constituencies will usually be given preference. On the other hand, as a representative imposed by the party's central bodies on his "constituents," he may not be acceptable to them, and the nomination will boomerang. This has happened more than once with the choice of candidates from the Eastern Communities, referred to variously as Sephardi or Oriental, who are in any case from origins as diverse as North Africa, the Balkans, Kurdistan, and Yemen. As a device to facilitate change of blood in the candidates list, the Labor and Liberal parties have required members seeking a third term in the Knesset to gain the support of at lest 60 percent of the party's Central Committee; the Liberals did away with this hurdle for the 1984 election.

The increasing tendency to concentrate final decision making with respect to the candidates list in a wider party group, such as the Central Committee, with a membership of hundreds, has not always proved satisfactory. According to a Liberal leader, the factions of whose party sought in 1983 to revive the small nominations committee so that it would order the candidates on the list after their choice by the Central Committee, that system is more honest and fair than internal election of candidates accompanied by manipulations and deals, which produces a list without the qualifications and balance of talent that the Knesset requires.[4] Lending some support for this view was the experience in 1977 of DMC, the composition of whose candidates list, elected by the rank and file of party members, came as a shock to many;

the first fifteen candidates (the number later elected), included only one Sephardi (a second was Israeli-born), no women, but two members of the relatively small Druze community.

Some early nomination practices would be illegal today. For example, there was nothing to prevent the placing of Golda Meir on a candidates list in 1949, while she was serving as Israel's ambassador to Moscow. Today the election law provides that a senior state employee or army officer who is to be a candidate for election to the Knesset must give up his position at least 100 days before the election.

No matter by what method a party has picked its candidates, if it is part of a political bloc, the finally ordered list of the alliance of parties will be determined by a prearranged agreement between the partners. Thus, when the *Herut* and Liberal parties formed the *Gahal* bloc in 1965 they agreed to a slate on which each would get eleven of the first twenty-two places, the very first going to a *Herut* nominee, the second to a Liberal, with continuing regular alternation; of the eighteen following slots, eleven would go to *Herut,* seven to the Liberals; the remainder of the list would revert to the parity arrangement. This ordering between the two parties remained unchanged through five elections, even after *Gahal* was joined by other political forces to become the *Likud,* the newer partners affecting only the overall composition of the candidates list. Only toward the 1984 election, at the insistence of *Herut,* was the ordering altered somewhat.

The composite nature of a candidates list will be even more rigid where a party, as well as being part of an allied bloc, must leave the initial choice of its candidates to the component wings maintaining loyalties to old political frameworks. The Labor party, while sharing the candidates list of the Labor Alignment with its ally, *Mapam,* had in a number of elections to provide for fair representation of each of its three historic wings, *Mapai, Ahdut Ha'avoda,* and *Rafi,* the formally disbanded parties who together had founded the united party in 1968. The formal constraints that may operate in determining a candidates list can be appreciated from the arithmetical regularity with which the four components of the Alignment list were arranged in the elections of 1969, 1973, and 1977 (see Table 4). In the 1981 election the same Labor-*Mapam* ratio was maintained. And in addition a safe slot among the Labor party candidates had to be reserved for a member of its Religious Worker faction. *Mapam* in turn nominated its candidates to the combined Alignment list according to a prearranged formula: after the party secretary-general in the first place, there were nominated alternately candidates from the kibbutzim and from the cities, with the fifth and eleventh nominations reserved for Arab candidates and the sixth or seventh for a woman.

Alongside of formal restrictions such as the above, the general assumption in a political party has been that only its leaders and central bodies, who

Table 4

Composition of the Labor Alignment Candidates List in 1969, 1973, and 1977*

The Two Parties	The Party Wings	Number Out of Every Seven Candidates in the Alignment List
Labor party	*Mapai*	4
	Ahdut Ha'avodah	1
	Rafi	1
Mapam		1

*For an explanation of Hebrew names, see Glossary.

command an overall view, can put together a balanced and well-rounded list of candidates. And they have often made choices of expediency. A list may include a distinguished academic or man of letters as a drawing card though he represents no particular sector and lacks genuine political drive. The poet U. Z. Greenberg, placed second on the *Herut* list and elected in 1949, was never again a candidate. Yizhar Smilanski, the novelist, who was induced to stand on the *Mapai* list in 1949, served in six Knessets though never an active parliamentarian; in his last term, as a *Rafi* member, he resigned midway, after going abroad to study. In 1965, *Mapai* secured the election of the universally respected literature professor, Dov Sadan, who resigned before completing the term.

Since the central party organization fixes both the composition of the candidates list and the candidates' order, it is natural that there should be a more real obligation of elected members to party leaders than to amorphous electoral constituencies. Hence the charge that the system of election to the Knesset separates between voters and representatives. In an effort to combat this charge a number of parties, early in the 1970s, instituted regional parliamentary offices. The Labor Party, with the inauguration of such offices in Tel Aviv in 1971, announced that they would be open twice monthly for one and a half hours to take up queries from the public, receive suggestions, and discuss problems. However, no party ever made this activity mandatory for all its Knesset members. Moreover, it was considered by some merely a move to anticipate electoral reform.

A further weakness of the centralized control of elections, notwithstanding the "balancing" of lists, showed itself in the signal failure, in the 1981 election, to accommodate divisions between Israel's ingathered communities. Candidates lists based on community of origin had long been a familiar phenomenon. In the elections to the pre-state Assemblies and to the First and Second Knessets, both Sephardi and Yemenite organizations won representation. However, from the 1955 election until 1981 no communal list secured a single representative in the Knesset although a few campaigned each time. Though there was a series of riots in 1959 by immigrants from Muslim countries, and there were protest movements in the 1970s that took a political turn, the overwhelming majority among the Oriental communities preferred ultimately to press their interests through established and integrated parties. Yet, though Knesset members of Sephardi origin were elected through those parties in increasing numbers over the years, the Eastern communities remained underrepresented and the socioeconomic gap between them and the rest of the population far from closed. In the 1981 election the smoldering communal issue injected itself with renewed passion. A half-dozen communal lists campaigned in the election, with *Tami,* supported chiefly by Moroccan Jews, winning three mandates. The voters for *Tami* came largely from the National Religious party (NRP), which had been torn apart by a Sephardi revolt that reduced its strength in the new Knesset by half.

Though most Sephardi voters in the 1981 election consistently supported one of the two large electoral blocs, *Likud* or the Labor Alignment, both these forces were bedevilled by the communal issue. The *Likud* was greatly embarrassed when overenthusiastic supporters resorted to violence against Alignment meetings and property in the course of the election campaign. The Alignment, though in opposition, was perceived as the "establishment" by the largely Sephardi population of the development towns whose depressed living standards were in sharp contrast to the prosperity of neighboring kibbutzim affiliated with the labor parties, and whose breadwinners often depended for employment on kibbutz industries. There resulted a polarization between the two large electoral blocs in communal terms which neither had sought. Sixty percent of Sephardim voted *Likud* and 30 percent Alignment, while approximately the same percentages in reverse were true for Ashkenazim (Jews of European origin).[5] And these results bore no relation to the composition of the respective candidates lists, since more Sephardim were in fact returned to the Knesset from the Alignment than the *Likud* list.

Though in the election of July 1984 the communal note was more muted in the contest between the two large blocs, the vote indicated a continued and even more sharpened division between Ashkenazi and Sephardi in respect of political alignment. Further, in 1984 the more traditionally Orthodox *Agudat Yisrael,* like NRP earlier, was riven, losing half its supporters to the Sephardi Torah Guardians, who garnered four mandates. With *Tami* back with one member, there were now two distinctly communal parties represented in the Knesset. Curiously, the religious parties, whose solidarity benefits from the strong cementing factor of faith, have been the most vulnerable to communal dissension.

REPLACEMENT OF A KNESSET MEMBER

A seat in the Knesset may fall vacant for any of four reasons: the member's resignation, his death, termination of his membership because of election or appointment to one of certain specified posts, or his removal from membership because of conviction of a criminal offense with a prison sentence of at least a year. In every case the seat is filled by the candidate next in order on the list of the resigned or deceased member's Group. Thus, even in the last days of a Knesset term, the new member will automatically take his place in the house and make his declaration of allegiance.

A member may resign by submitting a letter of resignation to the Knesset chairman, signed on the day of its presentation, or of its transmission through an authorized person. The membership of the resigning member ceases forty-eight hours after the letter has reached the chairman, unless the member has withdrawn his resignation before then; indeed the purpose of the interval is to enable a hasty member to relent in time. His successor becomes a member for purposes of parliamentary immunity immediately with the coming into force of the resignation. However, to enjoy other rights of a member—to speak and vote in the house, and to draw a salary—the new member must make the declaration of allegiance, which the chair calls him to do as soon as he first takes his seat. When a member dies, his successor becomes a member at once. But only after a memorial sitting for the deceased member, normally held by the Knesset after the seven days of mourning have passed, will the new member take his seat and make his declaration of allegiance.

If a member is elected or appointed to one of the posts whose incumbent is debarred from being a candidate for the Knesset, his membership ceases automatically upon election or appointment. (These posts include those of president of the state, state comptroller, judges, ministers of religion, senior state employees, and army officers.) Again, the new member has only to make his declaration of allegiance.

If convicted of a criminal offense and sentenced to prison for one year or more, a member, on the complaint of at least ten Knesset members to the House Committee and its consequent recommendation, may be unseated by a two-thirds majority of the Knesset after he has been heard in his defense both in the committee and in the house. Once the Knesset has resolved to deprive the member of his seat, it is filled as automatically as in the other cases. While the member's sentence is under appeal he may, on the proposal of another member, be suspended from the Knesset by a simple majority vote of the House Committee. A member sentenced to any prison term for a criminal offense may be thus suspended. The suspended member is replaced by the candidate next on his list for the duration of the appeal or the sentence.

In 1981, shortly after the enactment of the suspension provisions, the House Committee suspended a member while he was appealing a nine-month sentence on counts of election bribery. The District Court overturned the suspension because the sentence involved was under a year. (The final sentence came after the following election, in which the member failed to win a seat.) Since the sentenced member had been elected from a one-name candidates list, his suspension, if confirmed by the higher court, would have left the Knesset with 119 members and no way of bringing the membership back up to 120. However, the Basic Law only provides that the Knesset shall number 120 members on election, so that its function later with a smaller number would not be a formal defect.

The party-list system has enabled Knesset members to resign their seats for their own or their party's convenience in a casual manner, hardly intended by the electors. Mr. H. J. Zadok, a former minister and chairman of Knesset committees, finding little to absorb his energies when reelected in 1977, with his party in opposition for the first time, resigned that year. S. Wertheimer resigned his seat in 1981 after the Knesset had already passed a dissolution law fixing the next election date; though, as a busy industrialist, he had not given full attention to Knesset duties, his resignation so close to the end of the term, to make way for the popular Stella Levy, a former Womens Corps commander, had the appearance of a party tactic. There have been instances of prominent personalities nominated to grace a candidates list, with an understanding that they would resign from the Knesset immediately after their election to make way for candidates farther down the list. In such circumstances four former army officers of distinction on the *Mapai* list resigned immediately upon being elected in 1949. In 1965, the former chief of staff, Tsvi Tsur, upon being elected, did not even trouble to make the member's declaration of allegiance in the Knesset before he resigned.

Since ministers may be appointed from outside the Knesset, coalition parties have on occasion had some of their ministers designate resign from the Knesset to make way for additional rank-and-file members who were not in fact elected. The advantage to a party of such a move is twofold: while spreading the fruits of office more widely among party members, it brings a significant reinforcement to the parliamentary Group since a minister who is not a Knesset member has all the rights of one except that of voting. While a 1965 amendment prevents a minister from resigning from the Knesset without giving up his portfolio as well, he can easily circumvent this limitation by resigning from the Knesset before his appointment to the Government. Thus, for example, after the 1969 election five ministers designate from all three coalition Groups, by resigning their seats, enabled five additional candidates from their respective lists to enter the Knesset. To cite a more striking instance, the Independent Liberals, who returned only four members to the Knesset in 1973, effectively secured the strength of six when two of their newly elected members resigned to be made ministers. A minister who must leave the Government because he has resigned from the Knesset after his appointment may be reappointed to his ministry by the Knesset after debate; but this procedure would not be popular, and the demand for its application to the minister from the *Tehiya* Group in 1982 was turned down.

Small parties have sometimes arranged for rotation of candidates on their list during a Knesset term. In the well-disciplined Communist party rotation agreements were fulfilled without untoward results. In a less homogeneous political grouping, the left-wing *Sheli,* the rotation between M. Pail and S. Marziano in 1980 was carried out only after a delay and after a quarrel between the two was patched up. Bad blood was stirred up in 1980 between the Bedouin and Druze communities over a rotation agreement in the United Arab List. Refusing to honor his written commitment to resign in favor of Jaber Muadi, Sheikh Hamad Abu Rabiya claimed that emerging problems of Bedouin land in the Negev required his continuing presence in the Knesset. A suit by Muadi was rejected by the judge, who ruled this and all similar rotation agreements not legally binding, and that such an agreement depends on the Knesset member voluntarily vacating his seat in another's favor. At the same time the judge expressed disapproval of Abu Rabiya's refusal to vacate his seat, especially since he himself had gained the seat by a similar agreement with the first holder of the list's single seat. However, some months later Muadi succeeded to the disputed seat, after Abu Rabiya was murdered.

COMPOSITION OF THE KNESSET MEMBERSHIP

Centralized control of the candidates list, as we have already seen, is used by the party to produce a roster balanced at least in the representation of its main sectors—organizational, regional, economic, and communal. With regard to the actual composition of the Knesset membership a number of studies have been made in the past, employing criteria of membership turnover, community (in the Eastern/Western or Sephardi/Ashkenazi sense), region,

Arab representation, sex, and profession.[6] For our purpose their findings require to be modified only in the light of more recent Knesset terms.

With respect to turnover, the Knesset has on average convened after elections with a quarter of its members new, the proportion tending consistently upward since 1965. If changes owing to resignations and deaths are included, there were more than fifty new faces in the Knessets of 1977–81 and 1981–84. The average Knesset member has served two and one-half terms, one-third only one term. Yet, owing to a continuing preponderance of prestate political leaders in the house, it was described early on as an aging institution, the average age of members rising from forty-eight years in 1949, to fifty-five in 1969; when the Knesset celebrated its twentieth birthday in 1969, it was noted that there were twenty-nine members who had served continuously since the First Knesset.[7] However, as the number of founding fathers in the house steadily diminished, a turning point was reached with the 1973–77 Knesset, and the average age of members dropped back since then to fifty-two years by 1984.[8]

Historical perspective is needed also in considering the issue of Sephardi representation in the Knesset. At the birth of the state only 10 percent of the Jewish population were from Islamic countries, while 55 percent hailed from Eastern Europe. The great waves of new immigrants in the 1950s from North Africa, Iraq, Yemen, and other Islamic countries, arriving after the foundations of statehood had been laid, also lacked any notions of parliamentary government, while confronted with a system dominated by essentially East European political parties (see Chapter 1). Not surprisingly, they remained for a long time grossly underrepresented in the Knesset. However, as the process of acculturation proceeded, Oriental Jewish representation in the Knesset increased, albeit never fully correcting the disproportion between Sephardi electors and elected.

The number of non-Ashkenazi members (including both foreign and native-born Sephardim, and those of Bulgarian and Yemenite origin) rose regularly, with only an odd reverse, from seven in the First Knesset to thirty-two in the Eleventh (elected in 1984). Constituting a quarter of the house, though Eastern Jews and their children then accounted for more than half the population, the day was past when Sephardi members could be described as ''pseudorepresentatives'' because placed on the candidates lists by party leaders; it was indicative of the changed times that five of the six municipality heads returned to the Knesset in 1981 were of Moroccan origin, each an acknowledged champion for his locality—the development town settled by his fellow immigrants. Further, it could hardly be said any longer that non-Ashkenazi members got only junior parliamentary and cabinet posts. By 1983, Sephardi officeholders included: four ministers, holding between them the portfolios of Justice, Labor and Welfare, Immigration Absorption (the last two assigned to one minister), and Housing together with the deputy prime ministership, while one of the four was minister without portfolio; three of the seven deputy ministers; two vice-chairmen, commanding thus a majority of the Knesset presidium; and the chairmanship of the largest parliamentary Group (Labor Alignment).

Entry to the Knesset of native-born—both Ashkenazi and Sephardi—was blocked unduly long by the predominance of the East European leadership. The new generation of both groups have much in common; as more native-born replace their immigrant fathers, while there is equal educational opportunity for all and the intermarriage rate continues to rise, there is good reason to believe that the problem of Sephardi representation will soon disappear.

The increased parliamentary representation of immigrant towns has corrected only somewhat one of the more conspicuous distortions of the geographic factor by the electoral system. Regional considerations weighed only to the extent they went to adjust a candidates list to ensure representation of the party's particular constituencies. Composition of the Knesset's membership, in terms of home district, has usually conformed to a skewed pattern favoring generally certain localities and leaving others greatly underrepresented. Overrepresented consistently have been the Tel Aviv area, Jerusalem, and the communal villages (kibbutzim). Tel Aviv and its satellite cities, as the nation's commercial, industrial, cultural, and communications center, where most party headquarters too are located, has accounted for a majority in every Knesset. Jerusalem, the capital and center of government, has on the basis of population ratio fared even better, with a parliamentary contingent that grows further as long-standing members and ministers take up residence there.

The kibbutzim have been the most favored sector with respect to parliamentary representation. Comprising less than 3½ percent of the population, they provided up until 1977 at least fifteen Knesset members—nearly four times as many as their numbers warranted. There were two reasons for this prominence: first, the role of the men and women of the kibbutzim as pioneers and nation builders won them recognition in the labor parties as a political and ideological elite; second, the communal organization of the kibbutz, by its nature, fosters public spirit and frees its able individuals from other duties so they can give full time to political tasks. Two labor parties, *Ahdut Ha'avodah* and *Mapam,* were essentially kibbutz-oriented, each assigning a minority of slots to candidates from the cities though most of their voters were city dwellers. (*Ahdut Ha'avodah* merged into the united Labor party in 1968, and *Mapam* has been in the Labor Alignment since 1969.) After the reverse suffered by the Labor Alignment in the 1977 election there were fewer Knesset members from the kibbutzim; but with ten after that election, and eight in 1981 and 1984, the kibbutzim still remained very well represented.

The underrepresented areas have been the north and south of the country generally, excluding the kibbutzim. A comparison made in 1974 of returns under the present electoral system, with results to be expected through a reform that would divide the country into sixteen electoral districts, showed that the representation of greater Tel Aviv would drop by a third and that of Jerusalem by a half, while on the other hand, in the north Haifa's representation would rise by two-thirds and that of Safed would be doubled; in the south Ashkelon would return twice the number of members.[9] Most immigrant development towns are also located in the north and south. The recently improved parliamentary representation of the development towns, mentioned earlier, was partly balanced by the reduction of the kibbutz contingent. At the same time, there has also been an increase in the number of Knesset members from the cooperative villages based on private ownership (moshavim), many of which are in outlying districts. With an impressive pioneering history and a larger population than the kibbutzim, the moshavim did not enjoy the same status in party circles, and their representation in the Knesset had been far less; in 1984 they had five candidates elected.

While the geographic profile of the Knesset membership is of value in considering its composition, domicile is not to be absolutely identified with representational role. Thus, national leaders like David Ben Gurion, Levi Eshkol and Yigal Allon, whose homestead for a long period was the kibbutz, could not be said to represent that sector either in the Knesset or in the Government. On the other hand, Knesset Member Menachem Hacohen, though a resident of the city of Ramat Gan, bordering Tel Aviv, was, as rabbi of the moshavim, clearly a representative of those communities.

Essentially regional, two or three separate Arab, Druze, or Bedouin candidates lists have won seats nearly every Knesset term, sometimes numbering together as many as five. The candidates were generally scions of leading families, village notables, or prominent sheikhs, rather than representatives of true political parties. In the house they generally supported the Labor party (having backed also its predecessor, *Mapai*) and were invited in time to sit in at Alignment Group meetings; from among them might be appointed a Knesset vice-chairman or a deputy minister. However, as Arab voters shifted their support to established political parties the local and village lists were weakened. In 1977 only one Arab list won representation in the Knesset, and in 1981 none returned a member though a number campaigned. The Progressive List for Peace, with two seats won in 1984, was a Jewish-Arab group with a political outlook far removed from that of the earlier village lists.

While at first only *Mapam* and the Communist party admitted Arabs to full membership and placed them on their candidates lists, this became more and more the practice also in other political parties, the Labor party admitting them by 1981, with its two Arab Knesset members after that year's election serving in rotation on the Alignment Group's executive committee. Arab Knesset members have usually numbered six or seven. The figure would be significantly higher if the Communist party, whose voters are overwhelmingly Arab, would make up its candidates lists accordingly; but it has chosen to emphasize its Jewish-Arab character by always placing a Jew at the head of the list, and allotting half the slots to Jews. To further justify its mixed projection, the party in 1977 formed a Democratic Front for Peace and Equality with a fission of the panther movement, a protest group of underprivileged young people which had never on its own won Knesset representation.

Women in the Knesset have on average made up more than 8 percent of the membership, a proportion higher than in most western parliaments. However prejudiced many voters might be about female legislators, the party-list process of recruitment has ensured that a certain number will be elected. But not every party has taken the same view about women candidates. Most women members have come from the labor parties, where there is a traditional emphasis on sex equality. Religious parties have tended to frown on representation by women; however, since 1959 the NRP has placed a member of its women's auxiliary in a realistic place on the candidates list. Separate women's lists have failed to win any representation except in the First Knesset (1949–51), when a women's Zionist organization secured one seat.

More significant perhaps than the number of women members has been their parliamentary performance. Though in the areas of defense, foreign affairs, and finance their activity has not matched that of their male colleagues, they have more than made up in fields such as education, social welfare, and civil rights. Studies have shown that their activity generally exceeds their numerical strength in the Knesset, one indicating that they are almost twice as effective as male members in having bills passed.[10] Mrs. Geula Cohen's Jerusalem bill (1980) was the only member's initiative to result in a Basic Law.

Considering the small proportion of women in the house, the positions which they have held are impressive. Already in the First Knesset a woman chaired the Education and Culture Committee; she held the post through three terms. As well as chairing other committees, women have been prominent in the presidium, providing four of the eight vice-chairmen in the 1965–69 Knesset. Of the eight women members after the 1981 election (with a ninth admitted on a member's death) four assumed committee chairmanships (Education, Internal Affairs, and the important subcommittees on Basic Laws and Complaints from the Public), one became a minister, albeit without portfolio, and another was appointed deputy minister of Education and Culture. The two women members earlier in Government included Golda Meir, whose varied cabinet career, together with the premiership, spanned a period of twenty-five years (1949–74).

In the nomination of candidates for the Knesset, occupational and educational backgrounds have been of less consideration than sustained party activity or sectoral representation. Observers who look closely at the professional equipment of members sometimes lose sight of the fact that under district electoral systems, such as in Britain or the United States, one does not begin to expect on the whole more than "average" representatives. Yet the majority of Knesset members, at least in recent terms, with election in greater force of the younger generation, had some higher education; and it is relevant that studies have shown the great majority of active proposers of bills and motions to come from the formally well-educated legislators.[11] This does not, however, answer professional requirements that might be desirable in particular fields. For example, a need has often been felt in the work of the Knesset for more lawyers and jurists; but that situation has vastly improved with an increase in the number of legally trained members from eight in the First Knesset to twenty-six in the Eleventh, elected in 1984.[12] The parliamentary system, however, creates its own "brain drain," with a large number of the professionally most able members regularly drawn off by the Government as ministers or deputy ministers.

More important, though, than formal education or professional attainments is the specialization of a member in the course of his parliamentary work. Nearly every member of the rank and file is assigned by his Group to one or two of the Knesset's permanent committees, each of which concentrates its activities generally in one main subject area. Only a few members are on three or more committees; while on the other hand, the odd member who refuses to sit on any committee, without the best of reasons, will be denounced in his Group as a shirker.

Though occupational background is a factor in committee assignments, so that economists tend to gravitate to the Finance Committee, teachers to the Education Committee, and so on, more often a member learns the relevant subject matter thoroughly after his appointment to the committee, and his contribution may in time be as valuable as that of his more professional colleagues. In an interview survey in the 1973–77 Knesset that embraced eighty-six Members (72 percent of the house). fifty-seven (two-thirds) pointed to committee work as the source of their expertise.[13] It follows that members of the relevant committee are usually the most knowledgeable speakers in the floor debate and the most effective proponents of related bills and motions. In that respect the work of a member who constitutes a one-man Group is particularly arduous; while his committee opportunities to concentrate efforts in certain fields is like that of every other member, his right and obligation to speak in every floor debate as the only spokesman of his Group—as much as that position is envied by other members—demands of him individually the mastery of a much wider range of topics.

THE QUESTION OF ELECTORAL REFORM

The electoral system, no less than the question of a constitution, has been a subject of controversy since the birth of the state. Mounting criticism of the proportional party-list system as noted earlier has brought increasing support over the years for the introduction of constituency elections. If such reform is not yet certain of achievement despite an apparent majority in its favor in successive Knessets, this is due perhaps as much to the gingerly approach of would-be reformers as to determined opposition.

Doubts which existed at the outset about the suitability in the new state of the unqualified proportional system that had served the voluntary organization of Palestine Jewry were overridden by the requirements of expeditious elections. Thus an amendment to the 1948 elections ordinance, which would have provided for constituency elections, and a similar amendment to the Second Knesset Elections Bill in 1951 were easily defeated. However, while the 1948 ordinance applied only to the first election, and the Provisional State Council expressly left open the decision on the nation's electoral system for the future, by 1951 the lines between the partisans of proportional and constituency elections began to harden. The 1951 Elections Bill was reported from the Knesset's Law Committee with a clause requiring a two-thirds majority of voting members to alter the principle of countrywide proportional elections. Although the plenum deleted that clause, a later attempt to entrench the existing electoral system succeeded when in 1958 the Basic Law on the Knesset was enacted with a provision in its Section 4 making an absolute majority of the Knesset necessary for changing the principle of "general, country-wide, direct, equal, secret and proportional elections."

The entrenchment of the above elections clause resulted from an amendment moved by members opposed to any deviation from the existing proportional system. In the preceding debate Prime Minister Ben-Gurion, who admired the British electoral system and had persuaded his party, *Mapai,* to put electoral reform in its platform, said frankly that he wished to see a two-party system in Israel in the interests of a strong government and a responsible opposition. To that purpose a member of his parliamentary Group moved an amendment providing for 120 single-member constituencies (the bill having originated in the Law Committee). The General Zionists (today the Liberal party), then the only other party to advocate electoral reform, proposed a compromise system whereby most members would be elected in multi-member constituencies, the rest from nationwide lists; they hoped in this way to prevent *Mapai* from winning an absolute majority overnight. (A year later the General Zionists made their proposal more concrete: thirty three-member regions, with the remaining thirty members to be elected from central lists.) None of the other parties at the time countenanced any change in the proportional system. Small parliamentary Groups stood to disappear with such a reform. But even the middle-sized National Religious party, which could only foresee losses by any system other than perfect proportional representation, was opposed to change. The antireform groups argued that constituency elections, in leading to wasted votes, would distort the result; that such elections in a country of immigration and heterogeneous population would artifically emphasize local interests to the detriment of the nation; and that the country was too small anyway for electoral divisions. The debate on the Basic Law concluded with the adoption of the entrenching amendment following the defeat of the two reform motions.

The difference over electoral reform was not strictly between large and small parties, since other factors were often present. *Herut,* no less than the General Zionists, had prospects of becoming the leading opposition in the event of constituency elections, as the fortunes of both parties varied sharply from election to election. But there was a deep-rooted hostility between *Herut* and *Mapai* dating back to pre-state years when David Ben-Gurion headed the official Jewish Community of Palestine, while Menachem Begin, later to found *Herut,* led the dissident underground *Irgun Zevai Leumi.* Consequently, *Herut* was mistrustful of a reform that might chiefly benefit *Mapai,* even if only in the short run. On the other hand, the General Zionists enjoyed considerable political strength of long standing at municipal levels, which made them naturally sympathetic to a constituency system. Parties whose membership came largely from the kibbutzim, *Ahdut Ha'avodah* and *Mapam,* rejected any reform proposals; the kibbutzim, because of their political activism, enjoyed a disproportionately high representation under the party-list system which would surely drop with district polling. Then, again, there were in later years quite small political groups like the State List, the Free Center, and the Civil Rights Movement that pressed for electoral reform though this appeared certain to eliminate their parliamentary representation; but each of these groups was the creation of one or two leaders of stature who could expect to be elected also on a personal basis.

In 1959 two members' bills aiming at electoral reform along the lines respectively proposed a year earlier by *Mapai* and the General Zionists provided each for a referendum to decide the question. On preliminary consideration the Knesset struck them off the agenda, while neither reforming Group supported the other in the voting. On the other hand a counter-measure stipulating an absolute majority of the house for every stage of legislation that would touch the existing electoral system went forward then to be enacted as a further entrenchment of proportional representation in the Basic Law on the Knesset.

A full decade elapsed before the electoral reform movement again picked up momentum. A significant turn came in 1969 with the recommendations of the Joseph Committee, representing all wings of the newly united Labor party, for a combined constituency-proportional system, much like that put forward earlier by the General Zionists. Bills that in large measure embodied the committee's recommendations were brought forward by Labor members in 1972 and 1974. But neither of these bills, nor a Liberal member's bill, though accepted by the Knesset on preliminary consideration, proceeded to first reading. Though nearly at one now on a program for electoral reform, Labor and the Liberals failed to push their advantage together, each party insisting on its way of proceeding. In contrast with their procrastination on electoral reform, they supported up to the hilt the Bader-Ofer list-quotient bill described earlier, so that it went forward in the face of unprecedented opposition; tabled on the same day as the 1972 reform bill and aimed at curtailing tiny political groups, it appeared in effect much like a stratagem to forestall the more basic reform. However, both Labor and Liberal lukewarmness about reform, despite official platforms, was understandable. Inside Labor the renewed commitment to constituency elections was due chiefly to pressure from Ben-Gurion's *Rafi* members who had returned to the party, while outside, the antireform stand of Labor's three coalition partners, the National Religious party, *Mapam,* and the Independent Liberals, could not be ignored. The Liberals for their part claimed to be hamstrung by *Herut* warnings that any action by them to promote electoral reform would rock their joint *Gahal* bloc.

Parliamentary obstacles notwithstanding, public sentiment for electoral reform was growing. While in 1965 an opinion survey showed that only 29 percent of the public hoped for a change in the system of election, one made in 1974 showed that 62 percent were for such a change.[14] That interval also saw the organization of nonparty movements for electoral reform. In 1976 a new political party, the Democratic Movement for Change (DMC), led by Yigael Yadin who had headed the electoral reform movement for years, put such a reform down as its most important goal and urged that the next Knesset, after passing a law providing for constituency elections, dissolve itself immediately thereafter and make way for a Knesset elected under the new system. The meteoric rise in the popularity of the DMC as shown by the growth of its membership and by opinion polls induced *Herut* at last, at its convention in January 1977, to accept the position of the Liberal party, its main partner in the *Likud* bloc, and to agree to support a moderate electoral reform. Consequently, both Labor and *Likud* agreed on a joint effort to secure a mixed proportional-district electoral system; a House Committee resolution of 16 March 1977, providing for a possible special session of the Knesset on a bill for electoral reform which was then under consideration in the Law Committee, stated that more than two-thirds of the house demanded that first reading be given the measure before the 1973–77 Knesset expired. However, the Law Committee did not report the bill back to the Knesset.

The coalition agreement of October 1977 provided that beginning with elections to the Tenth Knesset the system of election was to be ''regional-proportional-personal.'' The antireform parties in the coalition signed this agreement with the understanding that whatever the new system adopted, it would not allow votes in the constituencies to go to loss but would apply them to central lists. Although in 1979 the Government reaffirmed its commitment to the coalition agreement, the members of the coalition committee which was to work out the details of the change failed to find sufficient common ground. Also, repeated legislative initiatives of members during that term were abortive. Thus, though more than three-quarters of its members represented parties committed to election reform, the 1977–81 Knesset made no concrete step forward in that direction. Even less promising was the 1981 coalition agreement, which merely undertook that election reform proposals would be presented only with the prior agreement of all member parties, and that no member's bill for reform would be supported unless it conformed to those terms. The 1984 coalition pact, though again providing for a committee to study electoral change, was even more restrictive, laying down that no change in election laws be made without the assent of both partners, Alignment and *Likud*.

For years the impulse for electoral reform had been fed by what seemed an inability of the existing system to produce a real change of government despite shifts in the vote. Every one of eight successive elections had resulted in a coalition Government led by the largest Labor party, and a composition rearranged each time only as much as required by expediency. However, the displacement of the Labor Alignment by the *Likud* in the election to the Ninth Knesset, in May 1977—which demonstrated the possibility of turning out a Government with the electoral system unchanged—seemed to rob election reform of urgency. Here indeed was a case of historic irony, for it was the DMC, with its undertaking to press uncompromisingly for constituency elections, that had cut into Alignment support and had made the change of government possible.

As if to weaken further the case for electoral reform, the 1981 election showed that perfect proportional representation is capable also of producing in effect the much admired two-party system. Although political fragmentation was greater then than it had ever been—with thirty-one lists of candidates and eight small parties winning representation—the two large opposed blocs, *Likud* and Labor Alignment, secured together nearly four-fifths of the mandates. While a coalition Government was still inescapable, there was no third ''middle-sized'' party on the scene; the Democratic Party for Change, which won fifteen seats in 1977, had disintegrated well before this election, while the National Religious party returned six members instead of the twelve it had earlier. If tiny Groups could still tip the scale, this was because the large blocs were exactly equal in strength, each numbering forty-eight members on election.

Fresh impetus was gained by the movement for electoral reform with the election of July 1984, which brought into the Knesset fifteen Groups, a number unprecedented since 1951 (see Table 2). Though it was clear that a new Government, as in 1981, could be led only by the Alignment or the *Likud,* the formation of one with a secure parliamentary base appeared so unlikely that most looked to a National Unity Government, as forced a solution as that might be. Political atomization had proceeded so far that reform of elections was urged on every side. Yet to many such reform meant the simple expedient of raising the 1 percent qualifying threshold for a candidates list. But to do so would virtually eliminate any chance of electing an individual of an independent turn of mind, while voters remain confronted with a ballot paper carrying only the symbol and name of the party, whose list has been slotted entirely from the center, often by a small nominations committee. It is significant that in the only other system which makes one constituency of the entire country for proportional-list elections, that of the Netherlands, the ballot enables the voter to indicate preferences for individuals. Most Knesset members are aware of the stigma of ''deputies appointed from above'' which the public increasingly attaches to them. And political parties are no doubt mindful of the contribution that a district basis of representation might make to the resolution of the communal discord described earlier in the chapter. It would be rash, however, to predict the outcome. After all, the problem of legislating for electoral reform is that the surgeon is also the patient.

FINANCING OF ELECTIONS AND PARTY ACTIVITIES

Election expenses of Israel's political parties, which have been among the world's highest,[15] became an acute problem in the 1960s. In 1969 the Knesset enacted an Election Financing Law whose purpose was the public funding of party campaigns in the coming election, while limiting the total expense and providing for scrutiny of party expenditures by the state comptroller. A Treasury allocation was made payable to each party according to the size of its representation in the outgoing Knesset; other parties contesting the election would not be eligible. Challenged in the High Court of Justice, the Law, which had been adopted with a simple majority of the members voting, was invalidated as offending against the principle of equality in elections which is entrenched by an absolute-majority clause in the Basic Law on the Knesset. While the attorney general argued that the principle of equality meant simply "one person, one vote," the Court held that it applied also to equality between contesting lists. The Court left open to the Knesset as alternatives reenactment of the Law with an absolute majority, or its amendment so as to remove the discrimination against new lists. The Court suggested further that the inequality might be removed, while the Knesset's declared aim of avoiding unrestrained proliferation of new lists would still be served, by basing the allocation to a new list on the number of its mandates in the new Knesset, without granting it an advance payment as provided in the case of a party represented in the outgoing one.

Both indicated courses were followed. On the initiative of the Government (the original bill was sponsored by six members, one from the opposition) the Knesset amended the Law as suggested by the Court, taking care also that it was passed with the required majority. At the same time, the somewhat discomfitted Knesset, seeking to protect earlier laws enacted by a simple majority against possible attack by the Court, passed the Election (Confirmation of Validity of Laws) Law, 1969; enacted with an absolute majority, it ratified all existing statutory provisions concerning Knesset elections. Nevertheless, the Knesset allowed itself twice again, in 1981 and in 1982, to be caught off guard in similar circumstances (as was shown in Chapter 3), when its election legislation, passed without an absolute majority, was found by the Court to violate the condition of equality laid down in the Basic Law.

The 1969 financing law applied only to the election of that year and was described by its sponsors as experimental. Once the public had been introduced to the idea of a state subsidy for political parties, and the state comptroller reported that the law had conduced to restraint and economy in electioneering, the members who initiated that measures were encouraged to bring forward legislation providing permanently for the financing of both election and running expenses of parties. Passed in 1973; the Political Parties (Financing) Law provided for the payment of election expenses to a parliamentary Group out of the Treasury, of an amount to be fixed by the Knesset's Finance Committee (the "Financing Unit") for every seat won by the Group in the new Knesset, and of a monthly payment to the Group of running party expenses equal to 5 percent of the election funding. Every Group receives

85 percent of its allocation for election expenses with the gazetting of the election results, and the remaining 15 percent upon a favorable report by the state comptroller. A party or electoral bloc with representation in the outgoing Knesset is paid an advance against election expenses according to 60 percent of its strength in that Knesset.

The Financing Unit in April 1984 amounted to IS 12,500,000 (equivalent to 74,000 US$), with the monthly party expenses paid each Group equalling IS 625,000 (3,700 US$) for every one of its mandates in the Knesset. Owing to rapid inflation the Finance Committee linked the Unit progressively to 60, 70, and 90 percent of the rise in the consumer price index, with quarterly adjustment, while increasing also its real value from time to time. When, even with updating of the Financing Unit, the political parties continued to be in financial difficulties, the 1973 Law was amended to permit higher party spending in absolute terms from independent sources: the ceiling on campaign expenditures by a party from non-state sources of one-third the amount of the Treasury's allocation, and on running expenditures, of one-half the amount of the allocation, was amended in 1980 to permit, respectively, one-half and four-fifths the amount; in 1982, permitted election expenditure from non-state sources was increased further to equal the amount of the allocation.

With the aim of assuring the freedom of political parties from obligation to special interests, the 1973 law forbade them to receive contributions from corporate bodies in Israel. The state comptroller who inspects party accounts both for running and election expenditures, noted in his statutory reports to the chairman of the Knesset that since there was no restriction on contributions from corporate bodies abroad, or from organizations at home affiliated with a party, and which may serve as a channel for its funding, the value of his audit was limited and the financing law did not completely fulfill its purpose. One report drew attention to three bodies that had sprung up in the 1981 election and campaigned for the Alignment, *Likud,* and National Religious party respectively, but over whose activities these parties claimed to have no control.[16]

The significance of "party affiliates" in the context of the state comptroller's strictures, beyond his mention of election-time organizations, can be best understood against the historical background. In the pre-state period the Zionist parties had assumed the chief pioneering tasks in the embryonic national home. Each party undertook substantial social and economic activities in the course of which it built up organizations to cater to every need of its members. Although with statehood there came a general tempering of partisan attachments due to mass immigration, to the sobering responsibility of government, and to the mutual accommodations necessary for lasting coalitions, many party-affiliated enterprises such as newspapers, sports clubs, teaching institutions, and publishing houses continued to flourish while advancing party goals.

The *Histadrut* (General Labor Federation), because it has held elections to its convention about two months before Knesset elections, has been problematic in a number of ways with respect to national polling and the Parties Financing Law. While it goes far beyond the sphere of trade union activity, and its social and cultural services, and industrial enterprises, make it the nation's largest employer after the Government, as well as the roof organization for 85 percent of all wage earners, its governing bodies are politically elected. And though most of Israel's parties are active in the *Histadrut,* it is controlled by a Labor Alignment majority, being in origin a social and pioneering instrument of Labor Zionism. The majority parties in the *Histadrut,* just fresh from their victory in that organization, would benefit from a "halo" effect when campaigning shortly afterward in the Knesset elections. Further, since a party uses the same letter symbol for its candidates list in both campaigns, parties in the *Histadrut* might start to display that symbol long before the forty-two day limit prescribed in the Knesset elections by the law on modes of election propaganda. Finally, though in point of time the two campaigns might virtually merge, the Parties Financing Law specifies that its restrictions on election expenditures are not to apply to amounts received by parties through the *Histadrut* for its campaign and other expenses. And the *Histadrut,* from its members' dues, sets aside a fixed percentage for the political parties, allocating to each an amount proportionate to its elected strength at the convention. In April 1981, after ordering the cancellation of a *Histadrut* electioneering program on television as constituting campaigning for the June elections to the Knesset, Chairman Etsioni of the Central Elections Committee recommended that *Histadrut* elections be forbidden within 150 days of the Knesset election, which is the time limit for most prohibitions and restrictions set out in the law on election propaganda.

The straitened financial circumstances of some political parties after the 1981 Knesset election, as well as the state comptroller's criticism of the loopholes in the state funding provisions, induced a number of members to initiate amendments to the Parties Financing Law. Adopted in 1982, the amendments doubled the amount a party might raise for electioneering from independent sources (from one-half that allocated by the Treasury to an equal amount, as mentioned earlier), and provided that the basis of state funding be a Group's strength either in the outgoing or new Knesset, whichever was the greater, while introducing a sliding scale of forfeits, instead of the flat 15 percent, for overspending parties. Basing the allocation on the term with larger party representation would be an inestimable advantage; no longer might the advance payment of 60 percent leave a party in serious debt, as was the case of the Alignment in 1977, when it lost nineteen of its fifty-one seats.

The measure also introduced new prohibitions and penalties: contributions might no longer be received from foreign corporate bodies, while election expenditures of party affiliates would count as those of the party; a person who made false declarations about party income or expenditures was made liable to imprisonment or fine. However, while the date of enforcing the restrictions on party affiliates was left to be fixed by the Knesset's Finance Committee (and was so fixed only in 1984), the new basis for calculating expenditures and forfeits was made retroactive so as to cover the 1981 election campaign.

The retroactive clause, whose purpose was to spare overspending parties so they would not forfeit their 15 percent balance, prompted state comptroller Y. Tunik to exclaim (in the words of his predecessor on the occasion of a retrospective enactment to finance municipal electioneering, when Knesset and municipal elections had not been held, as usual, on the same day) that the amending law "fixed the norms after the act."[17] Further, the *Shinui* Center Group appealed to the High Court of Justice arguing that the retroactivity provision rewarded those parties that exceeded the ceiling and effectively penalized those that observed the legal spending limits. The Court quashed the clause as violating the provision of equality laid down in the entrenched elections clause of the Basic Law on the Knesset while having been passed without the required absolute majority—the very defects which had invalidated the 1969 financing law, described earlier. Required to make good the 15 percent forfeit—with the judgment handed down in June 1983, more than a year after the enactment—the five Groups whose overspending would have been retroactively legalized were permitted to extend repayment, index-linked, over a period of twenty months in the form of deductions from their monthly state financing for current expenses.

An indirect result of the funding of political parties from the Treasury was the attention drawn to their management. In the absence of any legal restraints they could adopt any organizational framework and determine their governing bodies and Knesset candidates lists however they pleased. With public financing of the parties, the opinion gained ground that the state had also the right to regulate their constitution and activities. Criticism of party organization was compounded by widespread censure of the parties after the Yom Kippur War, when a deferred election in changed circumstances left them impervious to demands for revision of their candidates lists. There resulted a spate of members' bills which sought to provide for democratic internal elections in parties, with direct and secret nomination of candidates for the Knesset, and to divest the parties of their economic enterprises. Four bills to such purpose were tabled in 1974–75 alone, and others have been introduced since. A Government bill with similar aims was given first reading in 1980 but stalled in committee. However, the regulation of the affairs of political parties was brought a step closer that year when they were brought under the scope of the Public Bodies (Elections) Law, 1954, which lays down penalties for dishonest practices in connection with internal elections.

While the legal status of political parties awaits definition, there are provisions regarding a parliamentary Group in the Parties Financing Law as the Group is the channel for state financing of the party. (The Knesset chairman, who administers the Law, makes all payments to the bank accounts of the Groups.) The Law, with later amendments, seeks to discourage floor crossing or further political fragmentation. Unless the majority of a Group agrees to a split, at least three members must break away from it in order to receive running expenses as a separate Group or as a reinforcement to another Group which they have joined. However, two who break away from a Group of three will affect allocations accordingly. There is particular concern in these provisions to preserve the integrity of the component Sections of a federative Group, each of which represents a separate political party at the national level. (Such Groups are described in Chapter 8.) Running expenses are paid directly to each Section so that if it should separate from the Group, its state financing will remain unaffected.

A link has been noted between state financing and the long election campaigns.[18] Formally the four and one-half months that are needed from the day on which the Knesset votes to advance the elections until polling day are due to two provisions: the need to allow army officers and senior officials who run for the Knesset to resign 100 days before elections; and the longer process of updating the voters register, which also entails time for public display and allowance of appeals. It is held, however, that the time lapse could be cut to forty-five days, particularly as the voters register has since 1959 been annually revised anyway, and it is only the further updating that requires the additional time. Although the Knesset, by a special temporary provision, shortened the cooling-off period for senior officials to sixty-six days when it dissolved itself on 4 April 1984, with the election fixed for 23 July, nearly four months of effective campaigning were yet left. A shorter time lapse is considered desirable not only for the sake of economy, but also to limit the sharpening of antagonisms which is characteristic of an election atmosphere, and to reduce the length of time during which unpopular though urgently necessary measures are deferred. The availability of public money for electioneering, however, has made such reform less pressing on the campaigning parties.

It is claimed also that the Parties Financing Law tends to freeze the political status quo by its allocations to the parties on a purely proportional basis, without providing a basic minimum for every party. By contrast, the law on modes of election propaganda lays down minimums of radio and television time for all parties, with additional time to each according to its Knesset Group strength.

5

Knesset Members

ELIGIBILITY

Every Israeli national of either sex at least twenty-one years old is eligible to be placed on a candidates list for election to the Knesset (while the minimum voting age is eighteen) unless a court, pursuant to any law, has deprived him of that right or he was previously sentenced to five years or more of prison for an offense against national security and since their completion another five have not yet elapsed. Occupants of certain positions are barred by law from candidacy: the president of the state, the state comptroller, judges, ministers of religion, state employees above a certain grade, and army officers. A Knesset member who is elected or appointed to any such post, as noted in Chapter 4, automatically ceases to be a member. A senior civil servant or army officer, to make himself eligible for candidacy, must resign his post at least 100 days before the election. The service of any other state employee or member of the permanent force—except a teacher—whose name is placed on a candidates list is automatically discontinued until election day and for the duration of his membership if he is elected.

The only other statutory prohibitions of outside occupation for Knesset members, beyond a disposition that they may not receive remuneration in the form of salary, are set out in the Government Companies law 1975, which forbids a member to serve as a director, general manager, auditor, or legal counsel of a state corporation. However, Knesset members from the Labor party were further affected by a decision of its Central Committee in 1982 that they could not hold any other top party-related posts while in the Knesset. That decision, though taken only with the purpose of distributing positions more equitably within the party while making no judgment about compatibility, immediately affected, among other Knesset members, those with executive positions in industries of the *Histadrut,* where the Labor party is dominant. While the 1982 decision could be circumvented by switching from a role categorized as executive to the chairmanship of the board of directors, D. Rosolio, secretary of the *Histadrut*'s holding company, resigned his Knesset seat. Three Labor town heads then in the Knesset were allowed to hold both posts until the 1983 elections to local authorities.

The provisions adopted by the Knesset in 1981, enabling it to unseat or suspend a member convicted of a criminal offense, as described in Chapter 4, have not completely spared it the embarrassment which can be caused by a delinquent member. On 24 August 1983, a member sentenced on counts of fraud and misappropriation of public funds—with his appeal turned down by the Supreme Court and the date already fixed for him to begin his prison term—showed up in the Finance Committee, where his vote that day was effective in the rejection of Government requests; the House Committee had not suspended his Knesset membership though empowered to do so.

Members bills have been tabled that would further tighten the law so as to facilitate suspension or unseating of a sentenced member, or the debarment of a candidate convicted of felony whose term in prison has not been followed by a fixed time lapse. One of those bills, whose proponents claimed that party considerations might be a deterrent to suspension of a member by the House Committee, or to his unseating by action of both committee and plenum, provides for automatic suspension of a member until he has served his sentence, and for his ouster forthwith where the court finds moral turpitude involved.

REPRESENTATION

The Knesset member, in fulfillment of his distinctly representational role and to complement his activity in the house and its committees, maintains contact with and performs services for his constituents who, if not often a geographic district, are a definite economic, social, or ethnic community. He addresses their gatherings and takes part in their rallies, answering questions and providing information. Taking up the problems of groups or individuals frustrated by bureaucratic tangle who write, telephone, or visit him, he is often able to meet their requests successfully because he can bring the issue directly to the relevant minister.

Much of the above activity in fact takes place within the party framework, with the member expected to clarify policy positions. A distinct example are the regional parliamentary offices for discussion of citizens' problems and hearing suggestions. They are often located in party branch quarters and may be shared with the party's municipal representatives and other functionaries. Despite the frankly partisan sponsorship of these offices, members who volunteer to man them (though in 1970 the Knesset's Alignment Group set up a roster for the purpose, including most of its membership) are in a position to discharge their representational function individually, with initiative and imagination. Mr. Pesach Grupper, for example, "staked out" his area during the 1973–77 Knesset by manning five such bureaus at the Liberals' headquarters for the coastal and Samaria areas. Mr. Chaim Herzog, before his election as president in 1983, served as the "Knesset's ear" in this manner as an Alignment member in a number of centers throughout the southern Sharon as well as in his own town of Herzlia; and as a long-standing advocate of electoral reform he pursued the task as a model for regional representation.

Within the constraints of Group discipline described in Chapter 8, the individual member can act freely over a substantial range in the interests of his client groups. In addition to the freedom granted by some parliamentary Groups on religious questions and other matters of conscience, most legislation is in fact taken on a nonparty basis. A member is also free to put questions to ministers as he sees fit. On some issues of fundamental importance also a Group-basis debate may be followed by considerable cross-voting, as occurred, for example, on the Camp David accords with Egypt in 1978. The roll-call vote on the coalition motion for approval of the accords found many Government supporters voting against or abstaining, and it was only with a large reinforcement of opposition votes that the motion was carried. Moreover, it is not unknown also for an individual member to vote contrary to the party line even on a question of confidence, while his position in the Group remains unimpaired; such was the case, for example, of Y. Sarid of the Alignment when he refused to vote for the Budget in 1974.

The narrow Government majority which has been the rule during most of the period since 1974 has strengthened the position of the individual member. The Government was made more dependent on his support so that he could in effect sell his vote more dearly when approval of the Budget or defeat of a no-confidence motion might hang on it. One striking case was that of NRP Member A. Melamed in the 1981–84 Knesset who used his decisive vote in the Finance Committee again and again to defeat or alter tax measures or to hold back budgetary allocations. His Group did not replace him on the Committee, perhaps because his dissents were also useful to it for displaying NRP's independence as a coalition partner. However, none of Mr. Melamed's adverse votes—all in committee, where decisions may have a tentative character and are reversible—were such as to bring down the

Government. A member in such a position is well aware of his heavy responsibility should he press opposition too far.

Cross-party activity by members on behalf of interest groups is often carried on through lobbies. Subject themselves to lobbying with regard to every conceivable question, members also form and lead lobbies to press matters in government offices and with ministers. Since 1980 some of the lobbies formed were: for the development of Haifa, consisting of all members from that city under the auspices of the mayor; on social matters, comprised of most Sephardi members on the initiative of the Sephardi Federation; for Jewish access to the Temple Mount, headed by members from the *Tehiya* and Liberal groups and actively supported by a number of like-minded organizations; and a short-term all-party lobby to fight proposed cuts in the 1982 education budget, made up of members of North African origin whose communities would suffer most from the step. Lobbying activity also makes itself felt in the Knesset's proceedings, as for example, when the Haifa members on 3 January 1984 together presented a motion that the unemployment situation in Haifa be debated; normally a member's motion has only one proposer, and a motion from both coalition and opposition is rare (though parallel motions, presented in sequence, are common, as noted in Chapter 9).

It remains to add that members fulfill an important representative role abroad. As well as travelling on official missions at the request of ministers, and representing their respective parties at international political meetings, they serve on delegations to the United Nations Assembly, the Interparliamentary Union, and other international political bodies. Two members regularly attend the Assembly of the Council of Europe as observers, and dialogues between the Knesset and the Parliament of Europe are held every year through committees and members. In addition, members take part in a growing number of bilateral parliamentary friendship societies as well as in exchange visits of delegations. Such contacts with other parliaments are greatly valued by the Knesset and have meant much to Israel in view of the enduring hostility of most of her close neighbors. It has become practice for a delegation back from a conference to report impressions and results to the house; such an account is not debated.

IMMUNITIES

To enable members to perform their duties without being troubled by indictments filed in bad faith on the initiative of the executive, with the purpose of hampering their freedom to act and voice opinions as the nation's elected representatives, the First Knesset established a system of immunities by enacting the Knesset Members (immunity, rights, and duties) Law, 1951. To ensure further that the Knesset could conduct its affairs free from disturbance or undue pressure by any extraparliamentary factor, a law providing for immunity of the Knesset Building was enacted the following term, in 1952; it was replaced by a more comprehensive measure in 1968, two years after the Knesset had moved to its permanent home.

A member's immunity is absolute—and thus may not be withdrawn in any circumstances—with respect to a vote, oral or written expression of opinion, or any other act in or outside the Knesset, also while the house is in recess, if the opinion or act pertains to or is directed toward the carrying-out of his mandate. That is to say, in no such case does the member bear civil or criminal responsibility, and his immunity from a consequent legal proceeding will continue also after he has ceased to be a member.

With regard to charges against a member for acts unconnected with fulfillment of his mandate, in the case of a civil suit his status is like that of any citizen. Against criminal process he is protected procedurally. In order to be prosecuted for an offense allegedly committed by him while a member or before his election his immunity must first be withdrawn with respect to the charge in question by a procedure to be described below. He may not be arrested unless caught while committing a crime involving violence, a disturbance of the peace, or treason. In a case of arrest in any of these circumstances notification must immediately be sent to the Knesset chairman, and the member may not be kept under arrest more than ten days unless his immunity has been withdrawn with respect to the charge in question. Where a charge is pending against a candidate on the day of his election to the Knesset, any legal proceedings in process are discontinued and not resumed as long as his immunity has not been lifted with respect to that charge.

The Knesset member is shielded also by additional immunities. His dwelling may not be searched. His person or belongings may be searched only by the customs authorities. His papers and mail are immune from search or confiscation and may be opened in his presence only in enforcement of currency laws. If a member is required to give evidence before a court of law, the date for the hearing is fixed with the consent of the Knesset chairman, and he is not bound to state any facts learned by him in carrying out his mandate. A direction prohibiting or restricting access to any place within the state other than private property is not applicable to members except for reasons of national security. A member is exempt from regular army service, and though subject to reserve call-up, he can, if such duty interferes with his Knesset obligations, arrange through the House Committee for its deferment during his tenure of office.

Since immunity is granted to the member not on his own behalf but to ensure that the Knesset can properly conduct its business, he cannot himself waive it; it can be withdrawn only by the Knesset. By resolution the Knesset may withdraw a member's immunity with respect to a particular charge or any other of the above-mentioned immunities—except those described as absolute—as well as any of the rights granted him by the immunities law (which include mail, telephone, and public transportation privileges). However, such a resolution can come only as the last step of a procedure detailed in the law.

The right to make application for withdrawal of a member's immunity with respect to a charge, which initiates the procedure, is vested in the attorney-general. He submits the application to the chairman of the Knesset, who forwards it to the House Committee for consideration at its earliest meeting. Since the Committee's part, of weighing whether to propose withdrawal of immunity, is only one of the preliminaries meant to clear the way for normal legal processes, its tasks, in the opinion of jurists, are essentially two: to determine whether the alleged offense is outside the orbit of the member's office; and to ascertain that no political bias or other immaterial consideration has motivated the application. In practice, though, the Committee often goes into the substance of the evidence through many meetings, with the attorney-general, as it were, in the dock. The Committee's proposal to withdraw immunity will be taken up by the house after twenty-four hours' notice of the proceeding have been given. Following opening remarks by the committee chairman, the member concerned has the right to state his case (as he had in committee) before the vote is taken.

The same procedure is followed for withdrawal of some other immunity or right as mentioned above, except that its initiation is not restricted to the attorney-general; an application to set the process in motion may be submitted by the Government or any Knesset member.

Of the ten instances in which the Knesset has withdrawn a member's immunity—the first occurring in 1954, the most recent in 1981—about half involved violation of traffic rules, causing in most cases a serious accident, while the rest were mainly allegations of bribery. In a few other cases the House Committee decided not to recommend removal of immunity. A member elected in 1981, with criminal proceedings pending against him after his immunity had been lifted by the previous Knesset, appealed to the High Court of Justice to annul them on the ground that he had regained immunity from prosecution on reelection. The Court rejected the appeal, stating that it suffices for the attorney-general's motivation to be examined but once.

The categorical protection of members from legal process, whether the Knesset is in session or not, if the act or opinion in question is at all related to the discharge of their mandate, and the elaborate procedural immunity which serves a member charged with any other crime or misdemeanor, were both written into the law as a consequence of historical circumstances which in the First Knesset still exercised a great influence. Memories of the intense pre-state animosities between political parties, and their separate, mutually hostile undergrounds, were still fresh. Those deep divisions, which seemed hardly abated during the early years of the state, account for positions taken in debate on the immunities bill. While objection to the wide scope of inviolability came primarily from members of *Mapai* (leading the coalition then), the opposition speakers, to a man, manifesting a pervasive distrust of the executive and genuine fear of political persecution, insisted on the enactment of the bill—drafted by the House Committee—without serious amendment.

As the passage of time brought a moderation of partisan enmities and increased confidence in the state's democratic institutions, the extensive immunities seemed to lose their justification and came under attack from all quarters. The Knesset in 1970 itself commissioned a comparative study by legal experts, who reported that the immunity of Knesset members was wider than in any other parliament and recommended ways to reduce its compass. Though the report was shelved, the press and the public did not allow the subject to be forgotten and, given the distinct equalitarianism of Israel's society, looked upon the immunities as excessive personal privileges.

The absolute freedom of members outside the Knesset to say or publish anything without liability to prosecution has drawn criticism in cases involving libel or disclosure of security-sensitive matters. In one instance a member passed on to the press his parliamentary question, before it had received the necessary approval of the chairman (it was in fact subsequently disqualified), about a commission allegedly received by a minister in connection with oil acquisitions by the state, and its substance proved unfounded. The fact that the member could not be sued because of his immunity brought a general wave of protest that led to the appointment in 1982 of the Behor Commission to study the broader question of publication of names before indictment. The Commission included among its recommendations amendment of the Knesset Rules or of the Defamation Law so as to forbid a member to make public a parliamentary question disqualified or not yet approved by the Knesset chairman. While some members, both before and after the Behor report, have themselves initiated bills that would curtail their immunities, there is special reluctance in the house to allow core immunities—those touching members' freedom of speech and publication—to be gnawed into. Amendments to the immunity law drafted in 1979 by the justice ministry were vigorously rejected by members as improper intervention by the Government since the Law was designed to protect the Knesset against the executive.

Impinging the most often on his fellow citizens' sense of equality was the protection of the member by the 1951 immunity law with respect to traffic offenses. Parking tickets to members would be passed on by the Knesset

Officer to the police for cancellation; a number of repeating offenders brought the total of cancellations each year into the hundreds. In the 1977–81 term the Knesset Officer's routine was discontinued so that a ticketed member had to apply on his own to the police and invoke parliamentary immunity. Shortly after that the House Committee decided that members would pay the fines. But this did not affect violations of driving regulations; in such cases if the member identified himself, he was not given a ticket at all. When in 1982 the house voted not to accept the House Committee's recommendation to lift the immunity of six members with respect to traffic violations, it found itself momentarily arrayed against the entire press and public opinion. Consequently, later that year, though some members still held that any change in the immunity law would lead to its further whittling down, an amendment with regard to traffic offenses was introduced by the House Committee and passed into law. It provides that the immunities law will not apply to traffic offenses unless a member against whom a charge sheet has been submitted expressly informs the chairman of the Knesset that he wishes to invoke his immunity.

The occasional encroachment by law enforcement officers on the liberty of members attests to their need of immunity. There have been instances in which a member's freedom of movement was impeded, and more rarely, when his papers were rummaged or seized. A resolution adopted by the House Committee in 1953 provides that a member's complaint that his immunity has been violated will be considered by the Committee, and if it finds there are grounds for the complaint, it will request that the chairman of the Knesset forward the matter to the public prosecutor with an instruction to bring the offender to trial. In practice, the Committee avoids hasty conclusions. Through the relevant minister it will hear the authorities concerned and seek to clear up what may be only a misunderstanding. Hindrance to a member's free movement in some area may turn on interpretation of security requirements. When on 1 March 1982 while the withdrawal from Sinai was nearing completion the defense minister ordered that Yuval Ne'eman be kept out of the Yamit area, the House Committee acted quickly, and on instruction from the Knesset chairman the barrier to his entry was removed. Shortly afterward, Ne'eman was forcibly removed from the area; this time a ruling by the high Court of Justice enabled him to return within a few hours.

While official identity cards have always been issued to members, the House Committee, in order to help reduce infringements of immunity to a minimum, decided in 1983 to furnish every member with a special identity document containing the relevant sections of the immunities law.

The Knesset Building and Precincts Law, 1968, authorizes the chairman to take any step he may find necessary for the maintenance of security and order within the Building, grounds, and immediate vicinity, and in consultation with the vice-chairmen to fix areas to which entrance is prohibited. The law provides that entry to those areas shall be only with the chairman's permission and that, except with such permission, nowhere within the Knesset precincts may any person carry arms, hold a meeting or procession, or put up any signboard, notice, or placard; permission is also required by a public servant to perform any duty there. Liability to a specific fine or prison term is laid down for the contravention of any of the aforementioned provisions or for behavior interfering with the orderly work of the Knesset.

Order within the Knesset Building is maintained through ushers, while outside, the precincts are protected by a special guard force. Both ushers and guards are under the command of the Knesset Officer, who is appointed by the chairman in consultation with the vice-chairmen. The Officer, with the powers of a police district commander, is responsible to the chairman. An usher or guard may, without a warrant, search a person suspected of concealing a thing forbidden in the precincts, or arrest one who has committed there an offense involving use of force, theft, or disturbance of peace and good order. The arrested person must be handed over to the police within two hours. Thus while the Knesset itself exercises police powers in the maintenance of public order within its precincts, further legal process is left to the general law enforcement authorities of the state. However, a criminal charge may not be filed or proceedings discontinued save with the chairman's sanction.

Yet it is noteworthy that notwithstanding the comprehensive statutory protection both of Knesset premises and individual members, parliamentary privilege in general remains unregulated. The Knesset cannot take legal action against outsiders who offend against its authority or dignity, whether by speech or publication liable to bring it into contempt, or by refusal to testify before one of its committees.

ETHICS AND CONDUCT

Questions of conduct for a member can arise in different spheres. Since, as we have just seen, his immunity shields him against legal action for defamatory remarks, whether uttered against an outsider or fellow legislator, some norms are necessary to prevent abuse of the privilege. The need to set ethical norms with regard to members' outside occupations has proved more insistent. The Knesset Members Remuneration Law, 1949, only lays down that a member may not draw a salary from any other source. Thus, apart from the incompatible occupations enumerated at the beginning of the chapter, he may receive income from exercise of a liberal profession, a trade or business, ownership or partnership in an enterprise, or from any other form of self-employment. Nor is he barred from holding a managerial position (except in a state corporation, as already noted), so long as his remuneration is in a form other than salary. And while the immunity law prohibits a member from using his parliamentary title in any activity connected with his business or profession (a ban which continues to apply also after his tenure in the house has ended), there are no other statutory restrictions on his private activities. This wide freedom has raised problems of conflict of interests. Finally, in the realm of general parliamentary conduct, matters such as wrangles between members and verbal violence in debate have needed regulation.

The need to check collision of interests that may result from a member's outside occupation was first concretely brought home to the Knesset by a few instances in which a member belonging to the legal profession raised a matter concerning his client in house debate. There resulted a number of House Committee resolutions: in 1963, admonishing lawyer members to refrain from pleading a client's case on the floor or in a committee; in 1970, proscribing testimony by a member in a Knesset committee on behalf of an interest group which he represents—without barring him from appearing before the committee as an expert on the matter in accordance with the Knesset Rules; in 1973, urging legislators in the legal profession to refrain from acts that do not comport with their duties and status as Knesset members; and in 1981, asserting in general terms that a member is duty bound to manage his affairs so as to avoid any clash between his mandate and personal material interest, and that in a Knesset committee when a matter under consideration touches his private affairs he is obliged to so state, and to refrain from taking part in the vote. Only in 1984 was a fuller ethical code for members adopted.

The above resolutions, couched in general phrases hardly binding, or dealing only with particular situations, failed to provide members with adequate guidelines. Two of the resolutions concerned only lawyers, while the problem exists with equal force for members who are economic advisers, accountants, or businessmen. No less than sixty members in the 1981–84 Knesset were engaged in some kind of outside employment, according to one well-informed source,[1] but only five of them were professionally active advocates. But the Israel Bar Association had long urged that Knesset members of the legal profession adopt a strict code of self-restraint after receiving complaints that a few among them had taken advantage of their parliamentary status.

Extraparliamentary employment also raised problems beyond those of representing clients in the house or of speaking or voting on matters affecting them. Though barred from explicitly trading on his Knesset title, a member can attract business because his status and influence are known, and he can advance matters with relative facility through ministers and officials who are in effect subject to his oversight in the Knesset plenum and committees. Again, how can a member withhold useful information from a business associate though it was received in the confidence of a Knesset committee? No less ethical questions were those of a member's expenditure on private matters of time which properly belonged to the Knesset or his use of the Building and its facilities for receiving clients.

Opinion in the Knesset about the extent to which nonparliamentary activity of members should be restricted was divided. Against the view that there must be a total ban on additional gainful employment, it was argued that members should not be a cloistered group, and that complete freedom to participate in the workaday world enables them to discharge their mandate more effectively. It became clear that to chart a mean between the two extreme positions a comprehensive set of rules was necessary. The report in 1969 of the Unna Committee, appointed by the justice minister to examine relations of lawyer members with governmental bodies, urged the Knesset to appoint its own ethics committee to regulate all extraparliamentary employment of members. After some years the House Committee began to set up a subcommittee each term on norms of conduct and in 1983 the Kulas Committee adopted a code of ethics applying to all Knesset members.

The code lays on the member both prohibitions and obligations. He is forbidden to receive material benefit, directly or indirectly, for any act performed in his capacity as a member; to exploit for personal benefit information to which he is privy as a member; to acquire government property unless it is available on the same terms to the general public; to act for or to receive a client in the Knesset; or to represent or advise for payment a governmental authority. Some restrictions are placed on a member's representation of clients before a government body. He is barred from membership on the board of directors of a government corporation. Receipt of fees for lectures before Jewish groups abroad, which in 1980 was declared by the House Committee not befitting a Knesset member, is banned outright by the code.

Among the positive injunctions in the 1983 code is the requirement that a member declare any personal interest with respect to a debate or vote, and that he refrain from the vote in committee (a practice which had already become a tradition in the Finance Committee). He must file with the chairman of the Knesset a declaration of his assets, liabilities, and sources of income and those of his family, upon his election, at the end of each tax year, and on termination of his membership. The chairman may reveal the contents of a declaration only on the request of the member or of a court.

The code provides for enforcement of the rules of conduct by an Ethics Committee consisting of four Knesset members appointed by the chairman of the Knesset in proportion to Group strengths in the house. The Committee is empowered to deal with complaints about infringements of the code and may, according to their gravity, formally call the attention of the offending member to the rules, administer an admonition, a reprimand, or a severe reprimand. At its discretion the Committee may make any decision public. Given exclusive authority to interpret the code's provisions, the Committee may rule also in regard to a question of conduct which they do not cover.

The 1983 code, though recognized as a significant step in regulating members' norms of conduct, was regarded as inadequate for a variety of reasons. The restriction on representing a client before a government agency applied in fact only to a body not itself represented by an attorney; consequently, the attorney-general deemed it necessary on the basis of the code to issue regulations in 1984 obliging public servants who are approached by a member as a lawyer or economic adviser to refer him to the department's legal adviser, who may act only after informing the attorney-general's office and receiving written instructions directing him how to proceed. Other criticisms of the code were that the submission by members of financial declarations without their being disclosed to the public was meaningless, and that likewise, even the sharpest censure by the Ethics committee, when it need not necessarily be made public, hardly constituted sanction enough to meet a serious violation of the code. Moreover, some held that the most effective rein on extraparliamentary activity would be to limit a member's outside earnings to a percentage of his Knesset salary or to a fixed sum.

Requiring a member in general terms to devote to his parliamentary duties the time necessary, and to give them priority over other activities, the ethics code in effect leaves it to the individual member to judge what constitutes adequate fulfillment of his mandate. After Chairman Savidor's proposal in 1982 that the immunities law be amended to require attendance of members on the Knesset's three sitting days failed of acceptance, he sought to have the obligation written into the ethics code but without success.

A complaint about a member's insulting remark is within the jurisdiction of the House Committee, which often appoints a standing subcommittee to investigate such cases. The incident may involve an exchange of uncomplimentary epithets, usually in debate, between members or between a member and a minister, or it may involve a complaint of a committee witness or some other outside person or body of affront by a member. Such verbal outbursts are often politically motivated; abuse of a civil servant in committee may serve as an indirect way to attack his minister. The House Committee may formally express displeasure at the offending member's remarks or censure him with varying degrees of severity, seeking always to elicit from him an apology. However, the Committee has ruled that where a minister's parliamentary behavior is complained about, he is not obliged to appear before it, as would be the case where his ministerial responsibilities are involved. In every instance the aim of the Committee is to secure speedy reconciliation of the two sides and to rid the Knesset of an undignified squabble. In a debate on Knesset affairs in 1984 House Committee Chairman E. Livni told the house that of more than twenty complaints that had been before the Committee in the 1981–84 Knesset, only one had come to the public's attention, while the others were all settled amicably. Physical encounters between members which are also brought before the House Committee have been rare.

Unrestrained heckling and railing in debate and the generally lax manners of some members motivated Chairman Savidor in 1982 to set up an advisory committee of three members from different Groups on parliamentary etiquette. Some of its first recommendations were that a speaker is not to be interrupted unless he yields, and that men are to wear jackets in the chamber and members' restaurant; these in fact went to confirm norms already urged as desirable. Other proposals were that no debate be held unless at least one minister is present in the chamber, and that a quorum of twenty-five be laid down for votes on second and third readings of bills. While attendance both in the house and in committees continued nevertheless to be low (see also Chapter 6), alarming in particular the coalition managers, there resulted, according to observers, some noticeable improvement in decorum.

It would be mistaken to think that violent oratory and public exchanges of invective mar the mutual respect and even friendship which develops between members, though political adversaries, through collegial labors in the Knesset. Recalling from his experience of decades, Prime Minister Begin, who had served as a member continuously from the First Knesset, once remarked when addressing the house on the favorable transformation that had taken place in the Knesset's social atmosphere since its early days, when political antagonisms and cold personal relations were certain correlates.[2] And indeed, esteem and affection, even for a member whose views are unpopular with a great majority of the house, will find expression, especially marked when there is a resignation or death. To enable a resigning member to take leave of the Knesset with a touch of ceremony the house spontaneously adapted the Motion for the Agenda, which has a different purpose (see Chapter 9). With the same intent, the chair has allowed a departing member to make a personal statement at the close of a sitting though the Rules reserve this proceeding for removal of a misunderstanding or refutation of a charge; and immediately following, the chair has permitted a minister to make an address in reply.

EMOLUMENTS AND SERVICES

The Knesset Members Remuneration law, 1949, amended a number of times, provides for determination of members' salaries by the House Committee. Pegged since 1980 to the pay of deputy ministers, that of members is three and a half times the average national wage, and in March 1984 equalled IS195,055 (about 1,260 US$) monthly before deduction of income tax. Members' salaries, first fixed in a period dominated by forced austerity and stern pioneering and equalitarian principles, reached their present level only after many adjustments. Early on, the law itself specified the member's monthly payment, and for its improvement when it fell behind general wage levels an amending bill had to be enacted. In 1960 the salary was linked to 60 percent of a minister's, and later to 70 percent. (The present deputy minister's level is equivalent to 83 percent of a minister's.) All members whatever their parliamentary position receive the same salary, except for the chairman of the Knesset, whose salary is equal to that of the prime minister. At one time, vice-chairmen and committee chairmen were paid higher salaries than other members, but that practice was discontinued.

The Remuneration Law, enacted when the example of the Provisional State Council was still fresh—members of that body had received only reimbursement of expenses—laid on the member a positive obligation to accept his salary and allowances. Another provision of the 1949 law which is still in force—that forbidding a member to receive a salary from any other source—discriminates in effect between self-employed and salaried persons, permitting the former to continue in their business or profession while serving as members. The legislator's fear that a member who is a salaried worker might favor his employer's interest in the Knesset was hardly more justified than the consideration that a self-employed member might be under a compulsion there to advance his client's concerns. An attack in the House Committee in 1984 on this differentiation led to a recommendation that a member should not be in receipt of any income from extraparliamentary activity. However, the discrimination in law is mitigated by the possibility of receiving payment in forms other than salary.

While any adjustment of members' salaries will draw the attention of the news media, often implying criticism, the method adopted in recent years for updating that remuneration has proved particularly vulnerable. Linked like all salaries to the consumer price index, those of members have since 1980 been further adjusted periodically in relation to the average wage in the economy. This dual updating system, considered necessary in conditions of high inflation because members' salaries are eroded more quickly in the absence of general creeping wage rises, seniority increments, overtime payments and the like, has never failed, however, to arouse a hue and cry when the pay rise of members exceeds by a conspicuous amount that of other wage earners.

In addition to his salary the member receives a number of benefits and allowances. Some of these are services free of charge as laid down in the Immunities Law, and include travel by railway and bus within the country, telephone calls up to a number fixed by the House Committee (at present 2,080 local calls a month, or their equivalent in long-distance calls), and postage for letters from the Knesset Building to any destination within the country, except during the seventy-five days preceding an election. Other allowances, all authorized by the House Committee under the Remuneration Law, are essentially reimbursement of expenses, and though often in lump sum payments linked to the consumer price index are graduated according to outlay. Members' subsistence allowances consist of two parts: a monthly payment (equivalent to 100 US$ in March 1984) during the nine months overlapping the sessions; and a payment (10 US$) every nonsitting day on which a member attends a committee away from his place of residence, and 60 percent of that (6 US$) if the meeting is in his home town. Overnight stay of non-Jerusalem members between sitting days, whether of plenum or committee, is paid for by the Knesset accountant direct to the hotel. A member preferring to rent lodging in Jerusalem while performing his parliamentary duties there will be reimbursed up to a certain amount monthly. An automobile allowance is granted a member according to distance of residence from Jerusalem, with the highest of four levels paid to members living in Safed or farther north (equivalent to 235 US$ monthly in March 1984), and the bottom level if they are citizens of the capital (175 US$).

The House Committee may grant also other special allowances which it finds warranted. For example, in 1980, it authorized a monthly payment to members to help defray the cost of telegrams; in 1981, it decided to reimburse them partly for postage on mail other than letters; and in 1983, the chairman of the Foreign Affairs and Security Committee, though a Jerusalem resident, was granted a maximum automobile allowance to meet his extraordinary travel expenses. An allowance for a member's Report to the Voter twice a year on his activities was decided on in 1983 by the joint House-Finance Committee on the Knesset budget. Any allowance may, however, equally be abolished.

The medical benefits granted a member supplement the care provided through the Sick Fund to which he subscribes, and make available free of charge to him and his family during tenure, and after retirement from the Knesset (with endorsement by a medical unit in the Health Ministry) such things as scarce drugs and accessories, plastic surgery, special nursing care and, if necessary, treatment abroad. The broad and permanent entitlement to these benefits, given that the primary purpose of members' perquisites is to enable them to discharge their parliamentary duties with greater facility, has had a bad press, the moreso as most applicants for the supplementary care are former members. Zealous reformers in the Knesset, who wish to revise members' emoluments so as to remove any suggestion of a privileged class, have been especially critical of the medical benefits as well as of the telephone privilege which, too, continues undiminished for life.

Pensions for members were instituted in 1958 by a statute setting out their terms. Up to that date, the Remuneration Law laid down a specified monthly grant in lieu of a pension. The 1958 law was replaced by the Holders of Public Office (Benefits) Law, 1969, which provides for the determination of members' pensions, as well as those of other specified high office holders, by resolution of the Knesset, but permits the Knesset to transfer that authority to one of its committees. The rules for members' pensions are consequently fixed by the House Committee. Their main provisions are a pension right of 20 percent for every Knesset term served, even if it falls short of four years, and an additional 2 percent for each year by which a member's age exceeds fifty at cease of tenure—to a maximum total of 70 percent. A member not yet forty on retiring from the Knesset is not entitled to a pension but receives a nonrecurrent grant equal to 18 percent of his last salary for every month of service. For a woman member the stipulated ages are five years less: she is pensionable at thirty-five, and her 2 percent annual credits are counted from age forty-five. The accelerated accumulation by a member of pension rights when compared to the ordinary citizen, and the fact that his widow receives his full pension, unlike the 60 percent in the case of a civil servant's widow, have not escaped controversy, even inside the house, any more than other parliamentary emoluments.

But any decision with regard to members' remuneration must be invidious so long as the Knesset is in the position of itself fixing the level. For while the House Committee has linked the members' salary to that of deputy ministers, it is the Finance Committee that determines the level of salary for deputy ministers as for other holders of high public office. While only the Knesset can properly judge members' need of specific allowances in connection with parliamentary duties, their salaries and pensions might well be fixed by an independent public commission, as is urged from time to time on the floor of the house. The level of members' salaries has not itself often been questioned, no doubt because other occupations do not offer a useful basis of comparison with the Knesset members' calling. An objective outside body, while sparing the Knesset recurring embarrassment, would no doubt be as cognizant as a parliamentary committee of the substantial loss of income sustained by many members on entering the house and of the risk faced by some of finding no suitable employment after they leave—and might in the result be more generous.

Members are perhaps least well endowed with respect to services and facilities that affect their very functioning as legislators and scrutineers of Government decisions. Up to the mid-1970s, leaving out of account the Government's legal advisers in committees who continue to offer their services, a member had available in the performance of his multifarious tasks only the limited office help of his parliamentary Group, and in emergency of the Knesset staff, chiefly for simple typing or translation or for photocopying or duplication. Since then he has been paid a parliamentary services allowance, which in 1984 amounted to IS 24,000 (equivalent to 140 US$) monthly. He can use this allowance as he sees fit—for secretarial, research, publication, or other purposes. Many members use the entire allowance to employ a young person with academic training as a personal assistant. Such an assistant is expected to answer the member's mail, arrange his appointments, prepare background matter for his speeches and work on their preparation, assemble material on committee subjects, peruse the press for possible Questions and Motions and formulate them, and to perform any other task assigned him by the member. If members are lucky enough to find devoted and competent assistants who put in long hours through the three sitting days every week despite the scanty pay and heavy work load, it is because the job is interesting and an ideal apprenticeship for a political career. In not a few cases, however, a member's services allowance secures him only half an assistant since, to improve their pay, some assistants work for two members.

A Reference and Information Service to provide documentation and prepare notes and analyses for members was set up in the Knesset Library in 1973. But its entire staff consists of one permanent head and a few temporary employees who are graduate students; and some of them are assigned exclusively to committees. Legal, economic, and statistical questions are not included among its subjects as those are dealt with by the Knesset's legal and economic advisers.

A question has occasionally been referred to experts by arrangement with the universities, and from time to time academic specialists are among expert witnesses invited by a committee or asked to accompany certain of its deliberations. But the Knesset has chosen rather to reinforce its own staff with a few legal advisers and economists; and these too work chiefly for the committees (see Chapter 7). As a result a rank-and-file member seeking to pit his views against those of a ministry armed with expertise still remains seriously handicapped. If the Knesset has not equipped its members with sharper information and research tools, this is not only because coalitions do not feel a pressing need for them; the gradualist approach in making such facilities available is due as much to the prevalent view that while increased research assistance and staff may be of value, their importance is after all secondary to that of the members' own application and forceful assertion of the Knesset's constitutional right to oversee and influence the executive.

6

Knesset Organization

IN BROAD OUTLINE the organization of Israel's parliament is laid down in the Basic Law on the Knesset, passed in 1958. Beyond its general dispositions concerning the Knesset's composition, sessions, presiding officers, and committees, the Basic Law provides that Knesset procedure shall be governed by a hierarchy of three elements: statute law, rules, and accepted practice. To a large extent the Basic Law brought together existing provisions or gave statutory force to practice already followed.

The Knesset's membership of 120, prescribed in the Basic Law, was first fixed in the 1948 election ordinance. A proposal made in 1951 to increase the number of members to 151, after the number of voters had doubled since 1948, was not accepted by the Knesset. This was also the fate later of all such proposals. When in 1972 the larger parties considered an increase in the Knesset membership, it was viewed as a means to allow fuller communal representation and to admit to the Knesset more persons of ability and professional talent. The press then drew attention to a narrower motive of the parties—to ease the pressure on their nominations committees. Yet one argument put forward in the Knesset from time to time for the enlargement of its membership merits consideration: a small country, scarcely less than a large one, needs a parliament large enough to cope with the multifarious problems of modern government and legislation, and to facilitate among other things the manning and functioning of an increasing number of committees. And the number of Knesset members carrying the parliamentary load is appreciably smaller than 120. For instance, in the Knesset elected in 1981 there was an interval during which twenty members were ministers, and eleven deputy ministers, so that more than a quarter of the house was largely absorbed by the executive arm.

As the parliament of a nation without time-honored class distinctions and without requirements of federal accommodation the Knesset is unicameral. Voices for an upper house are heard occasionally in the Knesset, buttressed by pleas that the state has so far no constitution to which faulty legislation can be appealed, and that a second chamber would be also a useful way of employing the talents of aging statesmen while facilitating change of blood in the nation's elected bodies. Arguably, the case for a second house is strengthened by the absence of presidential veto powers and of any quorum requirement in the Knesset. However, the idea has not won substantial support, and checks to unsound legislation must be sought for in Israel's free press, in a vigilant opposition—and not least—in the restraints that are natural to coalition government.

TERM, SESSION, AND SITTINGS

The statutory term of the Knesset is four years, with elections fixed for the third Tuesday in the Hebrew month of Heshvan (which comes in autumn). A term may be cut short because of a falling out between coalition partners, deep differences within the leading coalition party, or the absence otherwise of a secure parliamentary majority for the Government. The Knesset elected in June 1981, since it came after a short-lived house, would have served until November 1985 had it run its full term; however, serious economic difficulties and a narrow Government majority brought on elections in 1984. A term can be shortened only by the Knesset's enactment of a dissolution law fixing also the date for a new election. Dissolution bills are generally initiated by members. When in 1981 the Government introduced a bill to dissolve the house, it was criticized for infringing the custom of leaving to the Knesset and its members all steps with regard to such a measure. Whether a Knesset completes its term or is short lived, it continues to hold office until its successor convenes; and in practice it will meet, as necessary, at any time after the closing of its last regular session. The Eighth Knesset met as late as 16 May 1977, the day preceding the election of its successor. The First Knesset held its concluding sitting in the morning and the Second opened in the afternoon on the same day, 20 August 1951.

Two regular sessions, which together total at least eight months, are held by the Knesset in a year. The longer winter session runs from midautumn until the week before Passover; the shorter summer session from May to midsummer. The exact dates of each recess are fixed by the presidium with the concurrence of the House Committee. Sittings of the plenum, which normally last from four to five hours, are held on Monday, Tuesday, and Wednesday. The sitting opens at 4.00 P.M. on the first two of these days, and at 11.00 A.M. on Wednesday. The chairman of the Knesset may change the times of sittings, and with the concurrence of the House Committee he may cancel or add a sitting as necessary. These powers are exercised by the chairman most often to meet the press of business in the last weeks of a session, when he may advance the opening of sittings or ask approval for a Thursday sitting; even with such steps, however, the house may still need to sit until past midnight during that period. In the summer and Passover recesses a special sitting of the Knesset may be called by the chairman at the request of thirty members, or of the Government. In recent years the frequency of such special sittings has increased.

Plenary sittings are open to the public and the communication media. The publication of any proceeding taken at these sittings, except something prohibited by the chair on the grounds of national security, does not entail any criminal or civil liability. However, the house may decide to hold a sitting *in camera* on the proposal of at least ten members, or on a request by the Government supported by thirty members. Publication of proceedings at a closed sitting may be allowed only by the House Committee. Though the provisions for a sitting behind closed doors are made in the Basic Law and detailed in the Knesset Rules, only one such sitting was ever held: on 26 December 1960 the house closed its doors to take up the resignation of the chief of staff.

The Knesset's three-day week (in the plenum) and Israel's dimunitive geography enable every member to be home most of the week to pursue his various local political activities. This convenience has deterred the Knesset from adding a fourth day to its work week and making also Thursday a plenary sitting day as urged from time to time. To avoid late evening meetings of the parliamentary Groups, the Knesset preferred to compress its effective work week still further: in 1962, after consultation of the Groups with the presidium of the Knesset, the dinner-hour break on Mondays and Tuesdays was eliminated so that the house could adjourn at nine instead of ten o'clock. In the session of 1967–68 the house reduced its Tuesday sittings still further, from five to four hours, so as to adjourn by eight o'clock. Because members wish to get home from Jerusalem as early as possible on Wednesdays, an arrangement for the meeting of the house on Wednesdays at 12.30 P.M. instead of 11.00 A.M., so as to allow for two rounds of committee meetings before the opening of the house sitting, had to be abandoned.

Although the Knesset has been meeting in Jerusalem continuously since December 1949, when it moved from Tel Aviv, and according to a Basic Law Jerusalem is its seat, pressure by committees for permission to sit in

Tel Aviv has been resisted by Knesset chairmen only with the greatest difficulty. More than half the members of every Knesset have been residents of Tel Aviv and the surrounding area; and since that coastal city is also more accessible than the capital from most other parts of the country, extensive use was made by committees of the Knesset chairman's Tel Aviv Bureau until 1967 when those premises were closed. Since the inauguration of the permanent Knesset Building in 1966 and the closing of the Tel Aviv Bureau, the Knesset's Tel Aviv connection has been somewhat less marked. Yet a few committees continue to meet in Tel Aviv on days when the Knesset is not sitting.

A new Knesset, without being summoned, assembles on a date fixed by law: the Monday of the second week following the gazetting of the election results. (It is, however, customary for the secretary of the Knesset to notify the newly elected members of the opening date by a letter citing the pertinent provisions of the Basic Law on the Knesset.) In the presence of former members and dignitaries invited for the occasion, the Knesset is opened by the president of the state, who after a short address turns over the chairmanship to the oldest member; the latter makes a speech, usually of a nonpolitical nature, and then presides over the members' declarations of allegiance and the election of the chairman of the Knesset. The chairman, immediately after he is elected, assumes his seat on the dais and offers a brief address of thanks. The house then proceeds to set up the Organizing Committee, a body on which all parliamentary Groups are represented and which has ranged in membership from twenty-one to twenty-nine. It is chaired by a representative of the largest Group, generally the member who will head the coalition in the house.

The tasks of the Organizing Committee are: to nominate the vice-chairmen of the Knesset after determining what are to be their number and political affiliations; to determine the number of permanent committees, the membership and party composition of each, and to nominate their members; to arrange the seating of the Groups in the chamber, and to assign rooms to Groups and members in the Knesset Building. Neither law nor rules take cognizance of the Organizing Committee. Yet a new Knesset could hardly get under way without it. In fact it meets a number of times before being formally set up, prior to the Knesset's opening. If, through it, the Groups come to an early understanding on the vice-chairmanships, the nominees for these positions will be elected at the Knesset's first sitting, immediately after the election of the chairman. The organization of the committees, which is a more complex task, will take longer, although it is not unusual for the Organizing Committee to bring its proposals concerning them for approval at the Knesset's second sitting. Among the committees which are set up is the House Committee, whose concern is with Knesset procedure. The House

Committee, when constituted, replaces the Organizing Committee which ceases then to function.

After the foregoing business has been completed, the Knesset will proceed to its regular activity, although it can begin to function fully only after a new Government is confirmed by it. (The formation of a new Government, which may take days, weeks, or—in extreme cases—months, is described in Chapter 12.) The opening of a session other than the first sitting in a new term is usually marked by a general debate following a Government statement on the current situation or a recent event, or by the consideration of some major piece of Government-sponsored legislation.

The regular sittings of the Knesset are attended by little ceremony. The chairman enters the chamber accompanied by the Knesset officer, mounts the dais to take the chair, and with three taps of a gavel on his desk announces the sitting opened. Visiting parliamentarians or other distinguished persons will be seated in a special gallery below and forward from the public gallery and greeted by the chairman at the opening of the sitting. They may have been received earlier in the forecourt with the ceremony of the Knesset Guard. A foreign head of state may address the Knesset from the rostrum at a special sitting to which former members as well as other guests are invited.

There is greater fanfare at the sitting called once in five years for receiving the declaration of allegiance of the new president of the state, elected at a previous Knesset sitting. He enters a full house, the galleries and alcoves packed with guests, to the sound of ram's horns, followed by song of a choir. The ceremony, which may include an address by the retiring as well as by the newly elected president, is followed by cheers and singing of the anthem. The president then departs to a flourish of trumpets. Except on this occasion, and when he opens a new Knesset, he will be present in the chamber only as a spectator in a special section of the gallery when he chooses to hear a particular debate. The house will then simply take note of his arrival and departure by rising to its feet on being alerted by the secretary's call.

A special sitting may be held to mark a national or historic event. For years, there was no settled practice for the proceedings at such a sitting. At the sitting of 1 November 1967, which marked the seventieth anniversary of the First Zionist Congress and the fiftieth of the Balfour Declaration, there were twelve speakers from nearly as many parliamentary Groups. After general agreement that repetitious speech-making only detracted from the occasion, a Rule was adopted providing that a commemorative sitting is to be addressed only by the chairman or by another member whom he has designated for the purpose, and may be addressed also by the prime minister or by a minister designated in turn by him.

Proceedings for the special sitting which is called in memory of a deceased member or minister were laid down in a later Rule. After opening words by the chairman, two members whom he has appointed for the purpose may speak. When a former member dies the house honors his memory at the opening of a regular sitting: the chairman calls on the members to rise and utters a brief eulogy.

The seats in the Knesset chamber are arranged in concentric half-oval rows with each member occupying a swivel chair and desk. The four rows for members are broken by two aisles which open from the back and narrow to a close at the center, where the ministers sit around a horseshoe table with the prime minister at the base (see Figure 1). The Government table was originally planned for twenty ministers. When the Government was increased to twenty-two Ministers in May 1967, only nine months after the Knesset had moved into its permanent abode, the swivel chairs around that table were replaced by smaller four-legged chairs whose number could be altered as needed. The members of each parliamentary Group (but not of the coalition as a whole) sit together in places assigned by the Organizing Committee. Within each Group seating is according to order of appearance on the candidates list so that leading members are in front. There are only 116 seats for 120 members, but there are always more than four members at the Government table, so that as a rule there are some vacant places.

For years the seats to the right hand of the chairman, who sits at the center of a dais facing the members, were shunned by some Groups. They could not forget the old European parliamentary tradition of a reactionary and often anti-Semitic right wing. At the same time, according to the first House Committee chairman, each Group "claimed it was more left-wing than the next."[1] Consequently, the Groups were seated according to size, starting from the left, an arrangement which generally brought immediately next to each other the largest coalition and opposition Groups. The first change was made in 1970, while there was a national unity Government. *Gahal,* the second largest Group then in the house and in the Government, was taunted by the tiny Groups that had remained in opposition; and with its economic and social policies remaining of an opposition character, it felt more uncomfortable than usual about its juxtaposition with the Labor Alignment. Both large Groups felt it desirable then to emphasize the basic polarization of the house in the seating arrangement, and *Gahal* was moved to the right hand, overcoming at last its old prejudice about that side of the chamber. The rearrangement was not made without protest from the small Groups, who now had to sit in the middle, at the back of the chamber, where they were less exposed to the television cameras and to the public gallery, and from where interjections are less convenient. In 1977–81, when *Likud* led the coalition

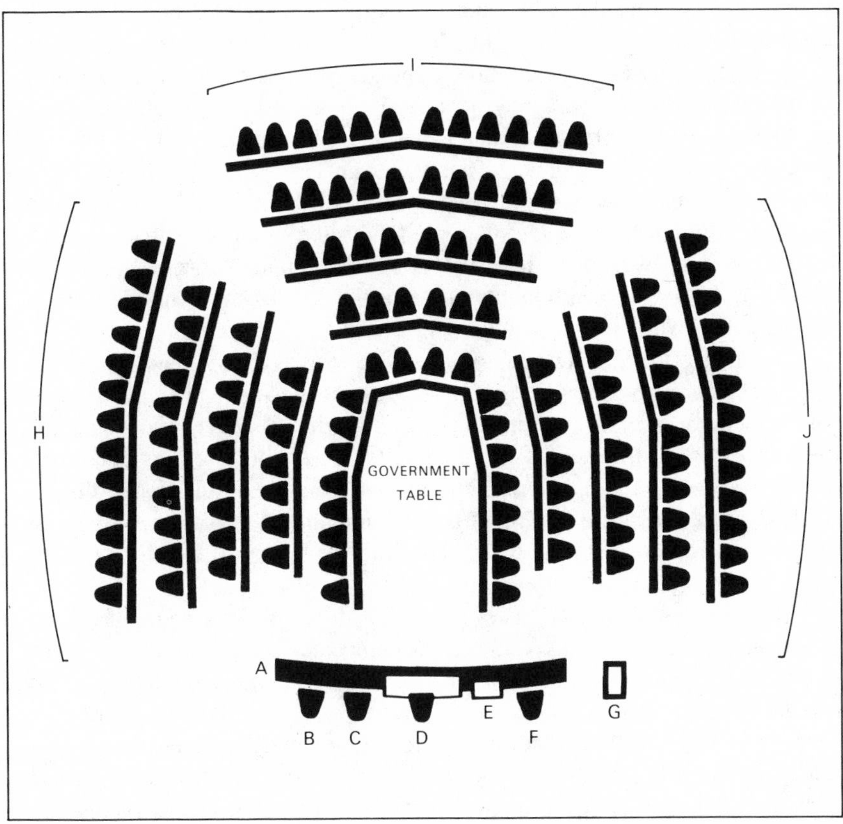

A- Dais
B- Knesset officer
C- Secretary
D- Chairman
E- Speakers' rostrum
F- Committee chairman (during second readings)
G- Stenographer's box.
H- Alignment
I- Smaller Groups
J- Likud

Figure 1

Seating Arrangement in the Knesset Chamber
(October 1984)

and elected to sit on the left hand, the displaced Labor Alignment would on no account move to the right-hand side with the result that the two largest opposed Groups again sat side by side, leaving the right wing to the small Groups. Only after the 1981 election, when the Alignment found itself a second time in the opposition, it agreed reluctantly to sit on the right after arrangements were made for the television cameras to photograph from the galleries on both sides of the chamber. Thus the main Groups of the coalition and opposition again sat face to face. Under the national unity Government formed in 1984, Alignment and *Likud,* though both in the coalition, still faced each other, this time with the Alignment on the left of the chair and the small Groups, whether of coalition or opposition, at the back—with spillovers in any direction where numbers required this.

To the right of the presiding officer on the dais is the rostrum from where speeches and statements are made. At his seat a member may only put a supplementary question to a minister, raise a point of order, make an interjection, or at most present with a minute's explanation a bill unopposed by the Government; a member who sits far back and wants to be sure that he will be heard clearly in one of these interventions will go to the nearest of the five microphones on the floor. Seated to the chairman's left, somewhat lower down, is the secretary.

The stenographers' box faces the end of the dais a few meters from the rostrum. A verbatim stenographic record of debates and proceedings appears in transcription about two hours after the words have been spoken for use by the press and by members, who have up to seven days to correct their speeches. A member may correct clerical and stenographic errors or other inadvertent discrepancies in his speeches but not their substance. In earlier years the House Committee authorized the presiding officer to expunge unparliamentary language from the record. However, the Basic Law and the Rules have empowered him to erase only what in his opinion is liable to harm national security. Thus, when he asks a member to withdraw an offensive expression and the latter does so, both expression and retraction will appear in the revised record.

The revised and printed official report, *Divrei Haknesset* (the Knesset Record), appears later as a weekly brochure including as appendices texts of bills, resolutions, and other documents such as committee conclusions and ministers' responses to them; these are documents which have been laid on the table of the house—that is, have been distributed to the members' desks and announced by the secretary, usually at the opening of the sitting. A minister may also have included as an appendix any document connected with his speech. *Divrei Hakensset* is published in Hebrew with an annual analytic index. For Arab members, of which there have been six or seven in nearly every Knesset, a simultaneous translation from the Hebrew is available, though most know Hebrew and use it in their parliamentary work. Speeches in Arabic are rendered in Hebrew by an interpreter from the rostrum immediately after their delivery. The Rules also provide for early delivery of bills in Arabic translation.

Plenary proceedings have been covered by the press and by radio since 1948, when the Provisional State Council was Israel's legislature. Occasional television broadcasts from the Knesset were begun in 1969. Since 1971, extracts of debates with comment have appeared regularly on television news. Noting that in certain instances the timing of a debate has been adjusted to coincide with television schedules, a Knesset secretary has observed also that the presence of television cameras in the chamber may have contributed to "more dramatic" performances in debate.[2] The Broadcasting Service, which is administered by an independent public authority, seeks to be objective in its parliamentary coverage. But since televising in the chamber is on a selective basis, it has been criticized from time to time as lacking balance in the newscasts and emphasizing the sensational at the expense of the workaday to an extent that brings the Knesset into public contempt. After a debate on the matter in 1980, the Knesset resolved that the House Committee, in consultation with the Broadcasting Authority, lay down rules for the coverage of parliamentary affairs.

Yet members have remained troubled by the preference of television for exceptional, rowdy debates as newsworthy, while overlooking much of the important but humdrum business which the house regularly transacts. Whenever the Knesset reviews the conduct of its own affairs—and this is done in a general debate nearly every year—the television problem is one of the most discussed.Though hardly anyone proposes that the house be closed to television, there have been hints that it might be well to confine the focus of the cameras to the speaker at the rostrum.

While the number of members present in the Knesset Building is notably higher as a rule than in the chamber, as attested by the electronic attendance board at the entrance to the chamber (which is used as a tool by the Groups in summoning their members to vote), television has exposed to the eyes of a large public, more than any other parliamentary blemish, rows of empty seats in important debates. The problem of poor attendance in the house, while aggravated by television coverage, had been a sore point also earlier on. In 1952, an attendance register was instituted but discontinued after three weeks because of members' objections.[3] The keeping of a register was proposed again in 1971 by Chairman Reuven Barkatt at a meeting with Group whips on the problem of attendance. A decision on the matter was deferred, while a proposal to pay a member his expense allowance only if he attended in the chamber was not favored then by the whips.

In the years 1979–81 the slim majority commanded in the house by the coalition compelled the parliamentary Groups to take notice of the attendance problem. As the coalition found Government measures voted down, while barely escaping defeat on a budget vote, and the opposition felt it narrowly missed toppling the Government on a number of occasions because of the absence of a few members, both the *Likud* and Labor Alignment Groups considered keeping black lists of absentees. Although the leaders of both Groups agreed at one point, according to a press report, "that the Knesset's work was being done by less than half the 120 MKs,"[4] it appears from repeated announcements that the publication of attendance records by the Group would be proposed that such a step was an ultimate measure which, while held out as a threat, could not be easily carried into effect.

Sparse attendance has continued to trouble the Knesset. On 17 November 1982, Vice-Chairman M. Shahal adjourned the sitting early, in the midst of a debate, in protest at the absence of all but three members. About the same time Vice-Chairman M. Cohen-Avidov wrote to the coalition chairman warning that thenceforth if none were present in the coalition seats while he presided, he would declare the sitting adjourned. In 1983, Chairman Savidor, noting that the Knesset Members (Immunity, Rights and Duties) Law of 1951 does not actually lay down a single duty, proposed that there be added to it a declaration that members are expected to be in the Knesset Building on the three plenary sitting days unless abroad on state or other public business. But members would not have the Immunities Law tampered with; nor did a suggestion that the requirement be at least included in the Rules win general support.

The Knesset Rules require members to attend sittings "as regularly as they can",[5] and when travelling abroad to inform the Knesset chairman with indication of time and destination. These provisions have not prevented members from absenting themselves from the house for extended periods. In 1967, after Y. Smilanski was absent from the house for more than a year while pursuing studies overseas, another member presented a bill that would deprive any member absent for a full month, or fifteen sittings in a session, of his seat. The bill was rejected, but less than a month later Smilanski resigned from the Knesset. Of a number of later members' bills aimed at deduction from the salary of a member absent for private reasons, one received first reading in 1981 after insertion of a clause that would authorize the House Committee to fix rules for the definition of "private business."

The attendance of ministers in the house is statutory only for the declaration which they must make, one by one, of allegiance to the state and compliance with Knesset decisions. The Knesset, by its Rules, further compels their attendance to answer members' questions; but any minister may be represented by another or by a Deputy Minister for any business in the house. Nevertheless, for its continuous dialogue of debate with the Government, the Knesset demands the presence of ministers at all times except when considering its own internal matters. Though the Knesset cannot enforce their presence, it may hold up or postpone proceedings—also Government business—in the absence of the minister concerned with the matter in hand. When no ministers are present, the presiding officer, at the urging of irate members, will send to find one and may interrupt the sitting until he shows up. Because of an empty Government table on 30 November 1981, Vice-chairman M. Shahal halted a debate on immigration and adjourned the sitting early.

Governments concerned for their part to expedite business, to provide leadership in the house, and to avoid embarrassment to the coalition, have sometimes undertaken to man the Government table on a rota basis, or to provide that in addition to the minister concerned with the subject under debate another always be present; but they could not always perform as promised. Opposition members were quick to rebuke Mr. Begin's Government, after the 1977 election for failing to abide by its early resolution to attend the house regularly in full strength.

Closely linked to the problem of attendance in the chamber is the question of a quorum. The Knesset has no quorum requirement for voting or debate. When the draft Basic Law on the Knesset was under debate in 1958, different proposals for a quorum were rejected as restrictions that would hamper plenary sittings. Since then a number of members' bills to institute a quorum have met with little success. A motion by Mr. Begin to consider the adoption of a quorum, less than a year before becoming prime minister, was referred to the House Committee. The Committee did not report back to the house. In 1979 a member's bill for a quorum on all votes appeared at first to make headway, though whittled down by the time it received first reading to a quorum (of thirty) only on second and third readings of bills. The committee which prepared the bill for second reading removed also the last provision, and instead of laying down a quorum merely added to Section 24 of the Basic Law (that "The Knesset shall hold debates and pass decisions whatever the number of Members present") the words, "if there be no other provision in any law concerning this matter."[6] In effect the house enacted the amendment as reported by the committee though it nullified the principle of the bill as accepted on the first reading.

Regarding a quorum as a potential encumbrance to expediting house business and as a possible weapon of obstruction, men in positions of responsibility in the Knesset have sought to ward it off, by the most tenuous arguments if necessary. Speaking on the last-mentioned bill, the committee chairman claimed that a quorum would hurt small parliamentary Groups, notwithstanding the fact that the two members who argued for the quorum provision, as well as the sponsor of the bill, were themselves members of small Groups.[7] The coalition chairman argued that instead of filling empty seats during debates, a quorum would lead to a defensive device like the holding of votes at fixed times; he did not consider a quorum for debate to be in question.

THE CHAIRMAN AND VICE-CHAIRMEN OF THE KNESSET

The chairman of the Knesset, who is charged by the Rules with the conduct of its affairs, ranks third in the state's order of precedence—after the president and the prime minister. He is elected by the plenum in an open vote, generally from the largest coalition Group after it has reached an understanding with other Groups in the house so as to secure the widest possible support for him. Only once in the past, when supported by a fortuitous combination of Groups, was a candidate opposed to that of the largest coalition Group elected chairman.[8]

After his election the chairman is expected to restrict his political activities though not to sever ties with his party. In the house he takes no part in debate and votes only exceptionally. Mr. Yitzhak Shamir, after being elected chairman in 1977, consulted the attorney general regarding party affiliation. He was advised that he could freely maintain his political links provided he held no executive position in his party. Certainly under Israel's electoral system a chairman who renounced all party links could not even hope to be reelected to the Knesset unless he formed his own candidates list.

Mr. Shamir went from the Knesset chairmanship to a more active political role and was made foreign minister in 1980. While the opposition criticized the appointment, curiously no one protested that the Government was depriving the Knesset of its chairman in midterm. Shamir's successor, Mr. Yitzhak Berman, served as chairman for the remainder of the term and after the 1981 election became minister of energy. Chairman Menachem Savidor (1981–84) declared in an interview that he would not consider interrupting his term as Knesset chairman to stand for a cabinet place. The chairman elected after him, Mr. Shlomo Hillel, had the career of a minister behind him as well as that of diplomat. Earlier chairmen too viewed their elections to the office as the crowning event of a public career. Kadish Luz, the Knesset's third chairman (1959–69), resigned as minister of agriculture to be eligible for the chairmanship. Both he and the Knesset's first chairman, Yosef Sprinzak (1949–59), were reelected twice, the latter dying in office.

The impartiality of the chairman of the Knesset as chief presiding officer is not often challenged; in emulation of British usage he is popularly termed "speaker." However, the chairman's situation differs in important ways from that of the speaker at Westminister. On top of his continuing party connections, his responsibilities with respect to the Knesset's order of business leave him open occasionally to charges of bias though his powers in this sphere are prescribed by the Knesset Rules. For example, Chairman Shamir refused to convene the house as requested by opposition parties for a special session in the 1979 Passover recess to discuss the High Court's rebuke of Government officials for contempt of court in the matter of land expropriation. He was criticized for confining the Knesset to the counsel of the Government's legal adviser, who had declared the matter *sub judice*. During regular sessions the agenda for the two weekly sittings which are reserved for Government business, on Monday and Tuesday, must be drawn up by the chairman in accordance with the Government's proposals. When he acts together with the vice-chairmen with regard to the recognition of urgent members' motions, he is liable to charges of partisanship no less than his colleagues. A ruling at a sitting, whether by the chairman or a vice-chairman, may be appealed to an Interpretations Committee of the house. While the Committee cannot change the ruling, the manner in which it resolves the question, even if at variance with the ruling, serves to guide the chair in future.

Nonetheless, the chairman of the Knesset has always commanded the respect of the entire house. On one occasion, when Chairman Savidor's remonstration with a minister at the rostrum led to a brush with the prime minister, members were quick to support Mr. Savidor.[9] The deference with which the chairman is regarded is reinforced by law, rule, and developing custom. He is generally in the chair on Monday afternoon when the Knesset begins its weekly sittings and on important occasions; at other times he is relieved by the vice-chairmen presiding in rotation. The predominance of the chairman was established in law when the Knesset provided for the election of a "Chairman and Vice-Chairmen" while rejecting an amendment that would prescribe their election formally as the "Presidium."* Statutes concerning the Knesset distinguish powers exercised by the chairman alone and in consultation with the vice-chairmen; the Knesset Rules state powers that are his alone and those which he exercises together with the vice-chairmen. More significant are the norms of practice. Unlike the vice-chairmen, who take part in debate and sit regularly with their respective parliamentary Groups except while taking turns in the chair, the chairman remains aloof from party strife and generally refrains from commenting on the issues of the day. Procedural rulings from the chair may not be disputed during a Knesset sitting. While this applies equally if a vice-chairman is presiding, the Interpretations

*However, in the interest of brevity the term "presidium," with a lower-case "p," is used throughout instead of the statutory name, "The Chairman of the Knesset and the Vice-Chairmen."

Committee to which a member may appeal is always presided over by the chairman of the Knesset.

As the guardian of its Rules and the dignity of its proceedings, the chairman influences the Knesset's procedure and decorum also by means other than rulings from the chair. Not infrequently he communicates the need for changes in the Rules to the House Committee. For example, at the instance of Knesset Chairman Yitzhak Berman the Committee set up a Subcommittee on Ethics in 1981 to fix norms of conduct for members. At the weekly meeting of the presidium, though held primarily to decide business for members' days, decisions affecting procedure in the house may be taken at the chairman's instance in matters not covered by the Rules, although to be binding such decisions need to be officially taken note of by the House Committee. To improve members' amenities, or to prevent disorderly debate, he may make changes in the Knesset Building or chamber on his own initiative. Thus to facilitate interjection in debate Chairman Reuven Barkatt had microphones installed on the members' desks in the chamber, in 1969. Ten years later, when interjections had become unruly and disruptive, Chairman Shamir silenced these microphones and in their stead placed five others in different parts of the chamber. Later examples were the regulations on attire issued by Chairmen Berman and Savidor in order to preserve a dignified atmosphere in the Knesset Building.

Finally, contributing to the great prestige which the chairman's office carries in the country generally is the statutory provision which requires him to act for the president of the state in the event of the latter's incapacity or absence from the country. When he is himself absent or otherwise indisposed, one of the vice-chairmen, usually from his parliamentary Group, is appointed by the House Committee as acting chairman.

The number of vice-chairmen has varied from two to eight. The absence of a permanently fixed number of vice-chairmanships has facilitated their use as political spoils with each new Knesset to take account both of the vicissitudes of party fortune and of emergent requirements in the negotiations and trading that take place between parliamentary Groups and between coalition and opposition. The coalition has always made certain that the vice-chairmen from its ranks, together with the chairman, were a majority of the presidium. Vice-chairmanships have generally been distributed among the larger Groups only. A Group with fewer than eight members has never received a vice-chairmanship except as part of a reciprocal arrangement with a larger Group, or as in 1977 when the four-man ultraorthodox *Agudat Yisrael* Group, refusing a Government portfolio in consequence of a ruling by its rabbinical authorities, was given a vice-chairmanship among other compensations. At the same time, a Group resulting from an alliance of parties may secure the allocation of a vice-chairmanship to each of its divisions, or, if commanding too few vice-chairmanships, may rotate them. It is accepted that the vice-chairmanships assigned to a Group remain at its disposal through the term. When Mrs. Hana Lamdan left the *Mapam* Group in 1952, she gave up the vice-chairmanship she was holding on its behalf.

There is some ambivalence toward the position of vice-chairman. Since political considerations may weigh more in the choice of vice-chairmen than erudition in Knesset procedure or ability to conduct sittings, vice-chairmen do not always enjoy the esteem and trust of the whole house though they generally seek to be impartial. In one instance, in 1979, a member charged that they were abusing their authority to approve urgent motions by allowing an undue proportion to one of their own colleagues; the house referred the subject to the House Committee. In the same year in a press interview Chairman Shamir conceded that parliamentary Groups do not always choose the vice-chairmen with due consideration for the qualities necessary in presiding officers.[10] Yet a vice-chairman, like the chairman, is elected by open vote of the Knesset. In the above case of Mrs. Lamdan, *Mapam*'s first nominee in her place did not become vice-chairman because the house refused to accept him.

RULE AND PRECEDENT

The First Knesset inherited the eighteen procedural rules of the Provisional State Council, an appointed body of fewer than forty members that sat little more than one hour weekly during its entire existence of nine months. Those rules were too few and too sketchy for the needs of the Knesset. Very early, therefore, the Knesset's House Committee, through a subcommittee, applied itself to the preparation of a comprehensive body of rules. As in much of its practice the Knesset drew inspiration for its written rules from the procedure of the two pre-state representative bodies described in Chapter 1, the Zionist Congress and the Elected Assembly of Palestine Jewry. Hence, to cite but two examples, the Knesset instinctively, as it were, adopted a collegial presidium and a system of time allotment on a Group basis for important debates.

The Knesset Rules of Procedure are the result of a long, ongoing process of regulation. It is convenient to distinguish between an earlier period when entire chapters of the rule book were first written and a later period, overlapping with the earlier, when new rules were adopted and existing ones amended as need arose. The earliest chapter, on the competence of committees, was adopted in 1949; the last, concerning members motions, only in 1971. Changes after most of these chapters had become part of the rule book and concerning specific matters were made in order to adapt existing rules to emerging needs and meet situations which had not been contemplated. For instance, continued neglect by the Government of Knesset committees' Conclusions prompted the adoption of a provision in the Rules in 1977 requiring the ministers concerned to inform the Knesset, within six months of receiving such Conclusions, of any action consequently taken. A later example is provided by the 1977–81 Knesset, when some exceptionally boisterous members moved the house to alter the Rules so as to increase the discretionary power of the chair.

For years the rule-making prerogative rested solely with the House Committee. A Rule or amendment adopted by the Committee would need only to be laid on the table of the house. Only in July 1967 were the Knesset Rules of Procedure adopted by a resolution of the house. Since then any change in the Rules proposed by the Committee has required such approval. Knesset members have fourteen days to submit objections to a proposed change. Objections not accepted by the Committee may be defended again in the house before it votes on the Rule or amendment.

The Knesset Rules provide further that procedural questions to which they contain no answer shall be settled by the House Committee. Hence alongside of the Rules there is a growing body of House Committee Resolutions. A decision of the presidium on a procedural matter is usually brought to the attention of the House Committee; the latter's "taking note" of the decision gives it the force of a House Committee Resolution. The Rules make the House Committee the final arbiter in many procedural matters. To give two examples: the Committee decides whether to confirm additional or cancelled sittings as determined by the Knesset chairman, as it does with regard to dates of session and recess fixed by the presidium; and Urgent Motions not recognized by the presidium may be appealed to the Committee. The House Committee is further empowered to lay down a manner of proceeding, in exceptional cases, that deviates from Rule and precedent. This power, when broadly construed, has laid the Committee open to the charge of setting the Rules at naught. Knesset Chairman Savidor in 1984 declined to accept the House Committee's permission to hold a secret vote on Knesset dissolution bills in face of an existing Rule that restricts such a vote to a few specified matters only. After calling an open vote as usual, he said that he would take the initiative to limit the Committee's power to decide on extraordinary procedures.

During a Knesset sitting procedural questions are settled by decision of the chair, the ruling of a presiding vice-chairman carrying authority equal to that of the chairman. However, these rulings over the years, though a valuable source of guidance in conducting a sitting, are not mandatory precedents. A ruling may be appealed to the Interpretations Committee, which consists of nine members, eight chosen by the House Committee, with the Knesset chairman presiding and the appellant present. The decision of the Interpretations Committee, though not affecting the ruling in question if in contradiction to it, is the binding precedent. An Interpretations Committee is set up in each Knesset; but there have never been more than a few appeals in an entire term.

A point of order may be raised by a member during a sitting by the proposal of a Motion for Order, for which he must receive permission from the Chairman upon a request made in writing. A request for a Motion for Order on a vote may also be made orally. The member, speaking from his place, has one minute to propose the motion. The chairman decides whether to accept it. The Motion for Order has often served as a device of procedural maneuver. Perhaps its most effective use in this way was made by small Groups in 1973 during debate on an elections bill whose purpose was to alter the method of dealing with vote remainders in a manner that would be detrimental to small parties. Although the Labor Alignment and *Gahal* carried the day by their large majority, the dilatory effect of Motions for Order from eight small Groups at every possible turn in the first and second reading debates prolonged the sittings of 1 January and 3 April 1973 well into the mornings of the next days. Further, the barrage of motions, by attrition, induced the chair at those sittings to resort to unprecedented and questionable procedures such as submission to a house vote of decisions of the House Committee and presidium on the order of proceedings; for the sake of progress against systematic obstruction the chair at one point waived the right to rule finally on Motions for Order and put them to a vote.

The Knesset Rules offer opportunities for parliamentary maneuver other than by Motions for Order. For example, vigilant opposition members, when they see that the coalition is momentarily a minority in the house, will waive their right to speak where a vote has then to be held forthwith; conversely, since the vote must follow immediately on the reply of a minister on first reading, and of the *rapporteur* on second reading, either of them, by deferring his reply if the coalition or the supporters of the bill momentarily lack a majority in the chamber, can save the bill. By such a move the Finance Committee chairman averted a Government defeat on a supplementary budget on 24 March 1982. A number of further illustrations of procedural tactics are furnished by the vote remainders bill mentioned above. To impede the bill's progress in every possible way its opponents also submitted no-confidence motions which had to be taken on the same days, and demanded roll-call votes at the different stages of the bill. The large Groups countered with other tactics: to minimize obstruction they voted in the House Committee for combined debate on no-confidence motions disparate in subject matter, and for a combined debate on the controversial bill and another virtually unopposed elections bill providing for a few administrative changes.

Among members who have skillfully employed the Rules to harass the Government and the coalition a name that stands out is that of Uri Avneri. In the years 1965–73 he represented, alone for the most part, the *Ha'olam Hazeh* list, the nucleus of whose supporters were the readers of his weekly of the same name. Sedulous in attending house sittings, though virtually boycotting committees, Avneri will be remembered for his marked parliamentary activism, which also influenced other members to utilize more fully every procedure open to them in the house. His example produced, among other things, a Question "explosion" whose effect continued after he was gone from the Knesset. His energetic submission of bills and motions for the agenda was checked only by the institution, a few months after his first election, of Group quotas for such initiatives.

THE AGENDA

The agenda of the house is the responsibility of the chairman. However, for Mondays and Tuesdays he must arrange the order of business so as to meet Government priorities, while the schedule of members' motions and bills, which are taken on Wednesdays, is fixed by him together with the vice-chairmen, acting as the presidium. Meeting at least once weekly, the presidium has also the tasks of granting recognition to urgent members' motions and of approving members bills' for tabling (Government bills need no such approval). The meeting is attended by a representative of the Government—a minister or deputy minister, to whom the duty is assigned on a regular basis, or the Government secretary—who states its position as to each item. But Wednesday is not a members' day in the first week of a session and in the last three weeks of the winter session when the budget is being taken.

The separation between Government and members' days is by no means rigid since the Knesset Rules further provide that the presidium may appoint another time in the same or following week for members' motions and bills; that Government business may spill over to a Wednesday sitting when there are no members' items on the agenda or when these items have all been taken; and conversely, that members' business may be taken on a Government day. Moreover, the chairman will at any time fit into the order of business, on a Monday or Tuesday, a member's bill that has been reported from committee for the first reading, or a debate consequent to a member's motion. There is similar flexibility with regard to the distinctly members' business of questions to ministers; the sittings and times at which they are to be answered are, under the Rules, fixed by the presidium. Also the oral questions instituted experimentally in 1983, though requiring to be taken on Wednesday normally, may as necessary be moved by the Knesset chairman to other days.

Precedence is given to certain proceedings at any sitting. The Government may deliver a statement or make a declaration in the Knesset at any time. On the request of at least thirty members a debate will be held the following day; but the Government may ask that it be deferred by forty-eight hours. An urgent and specially important Government statement will precede even a motion of no-confidence in the Government, which is itself taken ahead of any other item on the day following its submission. However, a debate requested on the supervening statement will be deferred until the no-confidence motion is disposed of. In addition, precedence over other items is given to a member's motion recognized by the presidium as urgent, to a debate fixed consequent on an urgent motion, and to any matter which must be considered or voted on pursuant to a law or to the Knesset Rules.

On Wednesday afternoon, while the last sitting of the week is still in progress, members receive at their desks the agenda for the following week listing the outstanding items of business. Since there is a continuing stream of bills laid and other subjects put down for debate, while only some items can be taken, the list on this agenda may swell from a few items early in the term to approach a hundred by the closing weeks. Items considered not urgent will appear again and again with each new weekly list. This agenda, which will almost never be followed exactly, nor its items all taken in the week for which it is drawn up, is all-inclusive—in effect the list of outstanding business for the session.

The items that are actually to be taken in the course of the week are set down on an order paper drawn up at the Monday noon meeting of the presidium. This paper lists the order of business for each sitting, the members bills approved for tabling, and recognized urgent motions. Since the Rules entitle the chairman to make later changes in the order of business, the items to be taken each day are listed again, posted on a notice board at each of the two entrances to the Chamber, and laid finally on the members' desks, after added items have first appeared as a supplement to the all-inclusive agenda; in the case of legislation, earlier listing in the all-inclusive agenda must meet the one- or two-day requirements for prior tabling as described in Chapter 10. But further last minute changes may still be necessary even in the course of the sitting.

At the request of the Government on a Monday or Tuesday, the chairman will transfer any item of business from the all-inclusive agenda to the order of the day, as well as defer any item. Should members profess surprise when confronted with such a change, the chair may remind them that the all-inclusive agenda is an official document, while the order paper issued by the presidium is just a press communiqué. However, during the 1981–84 Knesset when the Government seemed to make free with the order of business on members' desks by repeated changes without notice, and deferral of subjects which it was not keen to see debated, the chairman expressed protest in the house and proceeded to take the matter up with the prime minister.

Members motions and bills to be taken appear collectively as one item on both agenda and order paper and are enumerated only on a separately stencilled sheet. The seven or eight motions and bills put down for Wednesday are part of the sessional quotas allotted by the House Committee to the respective Groups of the sponsors. In any week there may be additionally a few urgent motions, not counted on the quotas, and more likely to be taken also on other days. The assignment of a member's bill or motion by the presidium to a Government-business day, with the approval of the chairman, generally causes no difficulty. When a presiding vice-chairman in 1983 inserted without notice in the order of business a controversial member's bill concerning archeological work at burial sites, which stood on the next day's agenda, Chairman Savidor took the unprecedented step the next day of ruling the vote out of order. He was moved to overturn a house decision, against the advice of legal counsel, also by the bill's presentation close to midnight in a sparsely attended house, an act which he regarded in itself as collusion.

VOTING

Since there is no quorum requirement in the Knesset, a simple majority of the votes cast is all that is needed to decide a question, except where a law designates an absolute or other special majority for alteration of any of its provisions. Voting takes place immediately at the end of the debate to which it is related, with a few exceptions as provided by the Rules. By custom, votes that come up in the Knesset while a national party conference is being held will be deferred if the parliamentary Group so requests; only questions that are not controversial will be put to a vote then.

There are three methods of voting in the Knesset: show of hands, roll call, and secret ballot. The usual way is by show of hands. If the result of a show of hands is not clear to the chairman, a count is taken by the secretary. If doubt persists, or if there is a request by a member before the chairman has announced the result of the vote, the chairman will appoint tellers from among the members, usually one from the coalition and one from the opposition, for a recount of hands. Should there be disagreement between the tellers, another recount is taken. In all cases the chairman's decision on the numbers voting is final, and once he has announced the result of a vote there may not be a recount. On the request of twenty members or of the Government a roll-call vote will be held. In practice such request nearly always comes from members. A roll-call vote, which is the only kind of recorded vote in the Knesset, is usually asked for on sensitive or controversial questions, when one side in the debate wishes all of its members to go on record, or seeks to compel those on the other side to commit themselves individually. The side opposed to a proceeding will occasionally use roll-call votes also as a dilatory tactic or demonstration. The chair has allowed roll-call votes on separate clauses of a bill though not on amendments.

A secret-ballot vote could at one time be requested on any question, like a roll-call vote. On 16 March 1971 an opposition Group called for a secret vote on a no-confidence motion, which was rejected by the house only because countered by a majority request for a roll-call vote. The realization that secret votes on no-confidence motions would be unfair to the public, while making coalition discipline unenforceable when most needed, led the Knesset in 1972 to change the rule on the secret-ballot vote: it is to be taken only where provided by law, as in election of the president of the state, or of the members to represent the Knesset on a civil or religious judges appointments committee—and when voting on the withdrawal of a member's immunity. And, as detailed earlier, when there was a proposal in 1984 to vote secretly on third readings of bills, Chairman Savidor decided against it. In a secret vote the members are called up by the secretary in alphabetical order to the ballot box placed near the dais. The votes are counted by three members chosen by the chair. The two representatives to a judges appointments committee are elected with one ballot carrying the list of all candidates. Sealed envelopes are used. In the election of the president a ballot slip of different color is used for each candidate, and a curtain is placed around the ballot box.

Abstentions in a vote by show of hands are counted only on a member's request. In a roll-call vote abstentions are listed and recorded in the same way as the "for" and "against." Beyond abstention, a member may by custom declare that he is not participating in a vote, as was done, for example, by M. Pa'il in 1977 on a bill to defer elections to the Chief Rabbinate. Opposed to involvement of the state in religious affairs, Mr. Pa'il sought in this way to put on record his objection to the entire proceeding.

Pairing arrangements between members of coalition and opposition Groups to neutralize the effects of absence on voting have been accepted practice in the Knesset. They took on extra importance in the period of the narrowly based Begin Governments when the need to recall members who were abroad, even ministers on state business, to stave off defeat on a no-confidence motion or on the summation of a policy debate became essential. At the sitting of 2 June 1982, twenty-eight pairs were noted.[11] A pairing agreement applies only to a specific vote and is arranged between Groups or individual members without any formal recognition by the Knesset. Misunderstanding about pairing arrangements sometimes gives rise to recrimination. A common practice, therefore, is to put an agreement in writing in the presence of a witness, or to arrange the pair with the approval of the whips concerned. There has even been a proposal for a coalition-opposition committee to arrange pairing. The importance of pairing as it affects votes has become well recognized. When the Alignment Group considered it had prospects of toppling the *Likud*-led Government, with a committee of inquiry investigating the September 1982 massacre in Palestinian refuge camps, it announced that its members would not pair; however, pairing continued.

When there is a tie vote the motion or bill is not adopted, and there is no recount. The presiding officer will vote to break a tie. He votes also on any question he considers important by asking the secretary to count him. If the chairman intends beforehand to vote on a question, he will make sure to preside when the question is before the house. A vice-chairman, when not presiding, votes at his seat like other members.

Five minutes before any vote or series of votes a warning bell is sounded throughout the Knesset Building. But the vote may be taken before five minutes elapse if there is no objection. Another bell rings for the final call to vote. The actual voting time may be up to five minutes in a show of hands, about twenty minutes in a roll-call, and up to a half hour in a secret vote.

It is recognized that electronic voting would save time and eliminate bickering about inaccurate counts. In a letter to Chairman Savidor in 1982 fifteen members from different Groups urged the introduction of electronic voting also on the ground that it would make the member more accountable to the public by recording his presence and indicating how he voted throughout the Knesset term. After looking into the budgetary and technical aspects Mr. Savidor announced that such a system would be introduced. In November 1983, the House Committee decided to publish a tender for installation of the equipment. The system as planned will have memory and print-out facilities and will be key-operated, with an individual console on each member's desk.

KEEPING ORDER

There are clear provisions in the Knesset Rules, which are often tempered by accepted practice, with regard to the conduct of house sittings. A member may speak only with permission from the chair. By pressing a button the chairman signals with a light at the rostrum when two minutes are left the speaker and when his time is up. If a member continues speaking though his time is up, or persists in a digression after the chairman has remonstrated with him, the chairman may have the stenographic recording of the speech discontinued. In practice, relevance cannot be strictly enforced. At most the chairman attempts persuasion to bring a speaker back to the subject. Generally too, there is lenience in allowing a speaker additional time. One vice-chairman told the house that he applied the time limit only to irrelevant speeches.[12]

With the permission of the chair and the consent of the speaker, a member may interrupt a speech with a question or comment. At the speaker's request, a question will be left to the end of the speech. Interjections have always been permitted and sometimes contribute liveliness and humor to otherwise colorless proceedings. However, the main problem of preserving decorum in the house has been the tendency for interjections in any debate with political import to deteriorate into unrestrained heckling and bandying of taunts, while the speaker is drowned in the welter.

But the Rules provide the chair with disciplinary means. Should a member act in a manner offensive to the dignity of the house or to another member, or otherwise disturb the proceedings and fail to heed the presiding officer (either the chairman or a vice-chairman) after being called to order three times, the presiding officer may deprive the member of the right to speak for the remainder of the sitting, discontinue the sitting for a short while, or order the member removed from the chamber until the conclusion of the sitting. In the last case the House Committee will consider the offense, hearing both the presiding officer and the member, and may suspend the member for up to five sittings. The presiding officer has in fact never simply deprived an offender of the right to speak for the duration of the sitting. It is not rare for him to break off a sitting for a few minutes when it threatens to become a shouting contest. But he is more likely to exclude the unruly member from the sitting.

The removal of a member from a sitting, until 1979, required approval of the house. After one instance that year in which the house refused to agree to a motion of the chair for the removal of a member whose conduct was disruptive it relentingly empowered the presiding officer, by a change in the Rules, to order at his discretion the ejection of a member, with the proviso that the member might rejoin the sitting for the purpose of voting. If force is needed to remove the member, it is exercised under the Knesset officer by the ushers.

A decision of the House Committee to suspend a member can be appealed by him to the plenum. The decision of the house, after hearing both sides, is final; it in fact has never reversed the Committee's decision. Suspension from the house does not affect the member's right to attend committees.

If at a sitting of the house a member or the chair is offended by the speech or action of another member, of if a member takes offense at any decision, remark, or direction of the chair, the final court of appeal is the House Committee, which may investigate the incident through a Subcommittee on Complaints. If the offending member will not apologize or retract, the House Committee may formally express displeasure at his behavior, and he may be reprimanded through the committee chairman from the Knesset rostrum. The complaint of an official about derogatory remarks of a member will likely be referred to the Complaints Subcommittee and if found justified, the member will be urged to send an apology.

The first member suspended from the house was Menahem Begin, in 1952, after the House Committee considered his speech against German reparations to contain threats of violence; since the five-session limit was not yet in the rule book he was suspended for some ten weeks—until the close of the winter session. The house has decided on suspension also for unseemly demonstrative acts in the chamber such as, for example, the throwing of a prayer book to the floor and a member's handcuffing of himself to the rostrum.

Commotion in the house, when not the result of organized obstruction, is often due to volatile temperaments. Certain proprieties, reinforced by rule and custom, will be only inadvertently breached. When addressed or mentioned from the chair or rostrum, a member is styled "Knesset member." A member's maiden speech will not be interrupted by interjections. Opinions or positions voiced in a committee or in private conversation between members will not be referred to from the rostrum, nor will the personal affairs of another member. A speaker will not criticize personally anyone who cannot reply from the rostrum. The House Committee has ruled a number of times against the mention of matters that are *sub judice*. Applause by clapping of hands is not permitted in the chamber except, with prior sanction of the House Committee, on a special occasion such as the presence of a distinguished visitor. There is no smoking or reading of newspapers in the chamber; the rare offender will need only a reminder from the secretary or an usher.

This chapter has dealt chiefly with the ordering of plenary affairs. Committees and parliamentary Groups, no less integral parts of Knesset organization, are considered in the next two chapters.

7

Committees

JURISDICTION

FROM THE FIRST the Knesset has turned over to committees all detail, whether in legislative or other matters. In the First Knesset the opposition Groups sought to have the committees set up according to government ministry, as in the Provisional State Council, for systematic surveillance of the executive. The Government, wishing to avoid any direct interference in its day to day administration, proposed committees by subject area and its view prevailed. Nevertheless, within their respective subject areas the committees are multifunctional, serving also as tentacles of the Knesset for scrutiny of Government performance.

No law is enacted that has not first been considered clause by clause in a committee: the procedure of "committee of the whole" is unknown in the Knesset. While a committee may not deviate from the subject of a bill referred to it by the house, it can amend the bill beyond recognition. Although the Knesset Rules require a committee to give precedence to bills, and it cannot decide against reporting a bill back to the house for second reading, it is not unusual for it to take up other business first and to leave a controversial bill effectively "buried." In the nonlegislative sphere, the subjects of most members' motions are referred to a committee, and the committee's Conclusions must be responded to by the minister concerned. The Knesset, with its remit to a committee, sets no time limit for the report. Only when six months have elapsed since the reference of a bill or other subject to a committee, and it has not yet reported, does it have to give any accounting; and this takes the form simply of a statement in writing by the chairman of the committee to the Knesset chairman giving reasons for the delay. Such a report is all that is required every time an additional six months have passed.

Every one of the ten permanent committees has also certain statutory powers and duties in its field. Many laws contain provisions making ministerial regulations or orders subject to the approval of a Knesset committee, while others stipulate prior consultation with or notification of the committee. A committee may consider any topic, also on its own initiative, within the range of subject matters assigned to it by the Knesset Rules; in such a case it does not report to the house but brings the matter to the attention of the minister concerned. Committees have also been approached directly by ministers to consider a particular question.

Permanent committees are appointed for the full term of a Knesset. The nine committees established in the First Knesset were reappointed each term through a quarter of a century, and only a few changes have been made since. The names of the ten present permanent committees, which tell also much about their respective subject areas, are: Constitution, Law and Justice (briefly "Law"); Economics; Education and Culture; Finance; Foreign Affairs and Security; House; Immigration and Absorption; Internal Affairs and Environment; Labor and Welfare; and State Control. Although the Knesset Rules confer equal status on all committees, the more extensive or special powers of a few call for some description.

The Finance Committee is a parliamentary watchdog in matters of budget, taxation, banking, and currency. In addition, it has been invested with a wide range of functions and duties set down in more than a hundred statutes, including such diverse responsibilities as the approval of electricity, water, postal, and telephone rates; of government guarantees of loans to enterprises; and of regulations for the certification of insurance agents. Since the Finance Committee has the most numerous statutory powers as well as some of the weightiest legislation to consider, it is the busiest committee and meets the most often. Until 1973 it had also to consider the state comptroller's reports to which end it regularly set up a subcommittee; only in 1974 was a separate State Control Committee established.

In the sphere of Knesset procedure it is the House Committee whose role is paramount. The Knesset will not consider an amendment to its Rules which has not first been taken up by that Committee. Until July 1967, when the Knesset by a resolution adopted its complete body of Rules, new Rules tabled by the Committee had not even required approval by the Knesset plenum. The Rules in turn confer on the Committee wide-ranging powers affecting the day-to-day proceedings of the Knesset. The Committee also initiates legislation concerning immunities of the Knesset and its members, and members' emoluments. In addition, the House Committee exercises important quasi-judicial functions in the consideration of election appeals, withdrawal of a member's immunity, suspension or unseating of a member, and removal from office of a president of the state, although in each case the Committee's recommendation must come before the house for approval. The House Committee's influence and importance in the parliamentary sphere can hardly be overstated, bearing in mind its decision-making role, on the one hand, in the conduct of Knesset business, and on the other hand, in matters affecting members' status, conduct, remuneration, and working conditions.

The Foreign Affairs and Security Committee is the most prestigious because its subject matter is considered to be in the sphere of "high policy," and the parliamentary Groups consistently send to it their leading members. The Knesset Rules empower the Committee also to come in place of the plenum to consider a member's motion whose open debate might be detrimental to the state's security or foreign relations. Since membership on the Committee is much sought after, a Group may decided to fill some of its places in rotation. A House Committee resolution in 1980 added further to the status of membership on the Foreign Affairs and Security Committee by forbidding the casual substitution of its members by Groups, a practice followed in other committees, and by providing that any change in its membership remain in effect for three months at least. The reputation of the Committee has remained high despite the recognition, as expressed by veteran chairmen and members of the Committee, that its chief role has been to legitimize Government policy choices on controversial issues rather than to articulate demands.[1]

The committees do much of their work through subcommittees. A few subcommittees have become virtually mandatory; since the early years of the Knesset a Petitions Subcommittee (of the House Committee) has been set up each term to deal with problems of individual disadvantaged citizens as well as with public petitions. A Subcommittee on Basic Laws (of the Law Committee) is also set up each term. Such too was the status of the Subcommittee on State Control (of the Finance Committee) before the separate committee was established. Other subcommittees have come to be set up with almost equal regularity for the full term of a Knesset, such as, for example, the Subcommittee on Sports by the Education Committee. But most subcommittees are set up ad hoc to consider a specific bill or other matter. In the Foreign Affairs and Security Committee subcommittees are a frank expedient for safeguarding secrecy in important political and security matters. However, the conclusions of a subcommittee will come before the parent committee for approval except where the latter, by a resolution adopted with a two-thirds majority, has delegated the subcommittee to decide finally on a question. Where the law confers a specific power on the committee such delegation cannot be made. In all cases members of the parent committee can move amendments to a bill.

The House Committee, most of whose time is taken up by emergent Knesset business such as appeals of rejected urgent motions, designation of committees to consider certain bills or motions, or allotment of time for debates, is dependent for most of its continuing deliberations on a system of permanent subcommittees. For example, at the beginning of the 1981–84 Knesset the Committee appointed seven subcommittees, ranging in size from three to seven members, on: Petitions; Complaints (about members); Members' Emoluments; Knesset Rules; Members' Technical Facilities; Parliamentary Delegations; and Members' Ethics. Their political composition, which could not be as representative as that of the parent committee, tells something about the limits of partisanship in the Knesset's committee organization. Most had a coalition majority. However, the three-man politically innocuous Subcommittee on Members' Facilities had only one coalition member; the six-man Subcommittee on Members' Emoluments had an equal number of coalition and opposition members. Since a change in the Knesset Rules has depended primarily on an understanding between the two large Groups, the membership of the subcommittee on Rules consisted of four—two from *Likud* and two from the Labor Alignment; they were joined by an observer from a small Group. In addition, of course, the House Committee will set up ad hoc subcommittees, like the one on the report of the Knesset's internal comptroller.

The subject matter of a bill or motion usually leaves no doubt about the committee to which it should be referred. However, if there is disagreement, the House Committee is charged with choosing the committee. The choice is sometimes political; if the coalition wants to expedite a bill that might be referred equally well to either of two committees, the bill may go to the one whose chairman belongs to the coalition.[2] Since as well as considering motions and bills referred to it by the house, a permanent committee also initiates its own debates, the organization of the committees by subject area has not completely prevented overlapping. It is not rare for a subject to be examined at the same time by two committees. In one instance, the problem of juvenile delinquency was simultaneously before the Labor, Education, and Public Welfare committees, with all three hearing the same evidence.[3] Such glaring duplication of work induced the House Committee to adopt a resolution (23 July 1974) admonishing the committees to keep to their respective subject areas as set out in the Rules. However, the effect of the resolution was not lasting. Other attempts to coordinate committee activity were made by Knesset chairmen, who set up a panel of committee chairmen for that purpose.

When a subject falls within the ambit of two or more committees a joint committee, with an equal number of members from each, may be set up for its consideration. The House Committee, which fixes the composition of a joint committee, also chooses the chairman from the committee to which it deems the subject to be more pertinent. Some joint committees are set up every session, a few with regularity; the defense budget is always considered by a joint Finance-Foreign Affairs and Security Committee, the Knesset budget by a joint House-Finance Committee. More rarely, on a ramified subject, a joint committee with members from three committees has been set up. However, a joint committee may be less efficient than a permanent one, failing sometimes to complete the assignment because its meeting times conflict with the members' regular committee duties. It has been charged that both joint committees and subcommittees are often a device for excluding members of smaller Groups who are on the parent committees.

The Knesset may at any time, on the recommendation of the House Committee, set up a special committee to consider a certain matter. Since the permanent committees are specialized and broadly cover together the entire field of government, special committees have been set up only seldom, on particularly problematic questions. The opposition of the elementary school teachers to the introduction of an intermediate level was the reason for establishment of the Committee on the Reform of the School Structure in 1966. In 1970, because the Complaints Commissioner (Ombudsman) Bill was found to lie within the subject areas of three committees, a special committee was resorted to. Controversial legislation concerning the status of members of cooperatives, though its subject matter under the Knesset Rules falls clearly within the ambit of the Economics Committee, was turned over in 1972 to a special committee with a chairman favorable to the bill. To expedite the consideration of the Government's health insurance bill in the face of determined opposition by the Labor Alignment, the Histadrut and the Sick Funds, a special committee of thirteen members, seven of whom supported the bill, was set up in 1981; in the last months of the Ninth Knesset, while the permanent committees were clogged with other legislation and diverse matters, the special committee could devote to the bill the time needed to hear delegations from the many interested bodies. Since elections cut short that committee's deliberations, a special committee on the bill, of like composition, was set up again in 1982.

Another kind of special committee is a committee of inquiry, which the Knesset may vest with powers to subpoena witnesses and call for documents. For the purpose of an inquiry either a special committee may be set up or a permanent committee may be empowered accordingly. Of the permanent committees only the House Committee has sat as a committee of inquiry, when considering charges of election irregularities. Proposals to establish a special parliamentary committee of inquiry have been opposed by every Government. Only once, when the Government itself made the recommendation and before provision was made for the Knesset to arm such a committee with investigatory powers, was a committee of inquiry set up; the committee to investigate the treatment of prisoners at the Jelemi penal camp, set up in 1951, was equipped with the necessary powers by the minister of justice under an ordinance dating from the mandate.

Although a permanent committee cannot subpoena witnesses it may call ministers (and through them the officials concerned), experts on a question, and interested groups or individuals on any matter which is before it, whether a bill or the subject of a motion. However, the committee cannot compel anyone to appear, give evidence, or answer questions. In 1979, when the Education Committee was not enabled by the management of the Broadcasting Authority to hear all sides on the question of telecasts in Arabic, it decided not to report conclusions on the subject to the house. In 1972 the court justified the refusal of the receivers in the Autocars affair to testify before the Economics Committee. If a witness does appear before a committee but conceals facts or gives false evidence, he is not subject to any penalty. Since the committees are in this respect without "teeth," and the coalition consistently rejects any proposal to set up a committee of inquiry on a particular matter, members' bills have been presented that would empower a permanent committee to subpoena public servants as witnesses if its members so wish. In replying to the sponsor of such a bill in 1979, Justice Minister S. Tamir, while pointing to the danger of putting a quasi-judicial procedure in the hands of politicians, undertook to present a bill to the same purpose on behalf of the Government so that it would be considered together with the member's bill in the legislative process. But no Government proposal came forward. Introduced again in 1982, an identical member's bill was struck off the agenda.

MEMBERSHIP

The membership of committees has ranged in size from nine to twenty-six, in the great majority of cases from thirteen to nineteen. The membership of a committee will be bigger if it is expected to be exceptionally busy or to work through a large number of subcommittees. There may be other considerations. In the early years of the Knesset, when the representation of every Group was considered necessary on the Law Committee, which was expected to deliberate also on a constitution, and on the House Committee, charged with the task of shaping the procedures of the nascent parliament, both these committees numbered twenty-three members. The membership of the Foreign Affairs and Security Committee was set at twenty-five in 1977 because of keen competition for its places; reduced to twenty-one in 1981, when most committees were made smaller than in earlier years, it was restored to twenty-five a year later. The State Control Committee, confined in principle to members from the large Groups, was reduced in 1981 from a membership of eleven to nine. After the 1984 election with the need to satisfy fifteen parliamentary Groups, the greatest change was the increase of the House Committee membership from thirteen in the previous term again to twenty-three.

Although the Basic Law on the Knesset prescribes only that committees of inquiry be constituted according to the political composition of the plenum, the Knesset Rules make this the ground principle in the organization of committees generally. However, the balance of parliamentary Groups in the house is to be looked for in the committee memberships taken all together rather than in the individual committee, since every Organizing Committee, in assigning committee places, has followed a rule that Groups with fewer than a certain number of seats in the Knesset cannot choose the committees on which they will be represented. This minimum number, fixed anew in each Knesset, has ranged from five to nine. The chief effect of the number rule has been to keep small Groups, among them the Communist and Arab lists, out of the two most confidential committees—Finance, and Foreign Affairs and Security. As a result, too, the large Groups have secured greater than proportional representation on these committees and on others which they consider important. After a boycott of all committees in 1955 by the six-man Religious Torah Group because it was refused a place on the Finance Committee, a rule was adopted that a committee may, by unanimous consent, invite to its meetings regular observers from Groups not represented on it.

A large Group may give up a place on any committee in favor of a smaller one as happened when Golda Meir of the Labor Party became prime minister in 1969; the place she vacated on the Foreign Affairs and Security Committee was given to Gideon Hausner of the Independent Liberals, a tiny Group then in the coalition but whose size had barred it from representation on that committee. Again, in 1977, as part of a coalition agreement when the small *Agudat Yisrael* Group waived the right to a portfolio, both the Finance and the Foreign Affairs and Security committees were opened to it on the *Likud* quotas.

The committee places allotted to a parliamentary Group remain its prerogative through the entire term of the Knesset. Since every permanent committee is in effect a specialist committee, the Group will send to it members who are competent or show a particular interest in the subject matter or who have gained experience on the committee in earlier Knessets. Thus, for example, the best legal talent of each Group is sent to the Law Committee.

However, a Group can rotate or shuffle members about in its committee places at will, and frequently does so, whether from expediency or according to the wishes of the members concerned. For instance, when the Foreign Affairs and Security Committee had to decide on the question of Jewish settlement in Hebron in 1980, a number of *Likud* members known to be opposed to the Government's position were replaced for the vote by other representatives of the Group. A committee member in disagreement with his Group's stand on a question may himself ask to be relieved of his place. A member who secedes from his Group will be divested of his committee memberships, which he has in fact held, on its behalf.

To effect a personnel change in a committee the Group gives notice to the House Committee chairman, and the latter in turn announces the change in the Knesset plenum with a request for its confirmation. In the absence of objection, the chair declares that the house has concurred in the substitution. Only rarely is there a debate leading to a vote; in one instance, in 1980, when a member at odds with his Group was replaced by it on the Education Committee, he attempted to dissuade the Knesset from concurring in the change, and the matter was referred back to the House Committee. The only result was a House Committee resolution to leave unchanged the accepted procedure by which the Groups determine personnel changes in committees.

In the temporary absence of a member, his Group, to keep up its committee strength, had been permitted by practice to send a substitute without formal Knesset approval, after obtaining permission from the committee chairman. This practice was further relaxed in 1972 by a decision of the House Committee enabling a Group to send a substitute to a committee without any prior arrangement. But the Foreign Affairs and Security Committee, as already noted, was later excepted entirely from this practice.

The manning of committees has been a problem. In the Knesset elected in 1981, for example, there had to be excepted from regular committee activity the twenty ministers who were Knesset members, as well as the chairman of the Knesset. Ninety-nine members were left to man the ten permanent committees with their various joint and subcommittees. (And in addition, a special committee on a state health insurance bill was set up.) Since a number of members did not serve on any committee, many others had to serve on two, some on three. Particularly acute was the personnel situation of the coalition, who, ranging between sixty-one and sixty-four members, had to provide from its ranks also all ministers and deputy ministers (the latter numbering eleven at one point, and who if on committees, could not be very active there). While keeping the precarious majority of one on every committee, the coalition had available for all committee work thirty-five or fewer members against the opposition's fifty-six to fifty. To compound difficulties, committee meetings are largely bunched together in the mornings of the plenum's three weekly sitting days. It is little wonder that while a standing complaint of members is that they must hop about between committees to an extent that prevents their doing effective work on these bodies, the press has called the thinly spread and mobile coalition members in the committees "voting commandos." Nor is it surprising that a proposal to set up a new committee on some special subject is usually countered with the claim that this can only further aggravate the tight situation of committee personnel. Only grand coalitions under National Unity Governments have been completely free of such manpower problems.

While there have been proposals for reducing the number of committees, the greater freedom of maneuver which a large number of committee places offers in a multiparty house has militated against such a reform. However, after the 1981 election the strained situation of the sixty-one-member coalition and the reduced political fragmentation of the house prompted a reduction in the membership of all but three committees so that the total number of places was brought down from 168 to 144. And continued low attendance in committees has given force to the argument that they should be further reduced in size so that no member need be assigned to more than one.

CHAIRMEN

The chairman of a committee is elected formally by the membership at its first meeting after he has been nominated by the House Committee. (The committee's first meeting is called and opened by the Knesset chairman). The House Committee, for its part, nominates the candidate put forward by the parliamentary Group allocated that chairmanship by agreement between the Groups. Also the chairmanships of important subcommittees, like those on Basic Laws and Petitions, are assigned after inter-Group negotiation. When elections have not altered the strength of a Group substantially it will generally claim the same committee chairmanships from term to term. The loss of votes by the Labor Alignment in the election which followed the Yom Kippur War compelled it to give up the chairmanship of the Interior Committee in favor of *Likud*. A further concession from the Alignment was called for, but its chief partner, the Labor Party, would on no account give up any chairmanship of what it regarded as the four key committees: House, Finance, Foreign Affairs and Security, and Labor, the last of special ideological significance for the party. Consequently, a new permanent committee—on State Control—was established and given a *Likud* chairman. It has been suggested that in the First Knesset foreign affairs and security were combined in one committee so that, among other things, a *Mapai* chairman would have both areas under his wing.[4] Within a Group a committee chairmanship may be rotated in the course of a Knesset term between members of its component political parties. Seniority is not an essential qualification for a chairmanship, which will sometimes go to a new member.

While a number of committees are always chaired by opposition members, the committee chairmanships, like the vice-chairmanships of the Knesset, enter into the calculations of the coalition when it is engaged in the distribution of government portfolios, deputy ministerships, and other positions. The process of negotiation within the coalition and between it and the opposition Groups may be so involved as to delay the election of committee chairmen inordinately. In 1955 the new Knesset, which first met on 15 August, did not have committee chairmen before December. After the 1977 election the chairmanships of the Finance, and Labor and Welfare committees, (together with a Knesset vice-chairmanship and a seat on the Foreign Affairs and Security Committee) were considered adequate compensation by the *Agudat Yisrael* Group, which chose not to accept Government portfolios though they entered the coalition. As a small Group, *Agudat Yisrael* would not normally have received any of these posts. And, of course, to an opposition Group too a committee chairmanship is a valued plum. When the Labor Alignment went into opposition in 1977 it gave all three of its committee chairmanships to former ministers.

The weight attached to committee chairmanships is not surprising if one considers the powers, both formal and informal, which they carry. The chairman fixes the committee's agenda and calls its meetings. His right to cancel or change the time of a meeting, or to call an extraordinary meeting, though sometimes a source of misunderstanding, is generally recognized by the committee. He decides who will be called to be heard and questioned, and his choice can be overruled only by a majority of the committee. He issues press communiqués which are the only official source of information to the public on the committee's activity. The draft Conclusions of the committee on the subjects of Knesset members' motions are drawn up by him.

The position of the chairman is further strengthened by the rule that he may hold meetings of the committee with any number of members present. Since attendance at meetings of a committee is often poor, the burden of its work will in any case fall largely on the chairman. While a committee member is registered as attending a meeting even if he only drops in to vote, the number of members on all committees taken together who consider themselves personally responsible for advancing committee business and who stay through to the end of meetings has been estimated at 20 percent.[5] There have been instances in which delegations appearing before a committee have found only the chairman present to hear them.[6] If a chairman must be absent for a short period, he will appoint a committee member, generally from his Group, to act in his place.

A committee chairman can use his powers to hold up or "bury" a bill, as a few examples will illustrate. In 1971 Chairman M. Surkiss of the Internal Affairs Committee managed to delay the progress of two bills on the rabbinate for months by refusing to put them down for consideration after they were referred to the committee; only the intervention of the prime minister moved him finally to bring the bills forward. The Law Committee chairman deferred indefinitely the consideration of a bill to regulate the practices of political parties, which was referred in 1980 to the committee; according to the press the bill conflicted with the interests of his party. The chairman of a committee in the exercise of his authority is able in some circumstances to frustrate the express will of its majority: for example, by not having a Finance Committee decision of 1980 concerning medical care for judges published in the official gazette, the chairman prevented indefinitely its coming into force. Even after the committee has reported back to the house the cooperation of the chairman is essential to advance the bill since under the Rules only he, if present in the house, can open the second reading, that proceeding requiring a statement by him on behalf of the committee unless he has appointed another of its members for that purpose. In one instance, when it was uncertain whether the chairman of the Law Committee had delegated his authority to open the second reading of an elections bill, proceedings were paralyzed until the presiding officer called him to the rostrum to explain his intention.[7]

The above examples are not simply instances of caprice. Ultimately a committee chairman uses his powers as a political leader. He is expected to do so. While every other Group appoints one of its representatives on the committee as coordinator of its affairs, the chairman's Group leaves it to him to look after its interest. Group coordination in a committee is necessary, for although party and coalition discipline is less rigorous there than in the house, and there is more openness to mutual persuasion, the committees remain important arenas of political confrontation.

CONDUCT OF BUSINESS

Committee meetings are held Sunday through Friday, most by far on the days when the house sits, on Mondays, Tuesdays, and Wednesdays. The average length of a meeting is two hours. The committees meet in the morning and early afternoon (except on Wednesdays) so as not to conflict with the plenary sitting. The attitude to overlapping committee with house sittings has varied. During the office of Knesset Chairman Joseph Sprinzak (1949–59), who did not favor such overlap, permission from the presidium for a committee to meet while the house sat was required. Practice today requires permission only from the Knesset chairman. Chairman Yitzhak Berman (1980–81), who believed anyway that the house should leave most parliamentary activity to the committees and deal itself mainly with second and third readings of bills, did not hesitate to permit committees to meet during plenary sittings. The volume of committee work has in fact increased over the years with the general growth in the amount of parliamentary business. Committees that would meet once weekly in earlier years now meet two or three times. More committee meetings are being held also in the Passover and summer recesses though their frequency is restricted. A committee may hold recess sittings only as empowered by the House Committee, unless such a sitting be called upon the request of the Government or one-third of the committee's members. A House Committee authorization usually includes a provision for the meeting in the recess of committees with statutory duties such as approval of ministerial regulations, and may specify that the Finance and the Foreign Affairs and Security committees be unrestricted in the number of meetings.

Meeting times are fixed by a committee after it has elected the chairman. In addition, urgent meetings may be called by the chairman, by one-third of the committee's members, or by the Government. Usually only the chairman makes use of this authority. Notice of meetings on his instruction, and with the agenda set by him, are sent to the members from week to week. A member, with the agreement of a majority of the committee, can add an item to the agenda, but it will be taken up only after the business fixed by the chairman.

When considering a bill, other matter referred to it by the house, or a subject it has chosen to examine on its own initiative, the committee will as a matter of course invite the ministers concerned, whom it is entitled to ask for information and explanation of policy. In practice, except when the minister appears in committee to give a review and answer questions about the Government's position or to follow proceedings that specially interest him, he will leave it to members of his staff to attend meetings to explain and defend the ministry's views. Out of concern to preserve ministerial responsibility and to assure that a civil servant's statements before a committee are authoritative, the Knesset Rules lay down emphatically that a state employee may be invited by a committee only through his minister. Informal direct contacts, which are in fact usually established between committee and officials concerned, are, it is understood, with the knowledge and consent of the minister.

Though the obligation of a minister to meet a committee's request for information can be fulfilled by his staff, he is expected to appear in person if requested on important questions. When, on 1 June 1983, Finance Minister Aridor refused to come before the Finance Committee to explain a projected tax bill, giving as the reason that the proposal still needed the Government's approval, the Committee decided to discontinue consideration of all other Government business until the new fiscal move was clarified. Should neither minister nor staff show up before a committee after being called, they can expect harsh reactions. When for a week during the 1982–83 campaign in Lebanon, the Foreign Affairs and Security Committee could get no report from the defense minister or any senior army man, criticism by the Committee's chairman, E. Ben-Elissar, and by its coalition and opposition members alike was unsparing. Condemnation was likewise general in the Labor and Welfare Committee on 14 April 1983, when nobody from the treasury appeared as requested to report on negotiations to end a prolonged doctors strike. And it made no difference in all foregoing cases that the committee chairman was himself from the coalition.

When the remit before a committee is a member's bill or motion the sponsor will be invited to its meetings. It is up to the committee to determine the extent of his participation in the deliberations. He has, of course, no right to vote. An amendment to a bill, when proposed by a member not on the committee, need not be considered by it, and if the amendment is considered and negatived, he need not be permitted, as would a committee member, to move it again in the plenum on second reading.

Experts and delegations from interest groups will be invited to appear before the committee after it has heard the minister or sponsoring member on the subject. The committee will seek to elicit all useful information from such witnesses but refrain from entering into debate with them. There are often more bodies seeking an invitation to the committee than it can reasonably be expected to hear. The chairman will invite those whose evidence he considers will be most material, being more restrictive when he wishes to expedite a bill. Members of the committee who oppose the bill may, as a dilatory move, seek to widen the circle of delegations. But the chairman usually has his way and will rarely put to a vote questions about hearings.

Information to committees is supplied also by their own advisers and staff. Though the essential staff of most committees is a secretary and a clerk-typist, they are also served by legal advisers and information compilers from the library's information service. In the Finance and Economics committees the secretaries are also economic advisers. A few committee chairmen have also personal assistants. Since the Knesset had for years only one legal counsel, mainly for fiscal legislation, members would often complain that in the committees they were completely dependent on the Government's legal officers. Today the Knesset has four legal advisers serving the ten committees and their members. In recognition of the Finance Committee's heavy work-load it is provided with more staff than other committees—two economists, a legal adviser, and two clerk-typists. Demands are frequently heard that the Finance Committee, particularly to cope with the annual budget, should be equipped with a larger staff including economists, auditors, and experts in administration, or alternatively, that it be enabled to call regularly on outside professional opinion. But judgment in the Committee itself as to the likely value of such expertise has been divided; some point to the experience of the Committee with the services of an economics professor whom it hired in 1971 as a consultant for several hours a week but kept only a few months as nobody actually turned to him.

To supplement its information from official sources, interest groups, and staff, a committee will tour anywhere within the country to study at first hand the operation of government or the problems of some locality or enterprise. Since the ministry concerned is usually prepared to pay the cost of the committee's transportation and accommodation, there was for years no provision in the Knesset budget for committee tours. But it came to be felt that this convenient arrangement cramped a committee's freedom and could affect its judgment where an investigation directly touched the Government. The House Committee consequently resolved in 1975 that any tour initiated by a committee in pursuit of an inquiry is to be financed from the Knesset budget. Tours of committees sometimes affect attendance in the house. In 1962 the presidium decided that such tours are not be held on sitting days. But this was in effect only a fond wish. Committees continue to go out on tours whenever they can be arranged. When two committees join forces for a broadly focussed tour the constraints in fixing a date are obviously greater.

With only few provisions in the Knesset Rules concerning procedure in committees, the proceedings there are far less formal than in the plenum, one committee differing sometimes from another in the manner of conducting business. There is no limit to the number of times members may speak. However, the chairman will impose orderly and connected discussion. He may, for example, arrange that members speak in two rounds on a subject. He may hold over the voting on clauses and amendments until the consideration of the entire bill is completed. But the last procedure is often a way of coping with the problem of absentees; when voting meetings are called Group and coalition discipline will be effective in securing full attendance and averting untoward surprises. A vote is deferred also when a member asks time for prior consultation with his parliamentary Group. Frequently on noncontroversial matters the chairman will declare the sense of the committee without putting any question. If the offhand manner in which he sometimes does so brings challenge or denial by members at a later sitting, he can point to the record in the protocol. In any case a decision of the committee not yet laid on the table of the house must be reconsidered if a majority of the committee so requests. Even when no reconsideration is requested there may be a revote if new pertinent information has reached the committee. The "revision" of a vote on a sensitive question is not, however, made casually. Notice is sent to the members, and the committee first votes whether to reconsider the earlier decision. If a revote is decided on, it is fixed for a certain date so that the committee's Group coordinators can muster a full turnout, resorting to substitutes where necessary.

But a committee can vote with any number present since it has no quorum requirement. As in the plenum, a simple majority of the members present can pass a resolution, with a few exceptions. The Basic Laws stipulate that a proposal to the house to remove the president can be made only with a three-quarters majority of the House Committee, and a proposal to expel a Knesset Member with a two-thirds majority. Certain approvals by the Finance Committee under the State Guarantees Act, 1958, require a four-fifths majority of members present. The Knesset Rules lay down a two-thirds majority for a committee to delegate power to a subcommittee and unanimous consent for its appointment of a regular observer.

The preservation of decorum in committees, with their informal and intimate atmosphere, was left to take care of itself for years. While sharp exchanges and flaring tempers are perhaps more rare there than in the plenum, Knesset Chairman Yitzhak Berman was prompted in 1980 to propose that a committee chairman be given order-keeping powers parallel to those of the presiding officer in the house. An incident shortly afterward spurred the House Committee to act speedily on the recommendation. On 24 February 1981 a member of the Immigration Committee, who had not until then attended any of its meetings, burst in with a stream of invective while the committee was hearing an immigrant from the Soviet Union. The House Committee, on finding it had power only to rebuke the offender, proposed six new Rules which the Knesset adopted. These Rules empower a committee chairman, like the chairman at a plenary sitting, after calling an offending member three times to order, to deprive him of the right to speak for the duration of the meeting or have him removed from it. If the chairman considers the misconduct serious, he can also take the matter to the House Committee, which after hearing both sides may exclude the offender from as many as five committee meetings. Unlike the case of an offender in the plenum, the House Committee decision cannot be appealed to the house. Disciplinary measures, however, leave the right of the Group to its affected committee place protected; it may send a substitute in place of the excluded member, and if the excluded member is a one-man Group, he may rejoin the committee for any vote.

CONFIDENTIALITY OF PROCEEDINGS

The protocol of a committee, according to the Knesset Rules, need contain only a summary of the proceedings, with the record of attendance, motions, and resolutions. In practice the stenograph is much fuller, leaving out nothing important that is said, its chief difference from the verbatim house stenograph being that the shorthand writer, who is supplied by the Knesset stenographers branch, has discretion to drop the irrelevant and repetitious. In a committee, remarks ''not for the record'' are permitted as well. Since full frankness and freedom of expression is secured in a committee through trust that what is said will be held in confidence, the stenographs are made available only to its members and to the ministries concerned. In 1977, when a member of the Interior Affairs Committee found that the stenographs of that committee from the previous Knesset term were not available to him, he objected, and this restriction was removed by the House Committee. In special cases Knesset members not on a committee are given access to its stenographs, as was done in 1968 by the chairman of the Committee on the School Structure, with the consent of the Knesset chairman, so that members could prepare for the plenary debate on the committee's recommendations. A delegation or witness appearing before a committee will, if requesting the stenograph, be given only the pages containing his evidence. The scruples about violating the confidential nature of committee proceedings extend also to the Knesset rostrum, where speakers are forbidden by a Rule to mention opinions voiced in a committee.

The public and the news media are, of course, generally excluded from committee meetings. Although the Rules permit a committee to hold open meetings, it does so only rarely, for instance, when conducting hearings of particular public interest. With the arrival in 1969 of television in the Knesset, cameras would be employed for interviews outside committee rooms after meetings. The invidious practice of the television men of consistently covering the prestigious Finance and Foreign Affairs committees while overlooking the rest, prompted the House Committee in 1976 to bar the cameras from the committee floor. However, with the consent of the Knesset chairman, television is sometimes allowed into a committee so that the public may catch a glimpse of the proceedings; subsequent personal interviews are then also televised.

The only official account of a committee's proceedings to reach the communication media and the public is the press communiqué which the chairman may issue after a meeting. But the committee need not issue a communiqué; there are few communiqués from the Foreign Affairs and Security Committee. The communiqué may report, in addition to resolutions, the highlights of statements by ministers, officials, or delegations who appeared before the committee. However, the committee's members too are a source of information to the press. They will be sought out by the press when there is no communiqué or when it is too terse to satisfy curiosity. Often a member may himself wish to give publicity to a subject that he has brought up in the committee or to his stand or that of his party faction on a certain question if he did not vote with the majority of the committee. There have been instances of a member's report to the press on his initiative in committee before the chairman has heard of it.[8]

Since the Foreign Affairs and Security Committee is privy to much classified information, it pledges its members to secrecy. This has not, however, prevented information leaks. Official witnesses appearing before the Committee have at times withheld information from the Committee on the ground of frequent leaks from its meetings. In replying in 1979 to a member's motion in the house on the subject of unauthorized disclosures of information given in the Committee, Chairman Arens said that it was up to the Groups to replace the offending members, who were usually well known. On another occasion he said that the only solution for dealing with disclosures was to use police methods, but that he could not get the prime minister to accept the idea.[9] A leak from the Committee in 1983 of remarks made by the head of the Security Services prompted Chairman Ben Elissar to suggest that a lie-detector test be administered. Later, Ben Elissar sponsored a bill that would deprive members of their immunity with respect to disclosures from the Committee so that an offender could be prosecuted. The Finance Committee has proved more successful in securing secrecy: by a gentleman's agreement an announcement by the chairman that what is being said is not for publication has the required result.

A description of the Knesset's committees would not be complete without a fuller account of their procedure on bills and on the subjects of members' motions, which are generally their main fare. But committee treatment is only one stage in the progress of a bill or matter, and these proceedings are considered in Chapters 9 and 10.

8

Parliamentary Groups

A PARLIAMENTARY GROUP in the Knesset comprises the members elected from one candidates list representing a nationwide party or electoral bloc; or the members elected from separate lists of parties formed later into a bloc; or a fresh combination of members elected from one or more lists, which requires authorization by the House Committee, who will first canvass existing Groups, particularly with regard to the name being chosen by the new Group. The further conditions for forming a completely new parliamentary Group after the election, if it is to benefit from state financing of running expenses, were described in Chapter 4.

Parliamentary Groups, as well as determining the nature and composition of the Government and functioning as the political agents in the parliamentary sphere, are a key factor in the Knesset's organization and procedures. The paramountcy of the parliamentary Group is recognized by the Knesset chairman, who will meet with their representatives when he wishes to improve attendance in the house, to persuade members to restrain their stream of Questions to ministers, or to introduce any significant innovation. Many a matter is left in abeyance by the House Committee until its members have consulted their Groups. While in some legislatures political groups, though an inseparable part of the parliamentary system, receive little or no formal recognition, the status and role of Knesset Groups are defined by statute and rule as well as custom; this could hardly be otherwise given the pervasive influence exercised by Israel's political parties as the midwives of the state and the carriers of its national and pioneering values, particularly during the Knesset's formative years.

FRAGMENTING TENDENCIES

The number of Groups in a newly elected Knesset has ranged from ten to fifteen. Notwithstanding mergers and the increasing trend to consolidation of Group alliances, simultaneous splintering has in recent years tended to increase their number in the course of a term, a phenomenon which can perhaps be accounted for on the one hand by the general falling off of ideological attachments and doctrinaire attitudes that has taken place since the birth of the state, and on the other, by the persistent attraction of a distinct party framework. Rather than continue fighting for their views from within, disaffected members of a parliamentary Group will often form a separate Group in the Knesset and organize a national party though their outlook at the polls is less than promising. The alacrity with which new groupings that have not yet faced the test of an election appear on the parliamentary scene once prompted a minister to speak of them as representatives of "ghost towns."[1] While it has been noted by observers that division may, paradoxically, bring a greater total vote than unity, this is true of old allied parties which again part ways rather than of fresh splinters.

Fissions and floor crossings, even if they do not reflect a corresponding political realignment of the public and scarcely affect the largest Groups may disturb the coalition. Their frequency sometimes lends to the Knesset's political landscape a kaleidoscopic quality which was well illustrated in the 1977–81 term. That term, which opened with thirteen Groups, had eighteen at dissolution, plus four independent members. Table 5 shows the Group membership changes, including the disappearance of two original Groups, the formation of eight new ones, and the dissolution in turn of one of these; but these were only the net changes. In the shifts of allegiance some Groups both gained and lost, while for some members a new Group was only the last stop after a number of previous moves. For example, Moshe Dayan, elected on the Labor Alignment list, left it immediately afterward to become an independent member while he served as foreign minister, and some time after he resigned, headed a new Group, *Telem*.

Not a few of the political switches in the 1977–81 Knesset were part of the disintegration process that overtook the Democratic Movement for Change (DMC). Organized in 1976 as a middle-of-the-road party emphasizing internal party democracy, efficient government, and electoral reform, it won fifteen mandates and formed the third largest Group in the house. It was, however, made up of disparate elements and, lacking the deep roots of the old established parties, its life was fleeting. Divided over joining the coalition in 1977, the parliamentary Group split into three a year later. The splinter Group which remained in the coalition as the Democratic Movement underwent further attrition until it completely disappeared in 1981. By the time of

Table 5

Changes in Composition of the Ninth Knesset (1977–81)

Group*	Membership on Election	Membership at Dissolution
Likud	43	40
Labor Alignment	32	33
Democratic Movement for Change (DMC)	15	0
National Religious Front (NRP)	12	12
Democratic Front for Peace and Equality	5	5
Agudat Yisrael	4	4
Sheli	2	1
Shlomzion	2	0
Development and Peace	1	1
Poalei Agudat Yisrael	1	1
Civil Rights Movement	1	1
Independent Liberal party	1	1
United Arab List	1	1
Groups Formed During the Term		
Shinui—Center party	—	5
Telem	—	4
Tehiya	—	2
Ha'ihud	—	2
Ahva	—	1
Yaad	—	1
One Israel	—	1
Democratic Movement†	—	0
Independent Members	—	4
Total	120	120

*For explanation of Group names, see Glossary.

†Formed in September 1978 with the break-up of DMC, it dissolved in March 1981.

the Democratic Movement's demise, the members of the original DMC were to be found in seven different parliamentary Groups (with three back in the *Likud* or Alignment) and as independent members (three).

While the protean political profile of the 1977–81 Knesset was perhaps the most marked, almost every term has witnessed defections, splits, or mergers, often coming in anticipation of the next election. But election results, in turn, frequently produce early realignments as a consequence of changed circumstances. Thus, for example, the Shlomzion parliamentary Group shown in Table 5 had almost no independent existence, merging with *Herut* in the *Likud* Group immediately after the 1977 election. Again, in the 1981–84 Knesset, the one-member Civil Rights Movement, though appearing in Table 9 as part of the Labor Alignment, had in fact been a separate Group upon election; joining the Alignment early on in the term, it reassumed independent Group status before the 1984 election. A striking burst of postelection regrouping occurred in 1984 when the formation of a National Unity Government led almost simultaneously to the affiliation of the centrist *Yahad* Group to the Alignment and the exit of the *Mapam* members to reconstitute a separate Group, while Y. Sarid departed from Labor to join the Civil Rights Group.

In the freedom of a Knesset member to defect from his Group despite the party-list system there is something of a contradiction. The voter, after all, chooses a party and a program not individual candidates. A member's change of party affiliation therefore usually carries opprobrium and brings demands from the adversely affected Group for his resignation from the Knesset so that his seat will revert to the list from which he was elected. Only a few seceders have done so. The first defection occurred in 1949 when a member broke away from the Communist Group in the Constituent Assembly (before it was renamed the First Knesset). When the Group demanded that his membership be annulled the Assembly accepted the conclusion of its committee on election returns that he could not be deprived of his mandate. When two Members left *Herut* in 1951, that Group sought to give effect to advance letters of resignation which it had collected from them before the election and so to unseat them. The House Committee considered their membership unaffected.

In the 1965–69 Knesset, when defections became more common, three members' bills with the purpose of unseating a member who leaves his Group were introduced but struck off the agenda. When by crossing the floor to join the labor Alignment in 1982 two *Likud* members temporarily deprived the coalition of a majority, remedies for Group splintering were again sought.

But in fact the federative rather than the fissiparous trend has become dominant in the Knesset; and the two large federative Groups about to be described, Labor Alignment and *Likud,* despite internal tensions proved the Knesset's most settled political elements, each in turn providing both parliamentary and Government leadership. Nor was this general course substantially deflected by the election of July 1984, when a Knesset with fifteen Groups replaced one that had ten. The two large Groups together managed to retain 71 percent of the mandates, and each, with certain small Groups committed to its leadership, in effect retained or exceeded its previous parliamentary strength. Though other small Groups might exact a high price for joining any coalition, the difficulty in forming a Government was again essentially one of closely matched opposing camps. The impulse to form a National Unity Government was due as much to an unprecedented economic crisis as to political fragmentation.

FEDERATIVE GROUPS

As the representative of a bloc or alliance of parties at the national level, a federative Group in the Knesset is itself a composite body made up of the several party Sections, each with its distinct political emphasis. Each Section, as well as securing proportional representation on the Group executive, will elect its own officers and meet regularly apart from the Group, often together with members of its party headquarters. The autonomy enjoyed by each Section within the Group has been facilitated since 1973 by the separate payments from the treasury to the Section of running expenses under the Political parties Financing Law. For all other purposes the Knesset recognizes only the Group.

Already in the First Knesset (1949–51) there was a federative Group: the United Religious Front, formed by four parties. The Group lasted as long as the alliance between those parties. Similarly, the Liberal Group in the 1961–65 Knesset, formed from the joint list of the General Zionist and Progressive parties, broke up when these drew apart again. Federative Groups have ceased to exist also where the allied parties ultimately merged.

Lasting federative Groups, embracing the main political parties, date from 1965. In that year, two new blocs, the Labor Alignment and *Gahal* (later, the *Likud,* in a broader alliance) each formed a parliamentary Group of two Sections. Though the number of Sections in each Group varied later according to changes in party alliances, both federative frameworks endured. As the two leading Groups in the house, well ahead of the others in strength, with each, generally speaking, on a different side of the left-right political spectrum, they have alternated in providing the main coalition element; in the years 1965–77 the Government was dominated by the Alignment, in 1977–84 by the *Likud.* (Table 9 shows their composition on the formation of the Shamir Government, in 1983.) They were the two chief elements in the coalition that gave rise to the National Unity Government in 1984, though the composition of the Alignment was altered in the process.

As pointed out in Chapter 4, the relative strength of the Sections within a Group, except when a bloc is formed between existing Groups, will result from the arranged order of candidates in the joint list drawn up by agreement between the allied parties before the election campaign. An example of such an agreement in the Labor Alignment, complicated further by the existence in one party of historic wings, was shown in Table 4.

The existence of Sections and other divisions within Groups, though not officially recognized by the Knesset (except under the financing law as described in Chapter 4), has at times encumbered its organization. For example, in the 1969–73 Knesset the Labor Alignment Group's desire to give representation on the presidium to each of the Labor party's three wings as well as to the Alignment's two Sections—while assuring preference to the large *Mapai* wing—brought the number of vice-chairmen to eight, though a smaller number, with the Alignment chairman, was enough to give the Group a majority on that body. In the 1973–77 Knesset a weaker Alignment Group, with only two of five vice-chairmenships, rotated them at midterm so as to satisfy the Sections and wings, though without showing preference any longer to the *Mapai* wing. In the same term the *Likud,* to be evenhanded with its Sections, rotated its four committee chairmanships as well as a Knesset vice-chairmanship. Intersectional calculations cannot be ignored with impunity in filling parliamentary positions. At one point the *Mapam* Section threatened to boycott meetings of the Alignment Group if it did not receive a subcommittee chairmanship.[2] Intra-Group differences following the 1981 election prevented the Knesset from electing the seven vice-chairmen that had been decided on; there were consequently only two vice-chairmen until 1984, when two more were elected.

Of greater moment to the working of the parliamentary system than disputes over representation on Knesset bodies were the deep-rooted differences of political orientation between the major partners within both the Labor Alignment and *Likud* groups. In the Alignment, *Mapam,* more radically left-wing, is also more strongly conciliatory in its position on Israel-Arab relations than its Labor partner. The resulting recurrent friction between the two Sections is illustrated by the following examples. When the *Mapam* Section voted against referral to a committee of a motion in 1972 for the settlement of Kiryat Arba at Hebron, it was charged with infringing Group discipline. In 1980 *Mapam* declared it would dissolve the Alignment if Labor initiated or supported legislation to annex the Golan Heights. In 1982, when the Labor Section sought to put forward an Alignment motion setting out areas of settlement that would remain unaffected by any peace treaty, *Mapam* objected, and there resulted a watered-down motion simply taking note of the Alignment leader's speech. While *Mapam* has always described itself as a Jewish-Arab party, with Arabs among its candidates both before and after it joined the Alignment, Labor, like its precursor, *Mapai,* had preferred to see separate Arab lists, with which it might cooperate later in the Knesset. Here the way of *Mapam* ultimately prevailed: while in the 1973–77 Knesset a Labor-affiliated Arab list was a third partner in the Alignment, in the 1981 and 1984 elections Labor, like *Mapam,* included an Arab candidate in a safe slot among the candidates which it presented to the joint Alignment list.

The *Likud* Group too has often been divided by intersectional differences. The *Herut* Section has placed greater emphasis on security and foreign policy questions, while the Liberals have stressed domestic and economic matters. Liberal members' loyalty to *Likud* has often come under strain over economic issues, and particularly over religious concessions which the Group was prepared to make to a coalition partner, such as prohibition of El Al sabbath flights or restriction on archaeological excavation of burial places. One Liberal, Energy Minister Y. Berman, whose dissatisfaction at the near absence of Liberal planks in the *Likud's* coalition agreement with smaller partners in 1981 was compounded by disagreement with the Government's Lebanon policy, resigned his portfolio the following year.

The existence within both federative Groups of Sections with persisting differences, and loyalties to separate party organizations, provides ready lines of cleavage on many questions that come before the Knesset. Some issues have found both *Likud* and Alignment split on sectional lines. While, in the *Likud, Herut* for a long time opposed electoral reform and any cooperation by the Liberals with the Labor Party on that question, *Mapam,* inside the Alignment, voted against any bill that would introduce district elections, despite the consistently positive stand of its Labor partner on that question. A more striking example, because it involved practical party needs rather than a question of principle, was the attempt in 1975 to secure state guarantee of bank loans to political parties for the consolidation of debts. The *Herut* Section in *Likud,* and Labor in the Alignment, whose parties were both in serious financial trouble, supported the step in the house, while their respective partners, the Liberals and *Mapam,* opposed it. (In the event, after a number of delaying court orders the plan was shelved.)

A Section is not amenable to Group discipline in the same degree as an individual. In the Golan debate cited earlier, for example, neither *Mapam* nor Civil Rights members were penalized, though they too participated in the vote contrary to the Group decision, because their entire Sections voted against the bill. The Labor Alignment, on some questions which divided its Sections granted the smaller partner, *Mapam,* the right to abstain in the Knesset vote, as was the case on strike restraint legislation in 1971, and on civil marriage in 1976. The concession was made to the *Mapam* Section though not to a number of Labor members. But such concession may be qualified: in the case of the 1971 bill it was stipulated that if there should be doubt about a Knesset majority for the measure, *Mapam* would submit and vote with Labor; moreover *Mapam* was refused the right to make a statement on the abstention. Where differences between the Sections of a Group are unbridgeable there may be agreement from the outset that on matters at issue each will have freedom to speak and vote independently. For example, in *Likud's* precursor, the *Gahal* Group, each Section retained freedom of action on German relations, religious matters, and electoral reform.

Sectional autonomy was given the most striking expression after the 1969 election, when *Mapam* refused to enter the coalition along with Labor because the National Unity Government included *Gahal,* whose positions it strongly opposed. Thus, for months, *Mapam's* two representatives in the Government would assume no definite responsibilities though Golda Meir of Labor was prime minister. They served as ministers without portfolio, they and their Group accepting discipline only with respect to foreign affairs, defense, and the budget. Only when *Gahal* left the Government, in August 1970, did the *Mapam* ministers take charge of the Health and Immigration ministries, held in trust for them until then by Mrs. Meir.

With the formation again of a National Unity Government in 1984, the six-man *Mapam* Section left the Alignment and renewed its existence as an independent parliamentary Group. It should be noted, however, that the Alignment continued as a federative Group, simultaneously taking into its ranks as a Section the *Yahad* Group of three, while still including as well one Independent Liberal. Further, there is reason to believe that *Mapam* will return to the Alignment as soon as the Unity Government, formed primarily to deal with a national crisis, comes to an end; it is significant that the Labor-*Mapam* Alignment in the *Histadrut* was not at all interrupted.

GROUP DISCIPLINE

A parliamentary Group is organized so its members can work out a common stand on questions as they come before the Knesset. Meeting weekly, the Group has a chairman and executive committee to conduct its day-to-day affairs and employs a small staff independent of Knesset control, which usually includes a legal adviser and a spokesman as well as secretaries. Of course, the smaller a Group the simpler its organization will be. As well as office space and facilities in the Knesset Building, each Group has since 1966 received a small monthly allocation from the Knesset budget to help pay for its parliamentary technical services. Linked to the consumer price index, the amount received by a Group was for March 1984, a flat sum of IS11,865 (about 74 US$), plus IS13,181 (about 82 US$) for every member in its ranks. (This allowance is not to be confused with the much greater sum mentioned in Chapter 4, for which the parliamentary Group is only a conduit, the funds serving to finance nationwide party activities.)

Group discipline (bearing in mind, though, the checks placed on its enforcement in federative Groups by underlying sectional differences, as noted earlier) is an ever present reality in the Knesset, with each Group, through one of its officers, seeing to the attendance and voting of its members. This discipline is reinforced in practice by the Knesset Rules as well a the member's dependence on his party leaders for reelection. The unquestioned right of the Group over committee assignments was described in the last chapter.

The Rules also place the Group in control of a member's right to speak in important house debates and to present bills or motions, Though any member who has registered may speak on matters not controversial in the party sense, when debates are on a Group basis—and these include most important matters, such as the budget, foreign and defense policy, and motions of no confidence—time is allotted proportionally to the Groups, and it is they who determine the speakers. Furthermore, the Rules require that on the demand of ten members, or of two Groups who together number at least eight members, the debate on any other matter be on a Group basis. Thus a member at variance with his Group's position on any question of moment is not likely to be chosen to speak. One Group was known to determine also who would speak first in debate on an individual basis.[3] Also the right to a statement on abstention in a vote belongs to the Group, so that a member who has abstained alone can speak only with its consent.

Though the Rules permit a member to submit any number of motions or bills, their chances of being considered depend very much on his Group. Every Group requires that such initiatives of its members be cleared with it. Some Groups have insisted on prior clearance also for Questions to Ministers, the practice in one being to assign formulated Questions, prepared by staff, to different members.[4] Further, a member's motions and bills are taken in the house only on the quota of his Group, which, as described in the next chapter, is largely a function of its size. The congestion of members' bills and motions which prompted amendment of the rule of consideration according to order of submission, in 1966, could have been met more simply by restricting each member to a certain number; but this would have given the individual member a measure of positive independence from his Group. A solution was preferred which further strengthened the Group, for clearly members' motions and bills when allowed only within its quota become its recognized domain also formally. Motions submitted as urgent, which are outside the quotas, are, however, likely to be under extra close supervision by the Group. For example, the Labor Alignment required the mover of an urgent motion to secure the consent of the Group chairman both as to its form and content and forbade him to appeal to the House Committee in case of refusal by the presidium to grant urgency, except with permission from the Group chairman.[5]

A Group is also likely to view with disfavor a member's unapproved joint initiative with members of other Groups, whether a bill or motion. It will see a more serious challenge, as also affecting the party, in the appearance of a ginger group in its midst: *Ometz,* formed within the Alignment in 1981 because it was dissatisfied with the Group's performance as an opposition, was discouraged from holding meetings. The case is otherwise with subjects politically more innocuous or enjoying a wide consensus in the

Knesset: there have been cross-Group members' "lobbies" representing special interests such as the city of Jerusalem, the Oriental communities, development towns, the protection of nature, and the advancement of industry. The most influential body of this kind was the virtually all-party group on environmental problems. Set up first in 1970 on the initiative of Liberal Y. Tamir, its subject won formal recognition in 1974 as a distinct area of continuing parliamentary interest with the establishment of the Committee on Internal Affairs and the Environment (previously just "Internal Affairs").

The member at odds with his Group's stand on a question will seek to cope with the requirements of discipline in one of a number of ways. He may ask the Group's permission to abstain from the Knesset vote; but this will not likely be granted in a close contest or matter of great principle. Not much different is a member's request not to take part in the vote so as to be excused from following the Group line. Absence from the chamber during the vote, though without permission it may earn a member the censure of his Group as much as abstention, is yet less conspicuous and a more prevalent way of steering between a vote for a position one does not honestly support and outright defiance of the party. A member denied permission to abstain may slip out before the vote. Since it is essentially the member's vote that is of concern to the Group, he may solve his problem by speaking against its position but voting for it; but such behavior does not go unnoticed and exposes him to ridicule. To plead that the question is one of conscience, particularly in religious matters, offers a member the best chance of being excused by the Group from a vote, or, in rare cases, of being permitted to record disagreement by a contrary vote. On a measure restricting the right to an abortion, Sarah Doron of *Likud* was granted the right to abstain on the ground of conscience. When a number of her colleagues claimed the same privilege hers was withdrawn. Though she nonetheless stayed away from the chamber for the vote, a party stalwart justified her, saying: "Doron is our one and only *Likud* woman member, and she has the right to be treated as a woman since only a woman can understand what an abortion means."[6]

An independent stand by a member in the face of Group discipline is not a rare occurrence. But the circumstances vary and sometimes help explain maverick behavior. Often there is an existing background of disaffection as in the case of A. Eliav in the 1973–77 Knesset. Earlier a deputy minister and secretary of the Labor party, he came to disagree sharply with Alignment foreign and security policy. Set anyway on a course that was leading him out of the Group, he voted against a supplementary budget and abstained in a no-confidence vote while the Alignment was the Government's backbone. Even before he left the Group he told his parliamentary leader, "I'm already out of your orbit."[7] Not far different was the situation of E. Weizman in the *Likud* in 1980. After policy differences led him to resign the defense portfolio, he did not hesitate to speak and vote against the Government on a no-confidence motion. A member may buck his Group leaders, as did H. Druckman of the National Religious party on the question of the Sinai withdrawal in 1982, when he is confident that he speaks for a considerable segment of opinion in his party. Y. Ben Aharon of the Alignment, who voted counter to the Group line on important questions in the years 1974–76, was an elder statesman near the end of his political career; he had been a minister in two Governments and secretary-general of the *Histadrut*.

When imposing a penalty on a noncomforming member, the Group usually takes account of the gravity of the infraction; on an opposition member's bill on national service for girls exempted from army duty in 1978, *Likud* member M. Shamir, who voted in support, was denied the right to speak in the plenum on behalf of the Group for two months; Mrs. Geula Cohen, who abstained, was denied the right for one month. Group leaders do not relish the task of meting out disciplinary penalties and prefer if possible to overlook a transgression. On a question not of prime importance, a member may escape sanctions even if he votes out of line with the Group, as in the case of *Likud* member B. Shalita who moved and voted on 21 June, 1982, to send back to the Government a bill to renew emergency regulations for guard duty at school buildings. When the offenders can claim that the Group line violates party tenets, disciplinary measures cannot easily be taken: this was in effect the situation on the 1976 bill providing for reduction of pay in slow-down strikes, when five Labor members voted against first reading and a sixth stayed out of the chamber.

However ticklish the disciplinary job may be, when a Group is seriously riven by a division in the house it cannot evade formal chastisement of the rebels. After the Alignment Group had decided to boycott the Knesset debate, and vote, on the 1981 bill to apply Israel law in Golan, eight of its members voted with the coalition and thirteen voted against the bill. Reeling from disarray, the Group appointed a committee of four to recommend sanctions. Consequently, with even-handed justice which did not discriminate at all between deviant doves and hawks, nine offenders were suspended from some sphere of Knesset activity for a month: three from the Group executive, two from committee chairmanships, and four from all committee activity; three others received a reprimand.[8] A month earlier, when eight Alignment members were barred from speaking in the plenum for periods of two and three weeks because they had failed to vote the Group line in a political debate, it was reported that they treated the penalties as a "big joke."[9] Another kind of penalty is for the Group to withhold approval of dissentient members' initiatives: when three *Likud* members voted with the opposition for a bill to end censorship in 1982, their own legislative proposals were refused clearance by the Group.

While summary punitive measures may be of slight deterrent effect on a member who has made up his mind to take an independent stand, the Group, through the party, wields also an ultimate power: when Shulamit Aloni, elected on the Alignment list in 1965, debated and voted against the Group's positions too often to be tolerated by party leaders, she was left off the candidates list for the following Knesset. However, such a penalty must await an election; though a Group has occasionally expelled a member demonstratively, the Knesset, in law, takes congnizance of Groups as elected from the candidates lists. Thus only when a member formally secedes from his Group, and this is noted by the House Committee, is he out, whether as an independent or member of another Group.

A member who breaks away from his Group and does not join another is the only kind of "independent" known to the Knesset. But unlike the member elected alone from a candidates list, who enjoys every Group privilege except the right to move no-confidence in the Government, a defector will find his parliamentary scope much restricted. Although according to a series of House Committee resolutions he is entitled to speak in the house in debates on a Group basis and is allotted a quota of motions and bills, he is denied other Group prerogatives. He cannot, for example, propose a motion on the summation of a debate. The committees are closed to him except by special invitation, when he is anyhow without a vote. The running expenses on account of his mandate, under the Political Parties Financing Law, continue going to his former Group. However, fresh one-man Groups have been given recognition by the House Committee in some cases.

While the Group restricts the freedom of its members, it is their most important parliamentary resource. As well as enabling them to assume duties and positions of responsibility and providing them with secretarial, research, and legal assistance to supplement what they receive officially from the Knesset, it will help to advance their initiatives. This is particularly important in the case of a coalition member to whose bill or motion the Government's attitude is equivocal. For example, the rules of the Labor Alignment Group in the 1973–77 Knesset, when it was the chief component of the coalition, set a limit to the study of a proposed member's bill by the minister concerned of thirty days; and of a motion, seven days. If the minister did not take a stand within those times, the bill or motion was submitted to the Knesset. If the minister expressed opposition to the initiative within the specified time, the member could appeal to the Group. Later, when the *Likud* was the main force in the coalition, it decided that initiatives of members would be considered first by joint ministerial-Group committees.

Conversely, since coalition Groups claim the right to preliminary scrutiny of Government measures, they have demanded, if not always successfully, that ministers consult with them regularly and before introducing legislation or taking any important step. The Government's failure to sound out their views may result in drastic amendment of its proposals, as happened, for example, with the 1971 Tenants Protection Bill, when the proposed increases in rents were halved as the result of a decision by the Alignment Group. Prime Minister Rabin agreed in 1976 to meet monthly with his own parliamentary Group (Alignment) and to its holding of political debates. According to one view, however, the value of such meetings was only psychological since the Government did not explain its tactical moves or submit basic decisions for approval by the Group.

Intracoalition strains and the continuous confrontation between the coalition and the opposition Groups are considered in Chapter 12. Here it remains to note that other inter-Group relations that cut across coalition and opposition alike also contribute a dynamic to the parliamentary scene. An example that is well remembered is the election of Nahum Nir as Knesset chairman in 1959, when a number of Groups differing sharply politically, combined to defeat the candidate of *Mapai,* then the largest Group in the house and in the coalition. Often there is an ad hoc realignment which pits the large Groups against the small, with the former seeking to confine or eliminate the latter. In 1976, when the two large Groups also sought to ration urgent motions according to Group size, several small Groups from both coalition and opposition issued a statement charging that their freedom of speech was being threatened. They were joined by the small Free Center Section of *Likud,* aware of its true interest, for it was to break away again from the *Likud* Group later that year. The 1973 bill to alter the allocation of Knesset seats that remain after the initial distribution found the small Groups from all quarters of the house united in opposition to the designs of the large. A natural antagonism between large and small Groups will, however, be overridden by the more pervasive conflict between coalition and opposition, as occurred in 1981 when the Alignment, in exchange for the support of two tiny Groups in confronting the *Likud*-led Government, undertook to oppose a bill to raise the one-percent threshold in elections (see Chapter 4).

The three previous chapters have dealt with the different aspects of the Knesset's organization. We now consider its forms of business.

9

The Knesset at Work

THE KNESSET PERFORMS a number of functions. It sustains a Government and oversees its activity; in partnership with the Government it legislates. The Knesset also serves as the nation's central forum for public debate of outstanding issues; though its scrutinizing function is performed largely in the privacy of committees. In its debates and decisions the Knesset's task is to influence the Government and instruct the public, while through the same proceedings the Government seeks parliamentary endorsement and legitimation of its policies and actions. The proceedings followed by the Knesset in discharging these duties are considered in this and the following three chapters. Not the least important function of the Knesset is representation of electors—both through coherent policy stands of parliamentary Groups and through positions taken by the individual member on behalf of an occupational or social sector whom he accepts as his constituency; and as we saw in Chapters 5 and 8, the two kinds of representation are frequently combined. The minor, elective and judicial duties of the Knesset—minor in that they take relatively little of the Knesset's time and are essentially of a formal nature—are described later in the present chapter.

DEBATE

A full-dress debate in the house is held on an individual or Group basis. Debates on an individual basis take place where no party lines are involved and there is a free vote. Many first readings of bills are debated in this manner. A member wishing to take part in such a debate has only to apply to the secretary. The speaking time, usually between ten and fifteen minutes, is fixed by the chairman, who also arranges the order of speakers, generally as they have registered, while meeting, where possible, the wishes of a speaker seeking a time other than that assigned him. The order of speakers is listed on the notice boards at the two entrances to the chamber. A member absent when his turn to speak is called by the chair, after failing to give notice of absence, loses the floor.

Group-basis debates, which provide the framework for confrontation between political forces in the Knesset, are of higher controversy and require greater organization than debates on an individual basis. Under the Rules they are held on the following matters: confirmation or resignation of a Government; the budget; foreign or defense policy; no-confidence motions; a subject regarded by the Government as a question of confidence; a subject on which ten members, or two Groups who together number at least eight members, have requested a Group-basis debate. Thus most debates on Government statements, on politically controversial bills, and on the subjects of members' motions that are put on the agenda, as well as on other important matters, are held on a Group basis.

The order of proceeding in Group-basis debates has been markedly influenced by the Knesset's multi-Group composition. After the House Committee has fixed the amount of time for the debate it is divided among the Groups in proportion to size, none receiving less than ten minutes. Since each Group may dispose of its time as it sees fit, it informs the Knesset chairman in writing of the names of its members who will speak, the order in which they will appear and the time each is to be given, provided that no speaker is to get less than eight minutes. For choosing its speakers a Group may have fixed rules; the Alignment's assignments panel in the 1973–77 Knesset had to give preference to members who were on the committee concerned with the subject.[1] From the lists submitted to the Knesset chairman, he fixes the order of speakers according to Group size, while providing that in the first round of speeches, in which every Group is represented at least once, the first speaker is from the largest opposition Group—and that the largest Group may put up four speakers, the second largest, two. Within these restrictions the chairman interweaves Groups as far as he can. In all cases the debate is opened and wound up by the sponsor, whether the Government, a committee, or a member; opening and closing speakers, including the proposer of a no-confidence motion, could speak at any length up until 1984, when the House Committee limited them to twenty minutes.

The rules for Group-basis debate, in their particularities, have been shaped to a large extent through experience. In the early years of the Knesset, all

Groups would appear once in the first round of speeches, with the result that most speakers from the largest Group, which disposed of the most time, would in long debates appear one after another in the second round. To correct this situation the rules were amended a number of times: in 1956, to allow more than one speaker from the largest coalition Group in the first round, and later, to allow that Group three speakers in the first round in a debate of at least eight hours; in 1969, the provisions described in the last paragraph, providing a more even distribution of speakers from the two largest Groups, without reference to coalition affiliation or length of debate, were adopted. There is also a history behind the eight-minute minimum for a speech, which was adopted in 1980. In fact a member at the rostrum may still be as brief as he likes. However, up until 1980 a Group could divide its time so as to give a speaker as little as three minutes. The chair would nearly always allow a speaker so restricted extra time far beyond the allotment to enable him to express himself. Consequently, a debate might take twice as long as scheduled by the House Committee. The eight-minute rule put a sharp limit to the number of speakers a Group may put up, while reducing the inevitability of spillover.

The time allotted for a Group-basis debate has ranged from one to ten hours, according to the gravity of the subject. While a debate ensuing from a member's motion may be set at one hour, the debate on a Government statement may be granted three hours, and on the budget seven. But even with such management the time actually taken by a debate may bear only slight resemblance to that fixed in advance. To cite but one example, after the House Committee allotted five hours for debate of the no-confidence motion on 19 November 1980, the time in fact ran to seven. The length of a debate is unpredictable for a number of reasons. First, the allowance of at least ten minutes to every Group and independent member effectively extends the overall time. Second, the chair continues to be generally indulgent toward prolix speakers, even after the adoption of the eight-minute rule. On the other hand, a debate may be foreshortened because a Group opts out. The views of coalition members are often adequately expressed by the minister. Interest in a long debate may flag so that members due to speak slip out of the chamber. Though a Group may put up another speaker in place of one who has lost the floor because of absence, in many cases it does not trouble to do so.

The allotment of debating time in the House Committee may on occasion be part of a parliamentary maneuver: for example, on 2 December 1981, when the coalition numbered only sixty-one members, its majority on the Committee allotted ten hours to a no-confidence debate to enable four ministers abroad to return in time for the vote; the opposition for contrary reasons had asked for a debate of one hour. Once the four were back and in the house, members who were registered to speak went up to the dais and had their names crossed off.

The Knesset has a number of procedures for economizing time in debate. Two or more related subjects may be considered in a combined debate if the plenum or the House Committee so decides; the vote on each is separate. A record number of eight bills on connected fiscal matters was taken in one debate on 10 June 1975. Such a debate may also combine proceedings that are formally different, like a bill and the subject of a member's motion or a Government statement. But views as to similarity of subjects may differ. Occasionally, in a combined debate the coalition has been charged with seeking to confuse issues in order to blunt criticism. Combined debate is based only on practice. Another expeditious procedure, Group statements in lieu of debate, is provided for by the Rules and gives less rise to misunderstanding. A debate may take the form of Group statements within limits of five to ten minutes upon a resolution of the House Committee. Every Group then gets the same amount of time and puts up one speaker. The order of appearance is according to Group size. The most frequent use of the Group-statements procedure is on no-confidence motions. In connection with members' motions, further ways of shortening debate are described in the next section of this chapter.

Over the years debates have become generally shorter, with smaller allotment of time by the House Committee. It was not uncommon for the Knesset in its early years to sit into the small hours of the morning, especially on budget debates. In more recent times all-night sittings have been rare: they occurred twice in 1973, when the small Groups were determined to stall a disadvantageous elections bill; in 1978, on the Camp David accords; and in 1982, on compensation to the Sinai evacuees. While debates have become shorter, there is more reading of speeches, which is generally deplored as inimical to genuine controversy. But if speakers today react in a less direct manner to words said at the rostrum by others before them, they are more often provoked into responding to abrasive interjections. The frequency with which sittings have been thrown into disorder by bouts of irrepressible trading of invective prompted the Knesset to hold self-searching debates in 1980 and 1982, among whose results were an advisory committee on a members' code of behavior set up by Chairman Savidor. One of the committee's first recommendations was that a speaker was not to be interrupted without his permission. But this had already been the accepted practice; the question was rather how to better enforce it. And many a raucous debate is in fact the result of the speaker's eagerness for a verbal duel with any comer.

The rule of relevance in debate has not been more strictly followed. Rarely exercising his full disciplinary power in this matter, the chairman may chide a speaker who strays unreasonably from the subject—but just as often, acknowledging the speaker's powerful sentiments toward a current issue and the fact that he may not have other occasion to voice them from the rostrum, the chairman will not attempt to check impertinent remarks. Chairmen will show understanding in allowing an unrelated but anguished preface to a speech, as they did, for example, in the case of the Arab member, T. Toubi, when he protested the expulsion of mayors in Samaria on a motion concerning rent control,[2] or at Jewish settlement there while explaining an amendment to a bill on autopsies.[3] The style of debate in the Knesset may itself invite irrelevance. A debate other than on a bill, or on the composition of the Government, is not focussed by a precise motion as in parliaments of English tradition. The subject for debate is couched in general terms. Only after the minister or sponsoring member in his reply has summed up the debate are Motions on Summation put forward.

A Motion on Summation of Debate may be brought from the rostrum by any Group or combination of Groups. The motion must be submitted first in writing to the chair, which has exercised the right to delete a part on grounds of security or has refused to put it to a vote because its subject was not debated. The first motion is proposed by the coalition and any momentary allies, and followed by motions of other Groups according to size. The coalition motion is often the shortest and simply "takes note of the minister's statement." Inter-Group negotiation is likely before motions are submitted or even before the debate, with the coalition seeking to secure the greatest degree of unanimity; in political debates it was the practice of Prime Minister Golda Meir to hold preparatory talks with the opposition leaders. Such efforts may produce a wide consensus and on occasion a united house. There can be no amendment to a motion once it is proposed from the rostrum. The voting of the motions is in reverse order, so that the coalition or majority motion is put last.

Each Motion on Summation is voted separately, for and against, a procedure which has resulted, though in rare cases only, in the adoption of two different motions, or in the adoption of none. An opposition Group, to embarrass coalition supporters, may ask that each paragraph of its motion be voted separately; the house will then decide by a preliminary vote whether to comply, unless there is no objection. The voting completed, with a resolution adopted, there may be a five-minute statement by any Group that abstained. An individual abstainee is allowed such a statement only with the permission of his Group and if he did not participate in the debate. At the close of the sitting any member whose speech led to misunderstanding or who wishes to refute an allegation made against him in the house will be given permission by the chair to make a personal statement of five minutes if he has first submitted its content to the chair in writing.

If the resolution adopted calls for some action by the Government, the chairman will transmit its text to the minister concerned, who within six months must inform the chairman in writing of any action taken in consequence. The minister's statement is laid on the table of the Knesset. The force of a resolution consequent on a policy debate is closely bound up with the question of Knesset sovereignty and considered in chapter 12.

MOTIONS FOR THE AGENDA

A Motion for the Agenda (more briefly, members motion) enables its proposer to speak for fifteen minutes on any matter within the Knesset's scope and to move that it be placed on the agenda for full debate. Two subsequent motions are then allowed in any order: to refer the matter to a committee, and not to include the matter on the agenda. The minister concerned, if Government policy is involved, will be first to propose a subsequent motion, and another member will move the alternate motion. The minister may agree that the subject be placed on the agenda. If he does so, or if he moves that it be committed, he too is confined to fifteen minutes; he may speak at any length if he moves not to include it on the agenda. A member moving either subsequent motion may speak five minutes. If the minister has agreed to a full debate, or if the Government has taken no stand on the subject of the member's motion, which is generally the case when it is properly a Knesset matter, such as for example, elections or the televising of house proceedings, both subsequent motions are left to members. The first subsequent motion may be proposed by the committee chairman concerned; a motion to debate information leaks from the Foreign Affairs and Security Committee has been replied to by its chairman, a motion concerning a quorum rule by the House Committee chairman. However, all three alternatives—plenary debate, committee consideration, or noninclusion on the agenda—are not always before the house for a vote, since a member's motion may be followed by only one subsequent proposal, or none. Further, the first mover often waives his motion for full debate in favor of a subsequent motion for a committee remit; if the original motion is rejected, and there was no motion for a committee remit, he may himself move that the subject be committed.

The Motion for the Agenda grew out of the early practice in the Knesset of proposing new business on the floor without notice. Though the proceeding had taken its present form by 1950, it rested largely on custom until 1971, when a chapter on members' motions was added to the Rules. The member's motion is analagous to interpellations in some European parliaments, but the result cannot bring down a Government.

As the only procedure available to a member for initiating a debate other than on legislation, the Motion for the Agenda is valued by him as a means of criticizing the Government, giving vent to a grievance, or making a constructive proposal. Although only in a small proportion of cases will the subject be placed on the agenda, most by far being either committed or voted down, the mover's goal is nearly always achieved. The response elicited from the minister in most instances, the third speaker, and Group statements on abstention that may follow the vote, together assure that the subject will receive an airing from all points of view, with attendant publicity. This will be all the more true when a number of members' motions provoked by one event are brought one after another, followed by subsequent motions allowed separately to each original motion. Members from eight parliamentary Groups proposed motions concerning the recommendations of the Etsioni committee on teachers' status, on 6 January 1981. One motion may be proposed by members from different Groups, but this occurs only seldom because a member's motion requires the approval of the Group and, where necessary, also that of the minister concerned, through the coalition executive committee.

In some circumstances the proceedings on a member's motion will be briefer than usual. Not infrequently they end with the mover's indication that he is content with the minister's reply, and there is no vote. Since there is no more appropriate vehicle available for the purpose, a member's motion may be used to make a statement, without much attention to the procedural form. To call the attention of the Knesset to the passage of forty years since the notorious Nazi Wannsee conference on the "Final Solution," two members' motions were made on 19 January 1982; the Government's response through a deputy minister merely voiced solidarity with the movers and with the solemn house. On other, similar occasions the sense of the house may be summed up by the chair. Resigning members have been permitted to use the motion as a parting speech for the restatement of a credo rather than for direct confrontation with the Government; in such cases the minister's reply, in turn, will be complimentary rather than contentious, with little thought on either side of formal motions. However, on 18 February 1981, a resigning member's motion on industrialization was referred to the Economics Committee where, it was hoped, he would still appear as a witness.

A member's motion must be submitted in writing to the chairman with a short explanation of its nature. He may refuse to approve it if it is couched in words implying an insult to or derogatory judgment about any person; if it is on a matter that stands to be debated that week, or that has come up for debate within the preceding month; or if its subject is *sub judice*. The chairman's request that a motion be reformulated to come within the Rules must be accepted. The presidium may at its own discretion alter the wording of a motion expressing a prejudgment. Rewording of motions, moreover, is the general practice when a number are placed on the order paper under one heading to be raised consecutively and replied to by the minister in one speech.

The chairman may dissuade a member from proposing an untimely motion. A motion has been refused because it raised an issue "too sensitive" for public discussion.[4] If the chairman, on consultation with the Foreign Affairs and Security Committee, should find that proposal and debate on the floor of a motion may be detrimental to the national interest, he may send it directly to the Committee for the entire proceeding.

The Knesset chairman notifies the Government of every proposed motion approved by him so that it may indicate whether it will take a stand on the matter. A member whose proposed motion has not been approved may appeal to the House Committee.

Early on, members' motions were taken in order of submission to the chairman without any restriction. As they were brought by members of some Groups in numbers that blocked others, the presidium introduced the practice of allowing one motion on a Wednesday to each Group; in the 1961–65 Knesset the two largest Groups were each allowed two. But since there was still no equitable distribution between Groups, an amendment to the Rules was adopted in 1966, making the size of a member's Group the chief factor determining how soon his motion (or bill) will be considered. The provision requires the House Committee to assign early in the session a quota of motions and bills to each Group while favoring, at its discretion, opposition Groups. In the application small Groups are favored over large. A motion or bill sponsored by a number of members from different Groups is counted on the quota of the Group whose member speaks on it. One Group may transfer to another the right to propose a motion or bill on its quota. However, since the Rules do not prescribe an incontrovertible formula for fixing quotas, a Group may not be satisifed with its share. The large Groups, on the other hand, often do not use up the full quota.

The quotas together provide for some 200 motions and bills of members to be taken in a session, so that seven or eight can come up every Wednesday. In practice the number taken that day varies and may be greater for two reasons. First, motions recognized as urgent (about to be described), being outside the quotas, may also be taken on Wednesday. Second, the frequency with which a number of motions on the same subject are taken in succession and replied to by the minister in one speech often make it possible to include a larger number of motions.

A proposed motion, at the request of the sponsor, will be recognized by the presidium as urgent if in its judgment consideration of the motion by the Knesset may prevent an irreparable act or omission or is of urgent public interest. Urgent motions are eagerly claimed because they can be proposed without restriction outside the sessional quotas, and must be heard by the house in the week of submission; in special circumstances an urgent motion may be deferred for one week at most. A growing stream of motions submitted as urgent has increasingly occupied the presidium and also the House Committee, to whom an urgent motion denied by the presidium may be appealed. While the House Committee not infrequently grants urgency disallowed by the presidium, and one finds, in any case, some urgent motions coming before the house that are scarcely on burning issues, both the presidium and the committee are accused from time to time by members whose urgent motions have not been recognized, of serving as a "rubber stamp" of the coalition or of supporting "dictatorship by the majority." Both the disproportionate amount of time spent by these two bodies in considering the urgency of motions and the unsatisfactory results have led to awareness of the need for a less cumbersome procedure. Chairman Shamir (1977–80) suggested one of two alternatives: that since the presidium as a political body could not be objective here, the chairman should himself have complete authority to decide on a motion's urgency; or that each Group should choose its urgent motions on a quota basis. Undoubtedly the duplication of effort in the examination of urgent motions by both the presidium and the House Committee was, among other things, at the root of one observer's suggestion that the Committee could be eliminated and all its work done by an enlarged presidium.[5]

In disposing of a member's motion, regular or urgent, the house votes whether and how to proceed further with the subject of the motion. So too with a number of motions on the same subject; the chairman will assign one general heading, the minister and the second mover of a subsequent motion may reply to some or all of the motions together, and if possible, the subject will be put to a vote as one, though the several motions were proposed from conflicting positions. However, separate voting will be unavoidable if a mover or a Group so requests, or if there were different consequent motions on separate original motions. Then the chair may have to seek accommodation between the movers or order the voting so as to avoid an anomalous result like that which occurred on 27 January 1982, when three motions on the flower-growing industry resulted in decisions for parallel plenary and committee debates on the subject.

When a current situation has drawn a number of members' motions—and seven or eight on one subject are not a rarity—their consideration itself approaches the dimensions of a general debate. To avoid the repetition and waste of time that would result from a further debate, there is a rule that in the case of motions on the same subject by members from different Groups who together constitute a majority of the Knesset, the presidium may, without putting the motions down for consideration, treat the subject as one which the house has voted to debate on the floor. In practice, the presidium will take such a step only with the consent of the large Groups. But even if motions are considered in the usual way, and there is a decision to put their subject on the agenda, the proceedings may be abridged, where there is wide consensus, by the proposal forthwith of Motions on Summation. A resolution is then adopted though there was no plenary debate. On subjects of unanimity the house may even proceed directly, without division on the member's motion, to a vote on a Motion on Summation as proposed by the minister, perhaps reformulated by the chair.

When a full, plenary debate is held on the subject of a member's motion, the house having voted to include it on the agenda, the debate is opened and summed up by the mover and followed by a resolution of the house, as described earlier in the chapter. However, this will be a gain for him only if the debate is held early, for, as we have just seen, he has made his point anyway with the original motion. As the date for the debate is fixed by the chairman in consultation with the Government, months may elapse before it will be held, if at all. The chairman may have difficulty fitting the item into the order of business, or it may tacitly be left in limbo; nor is there immunity from deferment for debates put down as the result of urgent motions. With the backlog carrying over from session to session, the last all-inclusive agenda in the 1977–81 term carried some thirty items consequent on members' motions, while the press of legislation and other matters left no possibility of taking even one before the session closed. Such accumulation every term of subjects for debate, some no longer timely, prompted the house to adopt a rule in 1979 which provides that an item on the all-inclusive agenda for six months, whose grounds are no longer found valid by the presidium, may be dropped by the house provided it has given a hearing to the original mover if he is opposed. However, it was not until 1983 that the new procedure was first followed, and a few stale items dropped; it is more often tactful to leave a subject effectively buried than to delete it by a positive act.

Where the house votes to commit the subject of the member's motion, the remit is according to the subject matter, which can be a straightforward step as the jurisdiction of each committee of the Knesset is defined by the Rules. But if there is uncertainty or difference of opinion as to the appropriate committee, which is often the case, the House Committee decides where to refer the subject. If the subject matter trenches on the jurisdiction of two or more committees, the House Committee may decide, if the Knesset has not itself so voted, to refer it to a joint committee. However, any committee remit is subject to change on the appeal of a member, usually a committee chairman. For example, in 1983, after the house had previously voted to refer the subject of a motion concerning incentives to teachers in development communities to a joint Education-Labor and Welfare committee, it accepted the House Committee's recommendation that the matter be taken instead by the Finance Committee.

Referred to a committee, the subject is not more certain of early consideration than it would be if put on the house agenda. The committee, as well as having other business which it may wish to take first, can in any case claim priority for bills referred to it, in accordance with the Rules. Though perhaps an extreme example, the subject of anarchy in labor relations, referred to the Labor Committee in 1965, was reported on to the house only in 1969, taking nearly an entire Knesset term.

Reference of the subject of a member's motion to a committee, though formally second-best to inclusion on the house agenda, will lead to investigation and deliberation such as cannot be performed by the plenum. The house has in fact opted for a thorough consideration of the subject behind closed doors instead of a more desultory debate openly held. The committee will hear the mover, the minister and his officials, and other experts or interested bodies, and terminate the proceedings with Conclusions which it will lay on the table of the Knesset. If the committee has good reason, it may decide not to make the Conclusions public, as is often the case of the Foreign Affairs and Security Committee. Occasionally, a committee may find it necessary to table Interim Conclusions, as occurred, for example, in 1979, on the subject of Yigal Allon's motion concerning development plans for the Jordan valley; citing the technological, economic, and political factors that were still unknowns, the committee, though constituted ad hoc from the memberships of three different permanent committees, resolved to continue its existence and to follow up with recommendations as necessary in the light of new developments.

The Conclusions of a committee, varying in length from one paragraph to a few pages, contain a brief description of its manner of proceeding and of the nature of the evidence and findings, followed by conclusions and recommendations. The process of drawing up the Conclusions, which start with the committee chairman's draft, may be protracted. It may necessitate consultation of committee members with their parliamentary Groups, or assignment of the task to a special subcommittee. The object will always be to arrive at a document on which the committee is of one mind. But in the absence of unanimity, a number of committee members or an individual member may insist on appendage of Minority Proposals.

In the Conclusions a committee may not depart from the scope of the subject as delimited by the discussion of the member's motion in the house. Should a committee member or the Government allege that the Conclusions go beyond that compass, the committee chairman will refer the charge to the House Committee, whose opinion must be accepted. On the other hand, a former minister has noted that the Conclusions may be inadequate because the committee, to spare the government embarrassment, has not carried the investigation far enough.[6]

The tabled Conclusions are transmitted by the Knesset chairman to the minister concerned, who, as in the case of a resolution of the house, has six months within which to report what action he has taken in their pursuance. In the Conclusions the committee may in fact call for an earlier report or for periodical reports. The requirement of a ministerial response, put into the Knesset Rules in 1976, went only a small way to meet demands of members who sought to give committee Conclusions greater force and to enable the Knesset to follow up the Government's implementation of recommendations. Still not satisfied that Conclusions were being taken with due seriousness by the Government, D. Zakin tabled a bill in 1982 that prescribed debate of the minister's response within two weeks of its receipt by the Knesset.

A committee's Conclusions may themselves be debated on the floor if the house has so resolved with the committee remit, or the Government has proposed such a debate, or in consequence of a member's motion to put the debate on the agenda. But a member's motion to debate committee Conclusions may result in circularity since the subsequent motion to refer the matter to the committee may instead be adopted, as occurred on 1 February 1984, when Conclusions of the Economics Committee on housing in Jaffa thus simply came back to that body.

QUESTIONS*

A question to a minister, submitted in writing through the chairman, must be answered within twenty-one days from the Knesset rostrum during a question period which is fixed by the presidium for most sittings. With copies of the questions on the members' desks, the answers are read by a minister or deputy minister. In response to the reply the questioner only is permitted one oral supplementary question, to which the minister may answer at once, defer the reply to the next question hour, or ask that it be resubmitted as a question; in the last case he is required to give the answer within seven days of receiving the question.

Though a light weapon in the parliamentary arsenal, a question can be aimed with precision. Submitted formally to elicit information, the question is used by members to expose administrative faults or weaknesses in Gov-

*The experimental adoption of an oral questions procedure in 1983 (to be described presently) does not render the opening account purely historical. The Rules respecting written questions remain unchanged.

ernment policy, to restrain or prod it into action, or otherwise to embarrass it. A question may focus on a grievance, whether of an individual or community, enabling the member to perform a distinctly representative function without the prior clearance from his Group which he needs for other initiatives. Nor is a member in any way restricted in the number of questions he may submit. On 28 January 1981, the minister of the interior answered 116 questions submitted by Mrs. Shulamit Aloni on grants to institutions. By putting this many supplementary questions to the minister, Mrs. Aloni was able to engage the minister in an unprecedented verbal duel in pursuit of the same subject—unapproved and unjustified payments, in her opinion, of public money.

Not to be left out of account are ''initiated'' questions, solicited from coalition members by ministers so they can, in replying, make a statement that by ordinary procedure might draw unwanted attention and entail a debate.

The early practice of the Knesset, inherited from the Provisional State Council, whereby question and answer were read out by the secretary, was replaced in 1950 by the procedure followed in essentials to this day. The 1950 reform, whose object was to liven up the question period, met with slight success. Questioners often did not trouble to be present for the answer, and the number who put supplementary questions was small. Yet so long as the number of questions did not put a strain on the house's time, boring and poorly attended question periods were not perceived as a problem. But the trend of moderate increase in the number of questions over time was upset in the 1965–69 Knesset, when a flood of questions from Uri Avneri, a new member elected alone from his list, and his emulation by a few other members, more than tripled the number of the preceding term. The number of questions continued nearly as high from that time forward (see table 6), always owing mainly to a few ''champion'' questioners.

An important change came about with a ruling by Vice-Chairman S. Z. Abramov in 1976, that in the absence of the questioner the answer need not be read and may simply be printed in the Knesset Record. Until then only in rare instances would the answer not be read at the rostrum, such as when the member, with submission of the question, had asked that the answer be sent directly to him or printed in the Record. Since more than half the questioners do not show up for the answers, the house, in following the 1976 ruling, has been able to dispose of questions in far less time. But the question hour never fails to find a small interested group of members present from among which there are frequent requests that the answer to an absent member's question be read; and the minister may not refuse. Sometimes the nature of the question itself induces the minister to give the answer orally in the member's absence. Question-hour procedure after the Abramov ruling

Table 6

Questions to Ministers (1949–84)*

Knesset Term	Number of Questions
1949–51	998
1951–55	653
1955–59	1,786
1959–61	998
1961–65	2,529
1965–69	7,898
1969–73	6,007
1974–77	6,939
1977–81	7,127
1981–84	3,631 †

*From sessional data issued by the Knesset secretariat.

† There were at least two reasons for this sharp drop in the number of questions; this was the shortest term since 1959–61, and the oral procedure followed in 1983–84 considerably reduced the interest of members in written questions.

was given binding force by a decision of the Interpretations Committee in 1979.

A question is transmitted by the chairman to the minister concerned if it conforms to the Rules. It must be on a factual matter and is not to contain any argument, judgment, or offensive expression or reflection. It must be free of any unessential name or disclosure. If it deals with a personal matter, the member must submit separately to the minister any details that reveal the identity of the individual concerned. Also inadmissible are abstract questions of law. The chairman, in his full discretion, has also ruled out questions he deemed no longer timely. In practice few questions are rejected by him. In some cases he will indicate how a rewording can bring the question within the Rules; or he may himself delete an uncalled for expression. A much decried weakness of some members is to publicize a question before it is approved by the chairman. In one instance, when a member gave early publicity through the media to a question subsequently ruled out by the chairman, he was roundly denounced by the House Committee after the allegation it contained, of acceptance of bribes by a minister, was found baseless.

The Rules also require questions to be strictly brief. But most questions to ministers have consisted of three or four, and sometimes as many as eight or nine, separate numbered queries. These usually come after a prefatory paragraph, often lengthy, which lays the basis for the question with a statement of source, facts, and motive. The minister, in turn, answers in a formalistic style to each part separately. Thus both question and answer are often verbose and lacking in edge, with the point of encounter not immediately clear. Further, such questions sometimes request innocuous facts and statistics which could more easily be obtained by private correspondence with the ministry. One member has dismissed the entire proceeding as an "exchange of documents."[7]

In the matter of content the minister's reply is subject to the same restrictions as the question but without the Chairman's prior inspection. A frequent complaint of the questioner is that the answer is inadequate or not pertinent. If he fails to receive the necessary elucidation by a supplementary question, his only recourse is to raise the subject as a member's motion. Curt answers, simply referring the questioner to some earlier reply, were resented by members and disparaged by the chair to an extent that checked such practice; further, the House Committee, in a resolution of 1980, called on ministers to be explicit in their answers. A minister may, however, still refer the questioner to an answer made earlier in the sitting. If the reply to a question may, in his opinion, harm the national interest, he need not answer at all, even privately; he is then required only to state that reason in writing. A long answer consisting of lists or tables will not be read but printed in the Record.

Late answers, of which there have always been some, are the most vexing to members. While it is accepted for a minister to hold questions until he can answer some twenty or thirty at a time, protest is certain when a reply is months over the time limit, for by then it is no longer of value to the questioner. But the dilatory character of the provisions in the Knesset Rules are themselves an inducement to ministers to put off answers. Given a time limit of twenty-one days to make a reply, a minister may receive a further three weeks upon a reasoned request and then an additional reprieve of seven days. If the question still remains unanswered, the chairman is to fix a date for the reply, and if the minister fails to answer then, to announce this to the house. In effect, a minister is given forty-nine days plus an indefinite extension of time at the chairman's discretion.

After proposals to streamline and give more vitality to the question period had been considered for some years, an oral questions procedure was introduced experimentally in the Knesset's winter session of 1983–84. A House Committee resolution provided for five questions, submitted up until Monday noon, to be put and answered orally at the opening of the following Wednesday sitting, with a supplementary question allowed from each questioner and then one each from the coalition and opposition sides of the house. The admissibility of a question is governed by restrictions identical to those for written questions, with the additional provisions that it may not exceed forty words, and that it is not to be published before it comes up in the Knesset. However, on the day of reply oral questions are listed on the notice boards and their texts laid in the house.

The oral questions procedure imposes extra vigilance on the chairman. In determining which questions are to be taken, he must assure that every member gets an equal share, taking care that two questions on the same subject do not come up within a month. Though within the prescribed limit of an hour for five questions he cannot be rigid about keeping the answer and the supplementary questions to their respectively allowed five minutes and half-minute, he has to be watchful that they do not depart from the restrictions that apply to the original questions, while being evenhanded in distributing the supplementaries between Groups. In great part because of the newness of the procedure, the main tasks of the chair have been to check irrelevant supplementaries and irruptions by other members; the microphones on the members' desks, open during oral questions, make it easier for anyone to break into the proceedings.

During the oral questions experiment, in accordance with the House Committee resolution, the procedure for written or "ordinary" questions was largely in abeyance. Answers to questions were nearly all sent to the questioner or, at his request, printed in the Knesset Record. Only in exceptional cases, determined by the Knesset chairman, was an answer given in the house. Consequently, the number of such questions dwindled sharply in the course of a few months. There came a demand from the opposition that oral questions be discontinued and the ordinary procedure fully restored. It was argued that written questions, which numbered about fifty-five weekly at the time of the House Committee resolution, were too valuable a parliamentary tool to be relinquished. Yet, while oral questions have not met the expectations of all members, competition for them has been keen, and the chairman, after making a selection from submitted questions each week, has had to send the rest to ministers for answer in writing. Oral questions were put also by members who had not bothered with questions before. Clearly, the experiment of 1983–84 will leave its mark on question periods whatever procedures are settled on.

ELECTIVE DUTIES

The Knesset's elective duties—like those which it performs internally in choosing the presidium and committee memberships—are prescribed by statute. However, unlike the open votes for those bodies, the elections here considered are by secret ballot. First in constitutional significance is the election of the president of the state for a term of five years. Ten members can propose a candidate. Where no candidate receives the required sixty-one votes on the first ballot, there is provision for further rounds of voting. However, a third or later ballot is held after the least successful candidate in the previous vote is eliminated, and a simple majority is then enough for election.

Each Knesset elects two of its members to the Judges Appointments Committee, which also includes the minister of justice and another minister, three judges of the Supreme Court, and two representatives of the Israel Bar Association. The Knesset also elects representatives to similar Appointments Committees for religious judges of the Jewish, Moslem, and Druze communities (the law of personal status in Israel being subject to the religious courts), taking care that the members elected in each case are, as far as practicable, from the community concerned. By resolution the Knesset fixes the number of Supreme Court judges. The Knesset has increased the size of that bench a number of times after referring the matter to the Law Committee and voting on its recommendations without debate. A minority view in the committee is, however, entitled to be heard in the house and replied to by the committee chairman. The Knesset, through its House Committee, also elects five members to represent it in the assembly, which elects the Council of the Chief Rabbinate and which consists of 150 rabbinic and lay members.

JUDICIAL FUNCTIONS

The Knesset exercises quasi-judicial functions as the final arbiter of its own composition and of the status of members. It must decide whether to remove from office the president of the state, whom it has elected, or the state comptroller, who was appointed on the recommendation of its House Committee.

Appeals over improper conduct of elections, after the results have been gazetted by the Central Elections Committee, must be made within fourteen days to the new Knesset, which may either reject an appeal, annul the balloting in a polling area and order it held again, or declare a different candidate elected. Any eligible voter may appeal. Faced with a number of election appeals in 1961, the Knesset adopted a set procedure. An appeal is referred by the Knesset to the House Committee, which is authorized for the purpose as a committee of inquiry to subpoena witnesses, allow them expenses, and take their testimony under oath. Appearing as the defendants are the chairman of the Central Elections Committee and the minister of the interior, within whose jurisdiction lies the supervision of elections; both may be represented by the attorney general. Where the mandate of a particular member is challenged, he and the candidates list from which he was elected are both defendants. They too, like the appellant, are entitled to representation by attorney. The recommendation of the House Committee is put to a vote on the floor after the committee chairman has explained the reasoning behind it. If a minority recommendation too was tabled by the Committee, the house will hear the sponsor's reasons and vote on it first. To date, all election appeals have been rejected.

The procedure on election appeals, which leaves the Knesset to sit in judgment on its own composition, has been questioned by many who would like such appeals heard by a more objective, nonpolitical body. Replying in 1965 to a member's bill for the submission of election appeals to the Supreme Court, Deputy Minister Y. S. Ben Meir argued that the Court, because of an irregularity, might annul an entire election. And indeed, even under the present procedure the grant of an appeal could touch the whole election result, since under the nationwide proportional representation a new election in one polling district would entail a full recount.

The judicial functions of the Knesset in deciding whether to unseat or suspend a member and whether to remove his immunity with respect to a criminal charge are carried out through procedures described in Chapters 4 and 5, respectively.

For the removal of the president of the state from office, a complaint must be lodged with the House Committee by at least twenty Knesset members, and a three-quarters majority of the membership is necessary both for the Committee's recommendation and the house resolution for deposition. The president, in person or by attorney, must be given opportunity to refute allegations in each body before a decision is taken. Ten days' notice by the Knesset chairman has to be given members of the special sitting of the house called to consider the deposition. Since the sitting must be called not later than twenty days after the Committee's recommendation, it will be held, if necessary, during a recess.

The statutory requirement for the removal of the state comptroller from office, in contrast with the more elaborate proceedings that are usual in the Knesset's quasi-judicial functions, is simply a resolution of the house by a two-thirds majority of votes cast. It may, however, be reasonably assumed that, as in the other proceedings, the house would act only on a recommendation of the House Committee; the more so as the state comptroller was appointed on its recommendation.

10

Legislation

IN LAWMAKING, the most distinctive parliamentary activity, the Government and the Knesset are both active agents, with the weight of the preparliamentary phase of Government-sponsored bills equalling that of the legislative stages in the Knesset; the latter, however, are our chief concern here. In 1981–82, a fifth of the Knesset's time went to legislation. A bill may be initiated by the Government, by a member or number of members, or by a committee. While the great majority of Government-sponsored bills become law, only a small proportion of members' bills, which may be more numerous than government bills in any term, have the same success; most are dropped from the agenda at an early stage. Committee-sponsored legislation, almost certain to reach the statute books, is negligible in quantity. Table 7 shows the relative weight of each of these three derivations in the legislative output of the last six Knesset terms. The procedure for bills from all three sources, after they are laid on the table for the first reading, is largely the same; the important differences occur before that stage.

BILLS OF GOVERNMENT ORIGIN

A Government bill is usually the product of a ramified preparliamentary stage in which its political, legal, budgetary, and administrative aspects have been scrutinized by the appropriate ministers, officials, and cabinet committee according to a set procedure.[1] In the process a memorandum drawn up by the minister concerned, with the assistance of the departmental legal counsel,

Table 7

Sponsorship of Legislation*

		Source of Initiative					
		Government		Members		Committees	
Knesset Term	Total Laws Enacted	Number	%	Number	%	Number	%
1961–65	281	247	87.9	31	11.0	3	1.1
1965–69	257	237	92.3	15	5.8	5	1.9
1969–73	318	300	94.3	14	4.4	4	1.3
1974–77†	347	287	81.9	56	16.1	7	2.0
1977–81	386	305	79.0	74	19.2	7	1.8
1981–84†	185	165	89.2	17	9.2	3	1.6
Total	1,774	1,541	87.3	207	11.0	29	1.6

*From *Reshumot* (Official Gazette), and sessional data issued by the Knesset secretariat.
†A shortened term.

results in Government approval of a bill drafted by the legislation officers of the Justice Ministry. The preparliamentary phase may be more or less drawn out accordingly as a bill is more or less controversial, and according to the nature and degree of the constraints operating on the Government with respect to it. The draft of a bill may need to be modified after interested and public opinion have been sounded, or to satisfy a dissenting coaliton partner or minister. A legislative undertaking by a coalition that faces strong resistance both within and outside its ranks may need to wait for an opportune time to be introduced in the Knesset. On the other hand, when a measure is urgent the Government will telescope the procedure of preparing the bill so that it will be ready in good time.

A bill is submitted to the Knesset chairman by the minister who initiated the legislation and will pilot it through the house and later administer the law. As soon as the chairman receives the bill he lays it on the table of the Knesset. (Printed on sky blue paper, bills form a separate numbered series in the official gazette published by the Justice Ministry.) Without delay, the chairman has the bill placed on the agenda for the first reading, to be taken at the Government's convenience on a Monday or Tuesday.

At least two days must elapse from the time a bill is laid on the Knesset table before it may be debated, unless the House Committee, at the request of the Government, should decide that it receive earlier consideration. Although both the House Committee and individual members have objected to frequent requests for a waiver of the two-day interval, the Government, when it is hard pressed as at the end of a session, or when important fiscal measures must be expedited, will not hesitate to ask for this concession; the House

Committee, with a coalition majority, can be counted on to grant it. The interval between the tabling and first reading may be cut short for tactical reasons. Such was the case, for example, in 1981, when the first Begin Government, concerned to bring forward a bill for the early dissolution of the Knesset—with five members bills of like purpose already on the table—so as to demonstrate its initiative while undefeated in the house, advanced the consideration of its measure by a day, after the House Committee decided to dispense with the early tabling requirement.

In the early months of the First Knesset, with the example of the Provisional State Council still fresh, bills of a noncontroversial nature, according to a decision of a subcommittee of the House Committee, were sent directly to a committee without any debate held first in the house. Very soon, however, it became the rule to give every bill three readings. The first reading, which is a general debate, is followed by consideration in committee. The second reading is a review of the bill as reported by the committee, with amendments which were rejected in the committee debated and voted before a vote on each clause. The third reading is a vote, without debate, on the entire bill as amended.

The first reading debate, held either on a Group or individual basis (as described in the preceding chapter), follows a speech by the minister concerned in which he has explained the provisions of the bill and has moved that it be referred to a committee. Although this debate is on the principle of the bill, the particulars of clauses are freely discussed by speakers. After the minister has replied, the Knesset's vote to refer the bill to a committee completes the first reading. The minister may defer his reply to a later sitting. But the vote, which must immediately follow the reply, cannot be deferred alone. When a bill has not drawn any speakers the vote will take place immediately after the minister's opening speech. The vote is usually taken "for" and "against" referring the bill to a committee. If the house should vote not to refer the bill to a committee, a reverse usually due to the momentary absence of a coalition majority in the chamber, the measure is defeated. In such a case the Government can and usually does present an identical bill shortly afterward and secures its passage. Thus, for example, the Emergency Regulations (Compulsory Payments) Extension of Validity Bill of 1967, which was rejected on the first reading, on 30 January 1967, was resubmitted by the Government on 1 February as a fresh bill. The Government will act as early as practicable to reintroduce a measure defeated at any stage. A Rounding of Sums Bill to simplify the collection of taxes was introduced by the Government three times between November 1980 and February 1981, before going forward to become law; the first two bills were defeated on the second reading, one when certain clauses were not adopted by the house, the other when a clause was negatived by a tie vote. A more adverse vote is the adoption of a motion to "return the bill to the Government." This was not rare under the Begin Governments, when they commanded a bare majority of the Knesset; in the summer of 1980 it occurred three times within the space of a few weeks.[2]

A bill is referred to the committee within whose jurisdiction its subject lies. Should different committees be proposed, the House Committee will make the choice. If the jurisdictions of two or more committees are involved, the plenum or the House Committee may decide on a joint committee. In the case of the Complaints Commissioner (Ombudsman) Bill of 1970, whose subject trenched on the jurisdictions of three committees, the Knesset set up a special committee. A special committee may be set up also to assure favorable conditions for the consideration of a controversial bill. As in the case of a member's motion, any committee remit may be altered on the recommendation of the House Committee following appeal by a member. Thus, for example, in 1960, when a Protection of Tenants Bill referred to the Labor Committee was found to contain unusual legal complexities, a motion was offered in the house by the chairman of that committee that the Knesset charge the House Committee with setting up a joint committee of the Labor and Law committees to consider the bill.

At the committee stage a bill receives full and detailed consideration. Before the committee begins to deliberate on the clauses of the bill it will, as necessary, hear and question the minister concerned and through him the appropriate officials. The committee may also ask outside experts on the subject matter of the bill to appear before it, as well as interested organizations or individuals who have petitioned it for a hearing, or whose evidence it wishes to hear. The committee to which a bill has been referred, and every one of its members, may become a focal point for innumerable pressure groups, so that not infrequently it must ask many who wish to be heard to make do with the submission of a written brief. The legal adviser and other officials of the ministry chiefly concerned will stay with the committee throughout its consideration of the bill as will the representatives of other interested ministries, most often Justice and Finance.

As the committee goes over the bill clause by clause, amendments, no matter how far-reaching, may be moved, provided they do not depart from the scope of the bill's subject matter. An amendment, if relevant on the face of it, can in fact nullify the principle of the bill. A claim by a committee member or the representative of the Government that an amendment departs from the subject matter is referred to the House Committee for decision. Should a Knesset member who is not on the committee considering the bill propose an amendment or charge that an amendment deviates from the subject matter, it is within the committee's discretion to decide whether to entertain the proposal or charge, and whether to permit the member to attend its deliberations. The minister or his representatives are on hand to preserve the bill intact so far as they can but will themselves move amendments as necessary, because of a change of approach within the ministry or differences between ministries. There may be a process of negotiation between the minister and the opponents of the bill in order to secure an amendment agreeable to both sides. Such give-and-take is facilitated in the committee by the absence of the public and the media; party spirit is often blunted there.

With the agreement of the house a committee may divide a bill so as to bring forward a part, whether because its provisions are found more urgent than the rest or because only it has prospects of being considered and reported within a reasonable time. The concurrence of the House Committee is sufficient for the committee to report two or more parts of a bill simultaneously as separate measures for the second reading. The committee requires only the agreement of the House Committee also to combine two or more bills into one.

In reviewing a two-year period (1959–61), Zidon found that more than 70 percent of all committed bills were reported back to the house within a month.[3] However, it is in the committee stage that a bill is most likely to get bogged down. Although the Knesset Rules require a committee to give priority to legislation over other business and to report a bill to the house once its consideration is completed, the progress of a bill in committee may be slow because of its length or complexity, because the committee is busy with other legislation, or because of determined obstruction. Not infrequently the Government, the committee chairman, or a parliamentary Group, may wish to hold the bill up in committee. Though a committee cannot decide against reporting a bill back to the house for the second reading, it is not uncommon for the bill to remain in the committee until the end of the Knesset term so that it is effectively killed.

That the committee stage is the most difficult hurdle in the legislative process is well illustrated by a few examples. The Succession Bill first came before the Knesset in 1958, when it received first reading and was referred to the Law Committee; there it remained until the Third Knesset ended. In 1959, in the Fourth Knesset, the bill was again tabled, read the first time and committed, but made no further headway. In the Fifth Knesset, after the legislative process had been initiated a third time, the bill emerged from the Law Committee after nearly a hundred meetings, held over a period of more than three years, had been devoted by the committee to its consideration. After the tabling of the bill for second reading on 12 January 1965, only a few weeks passed before it became law. The Judicial Courts Bill of 1955, after getting only as far as the committee stage in the Second Knesset, was brought in afresh in the Third after the Government had made some changes in it. Read a first time again and referred to the Law Committee, it was considered there for twenty months before being returned to the house in March 1957. After the bill was tabled for the second reading the committee asked for it to be remitted so as to enable the Israel Bar Association and some other bodies to offer additional remarks. After the bill was reported back a second time to the house and the committee chairman had already made a statement launching the second reading, the committee again asked to withdraw the bill, this time to receive further comments of the Supreme Court president. Released by the committee finally in mid-July, the bill received the second and third readings in a little over a week.

Today, unlike the Succession and Judicial Courts bills, a bill that has reached the committee stage would not need again to be tabled and read a first time in a new Knesset. While continuity of Knesset business from session to session within the four-year term had always been the rule, the Continuity of Debate Law enacted in 1964 provided that on the Government's request a bill may be taken up also in a new Knesset from the stage which it reached in the last. Consideration of the bill in committee can then be resumed directly. In 1979 the continuity law was amended so it can be applied to legislation initiated also by a member or by a committee, on the request of the committee within whose jurisdiction the bill falls. The application of continuity of debate to any bill can be opposed by a parliamentary Group. The Knesset will then decide the question by a vote after hearing both sides.

A committee's report to the house consists of the bill as amended in the committee and an appended list of amendments which the committee did not accept but whose movers wish to bring before the house for its final decision. An amendment negating the substance of the bill will not be appended. Duplicated in stencil, the report is laid on the table of the house by the Knesset chairman and then placed by him on the agenda. The second reading may be held on the day following the tabling or at a later sitting; however, as with the first reading, the House Committee can exempt the bill from early tabling. Once the report has been laid on the table no further amendments may be added unless the committee renews consideration of the bill. A decision by the committee to renew consideration of the bill needs only to be communicated by the Knesset chairman to the house. However, once the second reading has begun, a recommittal of the bill, or of certain of its clauses, requires the Knesset's vote on a proposal of the Government or of the committee chairman.

The second reading is a clause-by-clause review of the bill as reported by the committee, during which only amendments that fell in the committee are discussed, after an opening statement by the *rapporteur* of the committee; the only speakers are the movers of amendments and the *rapporteur,* who replies. The committee chairman serves as the *rapporteur,* unless, in disagreement with the bill or certain of its clauses, he has assigned the task of explaining the report, or of defending the committee's text in reply to amendments, to another member of the committee. In the absence of the chairman, the committee will appoint the *rapporteur*. The right of amendment is in effect confined to committee members, to other Knesset members whom the committee has permitted to register amendments for reconsideration in the house, and to the minister. Occasionally, a statement without proposal of an amendment may be made on second reading by the minister, as the Rules permit a member of the Government to speak at any point in Knesset proceedings, or by a deputy minister whose department will administer the proposed law. The rest of the house has only to cast their votes at this stage.

The opening statement by the *rapporteur* to the house is an explanation of the changes made in the bill by the committee. Each clause is then taken separately, except where a number of consecutive clauses to which there are no amendments are voted together. The mover of an amendment receives five minutes to explain it and is replied to by the *rapporteur*. Since there may be more than a hundred amendments to a bill, a chair beside the rostrum is provided for the *rapporteur* so that he need not go back and forth between his many speeches in rebuttal. To facilitate proceedings at this stage the chair, with the consent of the mover and the committee chairman, may have the explanations of amendments to a number of clauses combined; this has become a common practice. After the amendments to a clause are disposed of the house votes whether to adopt the clause—as amended or as reported by the committee. At this stage the house may also have to decide between alternate versions of one or more clauses since both versions appear in the report of the committee if they have received equal votes there. The second reading is completed when the last clause has been voted.

As long as the third reading has not been taken, the Government may withdraw the bill at any stage upon a statement in the Knesset to that effect, or by notice in writing to the Knesset chairman who in turn informs the house. If the Government withdraws a bill, it is barred by a Knesset Rule from bringing in another on the same subject for the remainder of the session unless permitted by the House Committee to do so. However, the Government may "retract the withdrawal of the bill."[4] On one occasion the Government exercised its prerogative to withdraw a free education bill after important paragraphs were voted down on the second reading; since it was the last day of the summer session (28 July 1982), and without the measure the authorization for an education levy would soon expire, the Government requested the Knesset chairman to schedule early special sittings so a newly tabled free education bill could be taken.

The third reading, which is simply a final vote on the entire bill, without debate, is the shortest stage in the legislative procedure. If the house, on the second reading, did not alter the committee text in any way, the third will be taken directly. If any amendments were carried or if a choice was made between alternate versions of a clause reported from the committee, the third reading will be held the following week. In the interval a stencil of the bill as amended is made so that members may see clearly the text on which they will have to vote. However, the Knesset Rules permit the Government or the chairman of the committee to request in special cases that the third reading be taken immediately despite changes made in the committee's text; in practice most bills are thus given third reading without delay. It is rather a deferment that has come to be the exception at this stage.

A resolution of the House Committee can make it possible to hold all three readings in one day, the committee stage being taken during a short break in the plenary sitting. With such quick treatment, a bill may pass with only a modicum of criticism if its urgency is generally recognized, or when the house finds it convenient to expedite the legislation process. The latter occurred, for example, with an income tax reform bill on 18 August 1975, and with a wage agreement bill on 3 May 1976; in both cases the Knesset had convened for a special session while in recess, a circumstance in which most members would wish anyway to complete in one day the business before them. On the other hand, the enactment of the highly controversial Golan Heights Law of 1981 within six hours during the regular session, after the opposition had received only a few hours notice of the bill, brought forth vehement charges that the parliamentary process was being abused.

The House Committee is most liberal in dispensing with the early tabling of bills in the last week of a session, when it may adopt one resolution to allow second reading without delay, of all bills to be reported from committees that week. By one dispensation on 27 may 1981, the Committee exempted from early tabling all bills relating to the forthcoming election. At other times the House Committee has appealed to the Government to refrain as far as possible from asking at any stage for dispensation from early tabling. Though it is expected that there will be an accumulation of bills toward the end of a session, particularly near the close of a term, and it is no surprise that at such times means to expedite the legislative process are employed, complaints are heard then not infrequently from members that they are being too rushed to do justice to measures before them, and that late tabling may not allow them time even to look at a bill out of committee before it is considered further by the house.

With its third reading a bill is enacted into law. There remains only the signing and publication. Certified by the chairman, the law is signed by the prime minister, the minister or ministers concerned with the law's administration, and the president of the state. However, any failure to sign a law would not prevent its coming into force. Within ten days from its adoption by the Knesset a law must be published in the official gazette, when it comes into effect unless it has specified an earlier or later date. Bills and laws are put on sale to the public like other parts of the gazette.

Should an error be discovered in the text of a law before its publication, and the committee which considered the bill determines on the advice of the minister of justice that the error is only of a clerical nature, the Knesset, may by a resolution correct the error. If the law has already been gazetted, the correction will be published in the gazette over the signatures of the chairman of the Knesset and the minister of justice.

Retrospective legislation, where necessary, came to the support of the executive authorities of the state in its nascent period. Since then the Knesset has from time to time provided that a law come into force earlier than the date of publication, but nearly always in face of opposition. Governments have found it necessary or expedient to secure retrospective enactments as remedies to court judgments, to impose taxation, or to meet other situations; neither have the large political parties hesitated to encourage members' bills to amend the parties financing law retroactively. On 9 April 1962, a bill came before the house to amend the Petah Tikva Agricultural Authority Law, which had lapsed on 31 March. The opinion of the attorney-general, who was consulted after objection was raised to the bill, was that the Knesset's sovereignty to enact the law was unimpaired. But he advised that a provision to make the measure retroactive to 31 March be inserted for the sake of administrative tidiness. Adolf Eichmann appealed to the Supreme Court in 1962 on the ground that the Punishment of Nazis and their Collaborators Law, under which he had been tried and sentenced, was an ex post facto statute which rendered criminal, acts done before the state was established. In this case the Court ruled that no constitutional restriction exists on the power of the Knesset to pass a criminal law with retroactive effect, though such a measure will be enacted only in extraordinary circumstances. The Knesset has more than once given retrospective effect to emergency regulations of a minister by measures extending their validity after they had been allowed to lapse; the legality of this practice was confirmed by a Court ruling in 1976.

MEMBERS' BILLS

A member in preparing a bill can have recourse to the services of the Government's draftsmen as well as to those of the legal counsel of his Group and of the Knesset. But since he can never command the full range of expertise which is available to the Government for its legislation, his bill is more likely to be of narrow scope or simply a proposal to amend an existing law. There are some exceptions. A detailed civil rights bill in 1964 and a comprehensive bill to regulate political parties in 1968 were the respective initiatives of the jurists H. Klinghoffer and S. Tamir; but both bills were removed from the Knesset agenda on preliminary consideration. The Klinghoffer bill, when reintroduced by his former student, A. Rubinstein, was committed by the house eighteen years later, in 1982. A substantial bill covering new ground, if submitted by a number of members representing both coalition and opposition groups and thus assured of a wide consensus, is likely to make more certain headway; some examples are the Pig-Raising Prohibition Bill, 1962, and the Political Parties (Financing) Bill, 1973.

Members are not barred from presenting bills that impose a financial burden on the treasury. However, a coalition member whose bill creates a public charge will take up his proposal with the minister of finance before introducing it in the Knesset. If the bill conflicts with the terms of the budget, the member will defer its introduction to the following fiscal year or drop the proposal completely. An opposition member will not hesitate to present a bill to amend the budget.

The progress of a member's bill up to the first reading is marked by a number of hurdles, some political, others procedural, the latter all absent in the case of a Government bill. For the presentation of a bill a member must first receive the approval of his parliamentary Group. A coalition member's bill is subject also to prelegislative scrutiny by the coalition executive and may be referred to the minister concerned. Having received the necessary political clearance for his bill, the member submits it to the chairman of the Knesset. From this point until the first reading, the bill, unlike a Government bill, is subject under the Knesset Rules to a number of checks, in recognition, as it were, that a rank-and-file member may not have the resources and may lack the necessary overall view to draft a bill competently. The checks are three: examination by the Knesset presidium, preliminary consideration by the house,and preparation by a committee for the first reading; the last proceeding may alter the bill drastically both in form and content. Thus a member's bill passes twice through a committee stage, generally in the same committee, after both the preliminary and first readings.

Submitted to the Knesset chairman, the bill is not laid on the table directly like one initiated by the Government, but brought before the presidium for approval after being scanned for correct form by one of the Knesset's legal advisers. Approval would be withheld in exceptional cases, for example, if the bill were not drafted as a law, or if it were worded offensively. After its approval, the bill is tabled for preliminary consideration by the Knesset and a copy sent to the Government. In fact a member's bill comes only before the ministers concerned with its subject matter, and they take a stand in the name of the Government.

Though preliminary consideration by the Knesset may take place after two days have elapsed from the tabling, the Government, if it does not wish an early debate (which is often the case), may hold up that proceeding. But the appearance of the bill on the agenda is regulated in the first instance by the sessional quota of motions and bills fixed for the sponsor's Group, as described in the preceding chapter. If the bill is above the quota, it will not come up before the following session. The preliminary consideration is a short proceeding. The proposer receives ten minutes to explain the need for the measure and is replied to by the Government through the minister concerned, who may support the bill or move that it be struck off the Knesset's agenda. Should the Government favor remit to a committee or avoid taking any stand on the bill, another member may speak against the bill for ten minutes and move that it be struck off the agenda. If either the Government or another member has moved that the bill be struck off, the proposer receives five minutes to make a reply. The house concludes the preliminary consideration by voting whether to commit the bill or remove it from the agenda. Not infrequently, if the minister has stated in his reply that the Government is preparing similar legislation, the proposer will agree that his bill not be put to a vote or that the vote be deferred.

According to a decision of 1979 by the House Committee, an unopposed member's bill is not counted in the Groups's quota if at the preliminary reading the proposer has spoken from his place and taken not more than one minute. But most members have preferred the normal manner of proceeding which permits a fuller exposition of their legislative initiative.

The committee to which a member's bill is referred after preliminary consideration will prepare it for the first reading or recommend its removal from the Knesset's agenda. The Knesset may commit a number of members' bills on the same subject after preliminary consideration at one sitting. The committee will then report for first reading only one bill in the name of all proposers. Their names will appear alphabetically on the bill, as they do when one bill is submitted by a number of members. Where the committee recommends that a bill be removed from the agenda, the house will decide the bill's fate by a vote, and should the house reject the committee's recommendation, the bill will be put on the agenda for the first reading in the version proposed by the member. The house will take the member's version for first reading also if the committee was evenly divided whether to prepare it for first reading or to recommend its removal from the agenda.

A member's bill need not be laid on the table two days in advance of first reading since that interval has already been observed on the tabling for preliminary consideration. The first reading debate is opened and replied to by the proposer of the bill or, if the bill results from a number of committed bills, by one of the proposers mutually agreed upon. If the several proposers do not agree who is to open the debate, it is opened by the chairman of the committee which prepared the bill for first reading, while the proposers are given the right to speak before other members. In all other respects the proceedings on the first and later readings are the same as for a Government bill.

It remains to note that compared with the Government the private member is a disadvantaged legislator yet in ways additional to those described earlier. He may not withdraw his bill after it has been through the committee stage which follows the first reading. If he withdraws it earlier, as permitted by the Rules, or it is removed from the agenda before the first reading, a bill deemed essentially the same by the Knesset chairman may not be laid on the table for the remainder of the session, except when the chairman determines that circumstances have changed sufficiently in the meantime to justify its tabling. Unless the House Committee should overrule the Knesset chairman's decision, on the member's appeal, the new bill may be tabled only in the next session, while its preliminary reading may not be taken before six months have elapsed from the day the first bill was withdrawn or removed from the agenda. Clearly, preferential treatment is accorded to Government bills in the provisions that the Government may introduce a bill parallel to that of a member which is down for the first reading, and they are taken at the same time, while a member may not submit for preliminary consideration an alternative to a Government bill which is receiving first reading.

In the exercise of its prerogatives and use of its majority in the Knesset, the Government has been criticized at times by members of intervening unfairly to deprive them of their right of legislative initiative. Yet, as Table 7 shows, through two recent Knesset terms members' bills accounted on average for more than 17.5 percent of the legislative output. There remains the fact, however, that while the great majority of Government bills pass through the entire legislative process, most members' bills fall by the way (see Table 8). And the members' bills that become law take much longer to do so; while the average time taken by a Government bill to pass through the legislative process is from one to three months, that for a member's bill is about a year.[5]

LEGISLATIVE INITIATIVE OF COMMITTEES

There have never been more than a few committee-sponsored bills in a term, and the Knesset Rules take no cognizance of them, though Government and members' bills are each given a chapter. Nevertheless, it has always been the practice for the House Committee to initiate legislation affecting members' emoluments, immunities, and other Knesset matters, for the Finance

Table 8

Government and Members' Bills Introduced and Passed*

	Government Bills			Members' Bills		
Year	Introduced	Passed	% Passed	Introduced	Passed	% Passed
1978–79	60	60	100	110	12	10.9
1979–80	101	82	81.2	122	13	10.7
1980–81	80	80	100	128	31	24.2
1981–82	57	53	93	254	3	1.2
1982–83	48	48	100	119	10	8.4
1983–84	72	64	88.9	103	9	8.7
Total	418	387	93.9	836	78	10.7

*From *Reshumot* (Official Gazette), and data issued by the Knesset secretariat. Since bills carry over from session to session and continuity may be applied also between terms, the figures are only general indicators.

or State Audit committees to initiate bills concerning the state comptroller, and for the Law Committee to sponsor proposals for Basic Laws or their amendment. The Law Committee's right of initiative with respect to Basic Laws rests on the Knesset resolution of 1950 which charged it with the task of preparing a draft constitution. However, bills concerning Basic Laws have been sponsored also by the Government and by members. Nor has the aforementioned right of initiative, of the House, Finance, and State Audit committees, been exclusively theirs.

Instances of bills initiated by other committees have been rare. A bill on dental practitioners' permits in 1957, sponsored by the Public Welfare Committee, and on the election of local-authority heads, in 1976, by the Interior Affairs Committee, both aroused some objection. The question of the committees' right of legislative initiative has in fact been bound up with their right generally to originate debate on a matter not referred to them by the house, some claiming that the Rules do not allow that freedom. But in practice every committee takes up matters on its own initiative as well as dealing with remits from the house.

Also after statutory mention of committee-initiated bills was made in the 1979 amendment to the Continuity of Debate Law, the question of such legislation exercised the house. When the Law Committee, in July 1979, resolved to bring forward a bill concerning criminal records if the Government did not request renewed consideration of its own, earlier bill of similar content, the Knesset chairman referred the entire matter of committee scope of legislative initiative to the House Committee. After drawn out discussion, the House Committee in 1980 resolved that a committee may originate legislation concerning Basic Laws, elections, and members, as well as other

Knesset matters, and the state comptroller. While designating no particular committee, the resolution provides that such a bill go on directly to first reading, thus settling another question that had always been raised, beyond the doubts about its very propriety, whether it should not first receive preliminary consideration, like a member's bill. The resolution essentially gave formal sanction to the existing practice while restraining general extension of committee legislative initiative.

DELEGATED LEGISLATION

The Knesset, like the parliaments of other technologically advanced and welfare-conscious democracies, has found it necessary to delegate law-making powers to the executive, and consequently, it too has been faced with the twin problems of drawing a line between primary and delegated legislation and of assuring scrutiny and control of the latter, which is many times more voluminous than the Knesset's own statutes. Though there can be no question of encroachment upon the sovereign legislative authority of the Knesset without its own complicity, as it were, safeguards have been required against inadvertent excess of delegation on the one hand, and overzealous use of secondary powers on the other.

Already in the state's first organic statute, the Law and Administration Ordinance passed in 1948 by the Provisional State Council, there was a general disposition concerning ministerial regulations for the administration of any law insofar as it should confer such power. Since then nearly every law enacted has contained a section conferring on the minister or ministers concerned the power to make implementing regulations. Only a small number of instruments of delegated legislation, of which there are well over a thousand every year, require approval by the house before or after promulgation. Prominent among these are the orders increasing indirect taxes under the Customs and Excise Duty (Variation of Tariff) Law of 1949, which lapse two months after their promulgation unless confirmed before then by resolution of the Knesset. Less often an order may impose a new duty. An order reducing or cancelling a duty remains in force after promulgation unless annulled by the Knesset within two months. Orders increasing sales tax require prior approval of the house, and increases in value-added tax require prior consultation with the Finance Committee and approval of the house within two weeks of promulgation. The publication of subordinate legislation is mandatory; even where the delegatory law exempts it from publication in the official gazette, the court has ruled that its publication otherwise is obligatory if it lays down a general legal norm.

The proceedings in the house on the above orders are brief and formal, with the vote taking place after a simple statement of recommendation by the *rapporteur* of the Finance Committee, where the order has been discussed, and sometimes up to a ten-minute speech by the spokesman for a minority opinion which has divided the Committee. Though an order may contain any number of provisions, and under a 1955 amendment to the variation-of-tariff law each may be separately deleted or approved, the practice has remained of voting the entire order in one.

The bulk of subordinate legislation never comes before the Knesset. In earlier years the practice had been increasingly to enact framework laws in which broad powers of regulation, often primary in nature, were delegated to a minister or other body without providing for any parliamentary control. Among statutes enacted in the 1950s and 1960s—ranging over the fields of economics, agriculture, labor, defense, transport, and health—some authorized an inferior rule-making body to lay down criminal offenses, impose taxes, and deny or curb free enterprise.[6] There has been a reversal of that trend in recent years. Addressing the house in 1979, on the Knesset's thirtieth anniversary, Justice Minister Tamir noted that in accordance with instructions from the Government, legislation was being drafted in greater detail than had been the case earlier, so that far less authority was being delegated to the executive, while any rule-making power conferred on a minister, if it affected matters of principle, was being made subject to approval by a Knesset committee.

The facts bear out Mr. Tamir's statement, particularly in the economic and social fields. In fiscal matters the Basic Law on the State Economy, enacted in 1975, lays down that rates of taxes, other compulsory payments and fees, left to be fixed by delegated legislation, require approval in advance or within a fixed period by the Knesset or one of its committees. As we have seen, fiscal affairs are within the jurisdiction of the Finance Committee. Illustrative of such scrutiny in other areas are: the Local Authorities Law (Discipline) of 1978, under which variation of civil service disciplinary regulations in their application to municipal employees require approval by the Interior Affairs Committee; the Secret Monitoring Law of 1979, under which orders of the prime minister regulating manufacture and distribution of monitoring instruments, and his regulations for the purpose of preserving or destroying information obtained by such devices, are subject to approval by a joint Law-Foreign Affairs and Security Committee; and the Chief Rabbinate Law of 1980, with ministerial regulation requiring sanction by a joint Law-Interior Affairs Committee. In its deliberations on a regulation or order a committee may hear affected interests as well as the ministry.

Yet the great body of regulations and orders, which are considered to be of a technical-implementing nature, are not made subject to any parliamentary control. And since the distinction between primary and secondary legislation is not always clear, inevitably some regulations will be made that trench on the Knesset's law-making prerogative. Furthermore, as the courts have pronounced, an administrative regulation affecting citizens' everyday life may be invalid not only because it is *ultra vires;* it may not comport with the purpose of the delegatory statute or may be otherwise unreasonable. Members' motions from time to time, raising the subject of an objectionable regulation, have been referred to a committee, while committees have also debated doubtful regulations on their own initiative. With the more general purpose of securing systematic parliamentary surveillance where substantive matters are regulated through instruments of delegated legislation, members' bills have been proposed over the years from all quarters of the house. The main argument of every Government against a measure that would subject the whole body of regulations to formal oversight by the Knesset has been that it would put the clock back and clog up both house and committees, while the purpose of delegation is to leave the primary legislator free to perform its essential tasks.

A proposal in 1964 that a special Knesset committee be established for the scrutiny of subordinate legislation, along the lines of England's Statutory Instruments Committee, failed to take account of a basic difference between the two committee systems. Unlike the House of Commons, which never set up a full range of select committees nor always sufficiently trusted those it might create to devolve upon them many regular duties, from the beginning the Knesset has had a system of specialized committees. Together these embrace the whole field of administration, and each would be eminently suited to examine secondary legislation as the body which has considered the details of the delegatory law, and is further the most knowledgeable about related subject matter as well as already having statutory powers with respect to some regulations. But ministers of justice also rejected bills later that provided for laying of all regulations before the appropriate committee, taking objection particularly to the power which they would confer on the committee of altering as well as annulling a regulation. The Knesset's right to alter ministerial regulations, it is held by the Government, would be a confusion of the accepted concept of separation between legislative and executive.

A challenge to the sovereignty of the Knesset and to the rule of law is undoubtedly posed where a statute can be brought into effect only with the enactment of administrative regulations and the delegated power is not exercised. A notorious example is the Nuisance Prevention Law of 1961 (the fruit of a member's initiative), which remained largely inoperative for ten years because the health and interior ministers failed to make the necessary regulations, which included, among other things, the very definition of "unreasonable" air pollution. Only a decision of the High Court of Justice in

1971 impelled them to issue the required regulations. Equally, where a minister has secured prior confirmation from a Knesset committee for a regulation, he may afterward defer its promulgation or drop it entirely. Regarding such action, too, as frustrating the will of the primary legislator, a member's bill was laid on the Knesset table in 1982 which would require a minister who changes his mind about a regulation to bring it again before the committee, where it might be reconfirmed and brought to the house for final approval.

While the Government has not responded positively to members' proposals for overall scrutiny of administrative regulations and orders, it has not been indifferent to the problems raised. In 1983, following recommendations made by a committee of experts appointed by Justice Minister M. Nissim to examine the whole procedure of secondary legislation, the attorney-general issued directives instructing rule-making authorities to publish draft regulations in advance in the daily press and to submit such drafts to bodies that stood to be affected. Retrospective regulations or orders, except in special cases, are forbidden.

Emergency regulations, provided for under a different section in the Law and Administration Ordinance 1948, are subject to a process of delegation unlike that just described. Their first condition is a national state of emergency declared by the primary legislator. A state of emergency, proclaimed by the Provisional State Council on 19 May 1948, early in the War of Independence, has continued uninterrupted down to this day, since its cessation would require a declaration to that effect by the Knesset. The state of emergency permits the Government to empower a minister to make emergency regulations at his discretion for the purpose of national defense, public security, or the maintenance of supplies and essential services. Such regulations can amend any law or temporarily suspend its operation but cease to have effect at the expiration of three months from date of issue, unless their validity has been extended before that date by statute.

There is no restriction as to the subject of emergency regulations, except that they must be for the broad purposes described, which are within the judgment of the empowered minister. Thus they have dealt with matters as diverse as security zones, compulsory payments, and essential services of x-ray technicians. However, defense matters have always preponderated in emergency regulations, with the minister of defense resorting to this form of rule making more often than any of his colleagues. Therefore, too, the number of such regulations has always been greater in the aftermath of war.

Emergency regulations vary in their course. Regulations whose purpose is of short term, if not rescinded by the minister within three months, will be left to lapse, or they may be extended once by the Knesset. If there is a continuing need for an emergency regulation or set of regulations, the Knesset may extend their validity again and again, each time by an act of legislation fixing the date of expiry. The extension may be for days, months, a year, or longer, or even until the Knesset should declare that the state of emergency has ceased to exist. (That declaration will also specify the date or dates when all other emergency regulations are to lapse.) An extending law often amends the regulations as well. There may also be amendments to regulations which have been previously extended to the end of the state of emergency. An extending measure may authorize the minister to rescind the regulations or part of them before the fixed expiry date, notwithstanding their embodiment in statute law. The Knesset has sometimes divided one set of emergency regulations into two parts, as it did with the Control of Ships Regulations of 1948 and the Foreign Travel Regulations of 1948; in each case some were extended for the duration of the state of emergency, others prolonged periodically by fresh enactment. Further, the foreign travel regulations which require periodic renewal were extended by statute only up to 1961, an amendment of that year making them renewable by the defense minister, who requires only Knesset approval. From that time on, the house has each year had before it for confirmation the minister's resolution, on which it votes after approval is recommended by the Foreign Affairs and Security Committee.

Extension-of-validity laws, though adopted by the normal legislative process, nevertheless attest to the Knesset's unreadiness to pass those measures in their own right. It is held that since they do nothing more than prolong the force of the minister's regulations, they would be as vulnerable to the courts. Vindicating further the view that extending laws are lesser statutes is the fact that a considerable number of emergency regulations, in the course of time, have indeed been made part of ordinary legislation, either by inclusion of their subject matter in other statutes or by enactment of specific laws. Some, like the prevention of Terror Regulations of 1948, were placed on the statute books before any extension of validity was due; others, like the Settlement Guard-Duty Regulations of 1956, after as many as eight extensions.[7]

The unlimited scope of emergency regulations and their power to override primary legislation, given as well the prolonged state of emergency, have raised problems. In broad construction of the terms "maintenance of supplies and essential services" in the 1948 ordinance, emergency regulations have been used for purposes such as the protection of local goods against imports, the maintenance of stable prices, the prevention of excess profits, and the issue to strikers of back-to-work orders. Criticism of the use of emergency powers by ministers for the regulation of matters having little to do with the state of emergency has been voiced both in the Knesset and in the Supreme Court. To assure that certain fundamental matters would not be affected by emergency regulations, the Basic Laws on the Knesset, President, and Government, as well as the Knesset Elections Law and other measures, have each been made immune from such regulations by a special clause. It has been suggested by Professor H. Klinghoffer, a former member (1961–73), that in view of the unforeseen long-drawn state of emergency, some measure of overall parliamentary scrutiny of emergency regulations would be secured if all those in force were brought every year before the Knesset to be reconfirmed.

CONCERNING THE LEGAL SYSTEM

One of the important legislative tasks of the Knesset has been to replace the heterogeneous body of law adopted outright with the advent of independence, by a legal system suited to a modern democratic nation and to Israel's needs. By a declaration of the Provincial State Council and under its first ordinance, the law in force in Palestine on 14 May 1948, when the British Mandate came to an end, was made the law of the nascent State, subject only to future Israel statute law and to the changed conditions of statehood. The mandatory legal system consisted of diverse elements: Ottoman law, which had been carried over from the pre–World War I period through the Palestine Order in Council 1922; English law; and enactments of the high commissioner for Palestine, in whom were vested both the legislative and executive powers. The Ottoman legacy itself consisted of dissimilar elements; Islamic civil, personal, and land laws which had survived in the Ottoman Empire; the French commercial, maritime, civil procedure, and criminal codes, which were adopted by the Sultan, mainly in the nineteenth century; and the personal law of non-Islamic communities.

Under the mandate many Ottoman laws were repealed and replaced by ordinances based on English common law or statutes codifying common law rules. While English law became the dominant element in the law of Palestine by the end of the mandate, important parts of the Ottoman statute law still remained in force. The newborn state thus inherited a patchwork legal system whose original languages furthermore were four: Turkish, Arabic, French, and English. But more serious than the motley character of this body of law was the inadequacy of some of its parts in the conditions of a modern progressive society. Its land laws, for example, were largely based on the Ottoman land code of 1858, suited to a preindustrial society with little urban land ownership. That code had already been repealed in Turkey itself and in some Arab countries, as had the 1869 civil code (the *Mejelle*), most of which too was in force in Palestine at the termination of the mandate.

The legal system taken over from the mandatory regime was, however, on the whole progressive and had already proved its adaptability in other countries where the British influence had been dominant. This was fortunate, as the replacement of Ottoman and mandatory law by the Knesset, which has gone hand in hand with the enactment of new legislation could only be gradual. Important progress was made particularly with the replacement of the antiquated Ottoman land code by the Israel Land Law 1969, and when the replacement of the *Mejelle,* chapter by chapter, was begun with the enactment of the Agency Law of 1965; the *Mejelle* was finally repealed in 1984. A comprehensive criminal procedure code adopted in 1965 replaced and unified a long list of mandatory, Ottoman, and earlier Israel laws. However, while the Turkish elements in the legal system have been largely swept away and will soon be extinct, the mandatory legacy has been more lasting. Not only was mandatory law ultimately based for the most part on British models, but pervading the Palestine legal system further were the substance of the common law and the doctrines of equity in force in England, which had been introduced through the Palestine Order in Council of 1922. It is relevant too that Israel's ministry of justice in its early years employed several of the Palestine Government's legal draftsmen. A good illustration of the persisting British influence was the Courts Law of 1957, which replaced a number of mandatory ordinances but retained almost in entirety the hierarchy of mandatory courts with the identical division of functions.

Because of the close attachment to English law, mandatory ordinances, some of which also adequately met the needs of the state, were more often amended, altered, and adapted than replaced. The basis of Israel's income tax law, for example, is the Income Tax Ordinance of 1947, as amended by the Knesset each year. However, to harmonize mandatory ordinances generally with Israel's legal system it has been necessary to issue them in new and more accurate Hebrew versions. (In case of a discrepancy between the earlier Hebrew translation and the English text, the latter would prevail.) Though a New Version embodies all changes resulting from statehood and any subsequent amendments, its adoption does not require the legislative process but follows a procedure laid down by law in 1964. The draft of a New Version, gazetted by the minister of justice, is brought by him before an Advisory Board of five legal experts, including a judge and the attorney-general. The Board, after examining whether the draft is substantively faithful to the original law and embodies the necessary changes, makes corrections as it sees fit and reports to the Law Committee of the Knesset. Employing a subcommittee regularly to consider such drafts, the Committee determines the new Version. With publication in the official gazette over the signature of the justice minister this version becomes the binding law, and no other version will thenceforth have effect. With the great body of mandatory law which can be expected to remain indefinitely in force, the issue of New Versions is far from complete.

At the same time, the process of freeing Israel law from subordination to foreign sources and evolving an independent legal system has gone steadily forward. In part this development was natural. In the Hebrew language, which is rich in its own legal literature and terminology, it was awkward to continue using English drafting techniques and patterns of legal thought; moreover, the British-trained draftsmen were in time largely replaced by persons of other backgrounds and eventually by a generation of Israeli-educated lawyers. More decisive, however, in the process of detaching Israel from the mandatory and English legal systems have been the positive legislative acts of the Knesset. Beginning with the Succession Law of 1965, statutes have been enacted from time to time with clauses expressly exempting the matters they deal with from the application of Article 46 of the Palestine order in Council of 1922–1947, which is the channel through which the English common law and rules of equity have been received by Israel's legal system. The Courts went further, interpreting without reference to English rules statutes that contained no such express clause. Further, in 1972 an amendment to the Law and Administration Ordinance of 1948 provided that any referral by a mandatory ordinance to English law was no longer binding.

A step of greater finality came in 1980 with the enactment of the Foundations of Law statute, which repealed the above mentioned Article 46, thus severing at its root the continuing link with English law, while putting in its place a provision that where the Court found no answer to a question of law in existing statutes or judgments, it is to decide "in the light of the principles of freedom, justice, rectitude and peace, of Israel's heritage" (Section 1). The measure also provided, however, that no law already absorbed into Israel's legal system was to be affected; in this way the substantial body of mandatory law, and even the Ottoman vestiges as well as judge-made law based on English rules and precedents, remained in force.

The dethronement of English common law and rules of equity by the principles of "Israel's heritage" was in reality the culmination of a process begun with the advent of the state. To religious Orthodox Jews there could be no greater anomaly than a Jewish state whose legal system was not based essentially on the comprehensive millenium-old Hebrew law whose elaboration had never ceased. The ministry of justice draftsmen began early on to pay special regard to the sources of Hebrew law and, where its provision could be adapted to present-day needs, it was given priority over the provisions of other law systems. Hebrew legal principles were the basis for a series of laws on matters of maintenance, adoption, guardianship, and succession, and later also on other matters. With regard to marriage and divorce, jurisdiction was left in the hands of the internal tribunals of the religious communities, as in the Turkish and mandatory periods; the positive law of the state strengthened the Rabbinic Courts in 1953 by extending their jurisdiction over all Jews resident in Israel regardless of nationality.

The secular-minded majority, on the other hand, resisted a more general application of Hebrew law, first, because it did not provide answers to many modern needs, and second, they sought to keep synagogue and state apart, for Hebrew law, though in large part of universal application, has been cast in a religious mold. The indefinite term ''Israel's heritage'' *(Moreshet Yisrael)* represented a compromise between the two positions. In any case, the Foundations of law statute merely provides a general directive to the Courts for the use of a complementary law source where a lacuna exists. The place of Hebrew law in the statutes of the state will continue to be determined empirically unless a written constitution ultimately settles the matter. And as we saw in Chapter 3, it was partly to avoid early answer to such questions that the writing of a constitution was postponed.

11

Scrutiny and Control

As we have seen, extensive surveillance of the executive is exercised by the Knesset through its debating and legislative procedures, question period, and committee system. And as will be shown in the next chapter, the Knesset's power to thwart the Government at any turn and to dismiss it at pleasure is alone an unremittent restraint on the latter. Yet the ability of the Knesset to monitor thoroughly the Government's ramified financial and administrative operations is perforce limited and fragmentary. The prospect of more systematic and rigorous parliamentary control lies chiefly in constant improvement of the Knesset's two scrutinizing instruments par excellence: the budget and the state comptroller. It is to these means that we now turn our attention.

THE BUDGET

The Knesset's supreme instrument for control of the Government's economic policy and order of priorities, offering members a chance to air views also on any other subject, comes before the house annually as the proposed state budget. Attesting to the weight and importance of the budget is its occupation of the house and the Finance Committee one way or another throughout the year, in addition to the many hours and days both spend in its consideration in the months preceding each new financial year, which begins on 1 April. The policies of ministries not debated in the house before the budget is approved are taken up later during the summer. Working all year, a Finance subcommittee considers all transfers of amounts of expenditure from one head or item of the budget to another, and the State Control Committee, whose main business is study of the state comptroller's reports, in effect a post-audit of the previous budget. Although a third of the budget goes for defense and a third for the repayment of debts, while most of the remaining allocations are statutory expenditures in which little change can be affected, the hundreds of items which are to form the schedules of the Budget Law present a challenge to members each year, requiring their utmost application, particularly in the Finance Committee. The very bulk of these schedules necessitate a separate Budget Laws series in the official gazette.

The proceedings on the budget, only broadly similar to those on other Government bills, are fixed every year by the House Committee as warranting extraordinary procedure. The procedure in recent years has been generally as follows. In the first-reading stage a comprehensive review of the national economy by the finance minister is followed by a seven- to ten-hour debate in which the number and variety of subjects that may be raised are of unlimited latitude. The debate may begin a week after the minister's speech so as to enable members to study beforehand the tabled budget books which include also the relevant accounts and other explanations. However, since the Finance Committee will need to sit six days week, meeting sometimes twice a day, so it can give adequate time to the estimates for each department, the budget is referred to it with the close of the minister's speech, before the first reading debate. The first reading over, the house proceeds concurrently with the detailed consideration of the estimates already in progress in the Committee to debate the policy and operation of each ministry, as it finds time, after hearing a review by the minister concerned; about two hours are spent on each ministry. To the movers of amendments on the second reading after the Committee has reported back, the House Committee has in recent years allotted together six to nine hours. Since the third reading of the Budget bill must be taken long before all floor debates on the ministries can be held, those held over are dispersed through the rest of the session and may each terminate with a vote.

Pressure of time on the Knesset in its consideration of the budget has been particularly acute some years when differences between ministers over allocations have delayed its tabling. To prevent such occurrence, an amendment was adopted to the Basic Law on the State Economy in 1982 which requires the Government to lay the annual State Budget bill on the table of the Knesset at least sixty days before the beginning of the financial year. Even this has been found insufficient, and there are thoughts of a further amendment for the tabling of the budget by 1 January to allow three months for its consideration. However, the Basic Law also provides that where it appears to the Government that the budget will not be adopted before the beginning of the financial year, it may introduce an Interim Budget bill.

For introduction of the 1984 budget the Government overpassed the sixty-day limit by more than three weeks because of the need to secure prior agreement to drastic cuts in every ministry. To make the late tabling lawful, the Government sought to amend the Basic Law by a temporary provision. But the Finance Committee, enabled to study the budget proposals for only three of the twenty ministries because of pressure of time, refused in protest to report the special amendment back to the house and instead, to give the enactment of the Budget bill certain force, inserted in it a ratifying clause.

The exclusive role of the Finance Committee in the consideration of budget details is often questioned. While members of the other committees are invited to participate in the discussion of departments within their respective jurisdictions, it is only the Finance Committee which has statutory authority with respect to approval of the budget items. Again and again proposals are made that equal status should be given to the appropriate specialized committee with respect to the items on which it is most knowledgeable about policy and can best judge the order of priorities. The example held up is the statutory joint Finance-Foreign Affairs and Security committee, which takes the defense estimates separately as their breakdown is not tabled in the house. Though a former member of this joint committee notes that its effectiveness is quite limited, he ascribes that situation to the secrecy which is necessary for its deliberations; the documents circulated at its meetings and gathered up at their close cannot be readily analyzed by the members, nor can experts be consulted outside later.[1] On the other hand, transfer of appropriations in the course of the year from one defense item to another, formerly without parliamentary surveillance, now comes regularly before the joint committee. The only other joint committee on budget estimates is that of House-Finance, for the consideration of the Knesset's own budget.

The heavily burdened Finance Committee, having to take its other pressing business while discharging its budget responsibilities, has been stimulated to organize itself internally so as to best perform its tasks. The Committee has worked regularly through subcommittees on taxation and on transfers between budget items. Its subcommittee on state control, for post-audit of the budget, ceased to exist in 1974, when the separate State Control Committee was established. But some think this separation detrimental to the consideration of the budget because lack of communication between the two committees prevents the application of lessons that might be drawn from the previous post-audit. Opinion has therefore been divided about the value of splitting the Finance Committee further into a number of small independent committees on the subjects at present within its jurisdiction—budget, taxation, banking, Government corporations, and so on. To deal with the budget adequately, however, has been the Finance Committee's greatest challenge and spur to effective organization. Some years the Committee split into a number of subcommittees, each taking a group of ministries, facilitating greater specialization and close study of estimates while sparing its own time. In 1983 the Committee set up a permanent subcommittee to oversee the implementation of the budget throughout the year and to bring items in line periodically with changed circumstances, whether by cancellation or reallocation to meet emerging needs.

Finance Committee Chairman Y. Kargman (1965–77) appointed each member as referent for one ministry, making him responsible for studying its estimates intensively together with any information requested from the treasury, so he would be first to speak and take a stand in the Committee's deliberations on that ministry. But most members did not take the scheme seriously. While a system of referents might be more successful if each followed his ministry's operations year in year out, some think that it would, in the nature of things, turn each referent into a spokesman for the ministry, seeking generally to enlarge its estimates.

While the parliamentary process of considering and approving the budget is open to experiment and entirely within the Knesset's control, some related problems are more intractable and have been a source of disquiet to members. Since coalition discipline is stringently applied in budgetary matters, few real changes are ever made in the Government's proposals, either in committee or on the floor. For the same reason midyear transfers of appropriations between items in the budget are invariably approved by the Finance Committee. Only in few cases, in committee, has the treasury agreed not to regard members' rejections of its budgetary demands on specific items as an expression of no-confidence in the Government.

Galloping inflation more than anything else threatened to render the annual budget deliberations meaningless. Not infrequently, the planned and estimated expenditures of the Government as set out were no longer realistic even as they came before the Knesset for approval. In case of necessity the Government is authorized to introduce an Additional Budget bill; and even during less inflationary times, the years when one or more such measures were not brought forward were few. Whether introduced because of unforeseen developments, inflation, or a natural disaster, Additional Budgets are regarded as a necessary evil, often permitting only ex post facto review of fresh expenditures by the Knesset.

As a way of securing budgetary flexibility in high inflation, a clause was inserted in the budget laws for the years 1979–83, providing that if it appears to the Finance Committee that revenues will exceed the forecast of receipts for the financial year, it might, on the proposal of the Government, authorize appropriation of additional amounts to cover cost increases or reduce the national debt. The provision was strenuously objected to by all opposition Groups as circumventing open debate in the house on Government expenditures and leaving the decision entirely to a committee from which some opposition Groups are effectively excluded. The opponents of the provision charged further that it encouraged the Government to present initially low, misleading estimates with the original Budget bill. Similar strictures are heard from time to time on predetermined use by the Government for specific purposes of the general reserves item in the budget.

While the above controversial clause no longer appeared in the 1984 budget law, another provision was included to help the treasury keep up with the marching rise of costs: the finance minister is to update the budget each quarter taking revenues and the various aspects of inflation into account. Items may be updated at different rates. And again, as only the Finance Committee's approval is required, no Additional Budget need be brought before the house.

Financial critics in the house have also decried the many other diverse means available to the Government for appropriations not included or only incompletely shown in the budget. For example, up to a certain limit the Government may use advance payments from the Bank of Israel to increase the amounts available to ministries beyond their budgetary allocations; estimates for public enterprises like railways or housing, which must be partly financed by the Government, are shown in the budget only to the extent of that support; while direct financing of a Government corporation appears as a separate item, indirect subsidies such as export incentives, for example, appear only as part of a general category.

The aim of the Knesset and the Finance Committee over the years has been to confine as far as possible the Government's capacity to exceed the budgetary limits they have fixed for its operations and expenditures. In this they have achieved a measure of success. Government subsidization of credit by indemnification against increases in the consumer price index or changes in currency rate, which would appear as debts in subsequent budgets, has been restricted since 1976 to undertakings of a certain amount (IS2.1m in 1983) beyond which approval of the Finance Committee is required. Similarly, sale of Government securities has been made subject to the Committee's approval. New emissions, to offer tax exemption, require such approval indirectly.

As the great majority of items in the budget represent statutory obligations not amenable to change, it has been suggested that the debate on it should concentrate on the central problems and goals of the national economy instead of on details of estimates, and that the Knesset should rather focus greater attention on the financial implications of bills, when, after all, the important commitments to later expenditures are being made. To this purpose some members have urged that every Government bill be accompanied by a statement of its budgetary aspects.

Finally, since most ministries work according to programs that stretch out far beyond one year, there is also a growing belief in the Knesset that effective oversight of the Government's economic policy will require multiyear budget proposals, enabling both house and committee to see the long-term estimates, updated annually, before approving expenditures for the coming year. The most frequently suggested terms are four years, corresponding with the Government's term of office, or five years, with the period projected by the Government's Economic Planning Authority. It has even been suggested that there might be several budgetary frameworks according to different, specific needs.

We next turn to the State Comptroller's office, whose annual report regularly gives first attention to treasury activities and, in particular, to the execution of the previous year's budget.

THE STATE COMPTROLLER

To monitor and effectively reach into Government offices the Knesset relies on the state comptroller. The State Comptroller Law was one of the Knesset's very first enactments, and since 1949 it has been a number of times replaced and further amended. The comptroller, appointed by the president of the state on the recommendation of the House Committee, is responsible only to the Knesset. His independence from the Government is complete; even his budget is exempt from prior review by the treasury and is submitted directly to the Knesset's Finance Committee. Appointed for a five-year term, which is renewable, he can be removed by the Knesset only. Subject to his inspection are Government offices, state enterprises and institutions, local authorities, and every enterprise or body in the management of which the Government has a share, or to which it gives assistance. In examining their workings, for which he employs a staff numbering in the hundreds including accountants, lawyers, and other professionals, the comptroller's broad objectives are to assure legality of financial transactions and to promote efficiency, economy, and ethical conduct in public administration.

The state comptroller is invested with broad powers. At his request an inspected body must submit reports of income and expenditure, balance sheets, detailed survey of operations, and any other information, documents, or explanations as in his opinion are necessary for purposes of scrutiny. He may lay down directives with regard to its accounting and audit system. With the approval of the Knesset's State Control Committee, he has the authority to summon witnesses and compel testimony under oath. Even a matter completely within a minister's discretion is subject to the comptroller's examination of procedures and method of investigation followed in the decision-making process, as was the case in 1983, when the State Control Committee requested the comptroller to examine the reasons that convinced the minister of the interior not to establish summer time.

The State Comptroller Law sets out the comptroller's reporting obligations and the order of proceeding to be followed by the Knesset and its State Control Committee with respect to his reports and opinions. A comprehensive annual report by the comptroller, leaving no ministry or state enterprise untouched, though only selected units and operations can be examined in any one year, is placed before the minister of economy and interministerial coordination within ten and a half months after the expiration of the financial year. Included in the report are follow-up findings with respect to recommendations made in the report of two years back for the rectification of faults. The minister must make his observations within twelve weeks of receiving the report, after which both are laid in the Knesset and stand referred to the State Control Committee. The Committee, given three and a half months to submit its conclusions and proposals to the house for debate and approval, informs the Knesset which chapters of the report it will consider to enable members not on the Committee to submit proposals; such proposals, even if negatived by the Committee, may be reported to the house and voted there as minority proposals.

In addition, the comptroller issues separate reports on every Government-assisted or jointly managed enterprise and institution, sending copies to the minister of economy, to the minister concerned, and to the body inspected. The State Control Committee, if it sees fit, may lay its conclusions and proposals on any such report on the table of the Knesset and may further ask for their approval, which will entail a floor debate. The same procedure is followed for an opinion given by the comptroller on any matter within his purview on the request of the Knesset, the Committee, or the Government.

The comptroller's responsibility to the Knesset is effected largely in close collaboration with the State Control Committee, the Law providing, among other things, that he shall report to it on his activities whenever he sees fit or is requested by it to do so. Where his inspection has revealed grave infringement of the law he may submit a preliminary, separate report to the Committee to enable it to consider the matter prior to his presentation of the statutory report. The Committee may consequently launch a commission of inquiry on his recommendation or through its own initiative. Such a commission is appointed by the president of the Supreme Court and enpowered to subpoena witnesses and compel testimony under oath. But equally the coalition majority on the Committee may prevent a matter from being submitted to the comptroller, as it did on 14 July 1983, with regard to private land sales in Samaria.

Up until 1974, the Knesset's Finance Committee was charged with the task of examining the comptroller's reports. That Committee, whose duties are mulitfarious, had to assign this work to a special subcommittee which it appointed for the purpose each term. While the subcommittee confined its deliberations as a rule to the subject-matter of the comptroller's reports, the separate State Control Committee, established in 1974, has itself generated much of its activity. Noting that study of the comptroller's reports is of necessity a review of the previous year's findings, Committee Chairman A. Katz-Oz stated in 1983 that investigation of fresher cases by the Committee, on its own initiative and often at the joint request of coalition and opposition members, made up 50 percent of its work.[2]

In 1971, the Knesset added to the comptroller's function that of commissioner for complaints from the public, so that any person can lodge a complaint against a body or official whose activities are subject to the comptroller's inspection, alleging an injurious act or the withholding of a benefit, which is contrary to law or good administration, or attributable to an inflexible attitude or flagrant injustice; a Knesset member can lodge a complaint also on behalf of another person. The commissioner may investigate the complaint in any manner he thinks fit and is not bound by the usual rules of legal procedure. If the examination reveals that the complaint is justified, he reports the findings to the complainant and notifies the body or official against whom the complaint was submitted, pointing out where there is need to rectify a fault. The body or official must notify the commissioner of measures taken to correct the situation. No court may entertain any application for relief against the finding of the commissioner. In practice, the commissioner has found nearly half the complaints received either totally or partly justified. Where an investigation has revealed a general shortcoming in the public service, the commissioner seeks remedial action so there will not be grounds for similar complaints in future.

The commissioner reports to the Knesset each year with a survey of his activities and an account of the handling of selected complaints. The Knesset's procedure on his report differs from that on the state comptroller's in that it is not accompanied by ministerial observations and that since 1982 its detailed consideration has been assigned to a subcommittee of the State Control Committee set up for that purpose alone. The subcommittee also conducts a follow-up of the commissioner's earlier recommendations to assure that they are implemented.

The discharge by one official of the functions of state comptroller and of complaints commissioner is considered a mixed advantage. Since the law empowers the commissioner to call for any information or documents likely in his opinions to assist in the investigation of a complaint, and at the same time expressly permits him to make use of any such material in his other activities, his monitoring of government operations will be facilitated by closer acquaintance with the more rampant bureaucratic evils. On the other hand, it is held by some that with the two offices combined certain areas are of necessity neglected, and that their separation would also reduce the average time of about five months taken for dealing with a complaint.

Since the creation of the state comptrollership in 1949, only three men have held the office, the second, Mr. Y, Nebenzahl (1961–81), serving four terms. The extended periods of service of the first two comptrollers enabled each to leave his imprint and to bring the office to high standards of competence and objectivity. The integrity of all three beyond question, criticism of their performance has been only rare, and their reelection by the House Committee certain. Nevertheless—or perhaps in reaction to this very idealization of the comptrollership—members' bills were submitted, as Mr. Nebenzahl's fourth term came to a close, that would assure more frequent rotation by limiting the comptroller to two terms of office, equalling ten years, or to one term of seven years. The last proposal would also free him from any political pressures, as the Knesset would no longer be in a position to deny him reelection. The intensive party activity and negotiations which preceded the choice of Mr. Nebenzahl's successor prompted some members to propose amendments to the State Comptroller law that would bar from candidature persons who had not been divorced for some years from political life.

Though the comptroller's scrupulous fulfilment of his duties is seldom called into question, his authority has been considered deficient for its lack of "teeth." Beyond his demand to the inspected body for the rectification of a flaw, all he can do is bring the matter to the attention of the minister concerned and of the State Control Committee; where there is suspicion of a criminal act he informs the attorney-general. While the comptroller's reports, specifying administrative faults and any infringements of the law or of moral standards, do not fail to receive a response from the Government, and their impact is strengthened through publication and prominent feature by the communication media, his follow-up findings each year indicate that not a few recommendations are without results; and while it is the finance ministry that has the means of applying sanctions to an incorrigible body, the responsibility for dealing with the comptroller's reports was transferred in 1981 from the finance minister to the minister of economy and interministerial coordination.

A member who considered also the authority of the complaints commissioner deficient submitted a bill in 1981 that would empower the commissioner, where a justified complaint involves damage greater than may be normally ascribed to maladministration, to fix a payment in compensation. The bill was committed in 1983 to be prepared for the first reading.

12

The Knesset and the Government

THE SUPREMACY OF THE KNESSET

THE KNESSET, elected by popular vote, is the vital organ of the state's constitution. A new Knesset brings on the formation of a Government determined by the changed parliamentary array of political forces, with the incumbent Government seen as having resigned on the day of the election and serving only until replaced by its successor. Even should the personnel of the proposed Government be identical with those of its predecessor, the prime minister designate must outline its basic policies and state its composition before the Knesset so as to receive there a vote of confidence; only after this investiture (and after the ministers have each gone up to the rostrum and made a declaration of allegiance which includes the undertaking to abide by Knesset decisions) does the Government take office. The Government, collectively responsible to the Knesset, must continue to look to it for legitimation; only so long as the Government enjoys the Knesset's confidence will it hold office. The Knesset may at any time topple the Government by a vote of no-confidence, upon which it is deemed to have resigned, as is the case when an election is held or when the prime minister resigns or dies; in every such instance, or when it resigns as a whole, the Government assumes caretaker status until replaced. In contradistinction, the Knesset's four-year term can be cut short only by its own enactment, whether initiated by members or the Government. Moreover, an outgoing Knesset continues in office until its successor convenes, so that even the caretaker Government is subject to parliamentary surveillance.

Legislation by the Knesset is not open to challenge except where the

Court finds that the Knesset is infringing a self-imposed constraint which it has previously enacted, without being explicit about the intention to do so (as occurred with the three election laws mentioned in Chapter 3). Though as will be presently shown, the Government nonetheless has the upper hand in many ways, the supremacy of the Knesset is both formal and real.

The procedure for forming a Government is set out in the Basic Law on the Government. After consultation with representatives of the parliamentary Groups, the president of the state assigns the task of forming a Government to the Knesset member with the best chance of rallying a majority of the house, and who will himself become the prime minister. (Other ministers do not have to come from the Knesset, and there are often one or two nonmembers in the Government; the Rabin Government, with seven extraparliamentary appointments to a cabinet of twenty, was an exception.) If the designated ''cabinet maker,'' who has up to forty-two days for the task, is unsuccessful, the president may assign the task to another—again and again if necessary. If there are still no results, parliamentary Groups comprising a majority of the Knesset may designate the member to whom the president is to assign the task. The law thus envisages the possibility of protracted negotiation for the formation of a Government, taking account of the realities of the coalition system.

The transfer of initiative to the parliamentary Groups in the event of an impasse in the president's attempts to advance the formation of a Government (a provision adopted in 1962) is designed to avoid prolonged periods of caretaker government where the president has not exhausted every possibility, such as occurred in 1951 and again in 1961 when Prime Minister Ben-Gurion, following his resignation, did not accept the assignment to form a new Government; on neither occasion did the president make a further attempt until after the next election, and there was no regular Government for nearly eight months in the first instance, and for more than nine in the second.

The president (whose duties are generally of a symbolic and representative nature) has, at any rate, little substantive power with respect to the choice of prime minister designate, since that is predetermined by the political constellation in the Knesset. Just how limited the president's discretion can be in the determination of premier designate was illustrated by the sequence of events that led up to the change of Government in 1983. After Prime Minister Begin declared his intention to resign, but before doing so, the *Herut* Central Committee nominated Yitzhak Shamir to succeed him, and Mr. Shamir at once met with the coalition partners of the outgoing Government and secured the necessary Knesset majority by a signed agreement. On Mr. Begin's resignation, shortly afterward, the president duly went through formal consultations with the parliamentary Groups, while his choice of Mr. Shamir to form the new Government was in fact a foregone conclusion.

The Knesset vote of confidence which invests the Government with the power of office, constitutes approval of the cabinet as presented by the prime minister designate. Thereafter, any change in the Government's composition or structure requires further Knesset approval—whether appointment or reassignment of a minister, establishment of a new ministry, unification or division of ministries, or transfer of authority between ministers. Knesset approval, in all such cases, like the initial vote of confidence, follows a Group-basis debate. Only when the prime minister himself assumes the portfolio of a resigning or deceased minister, or other ministerial functions, is recourse to the Knesset unnecessary.

A motion of no-confidence in the Government, proposed by a parliamentary Group of at least two members, if carried, brings the Government down at once. When an unprecedented tie vote on a no-confidence motion occurred on 23 March 1982, though it meant nonadoption of the motion, Prime Minister Begin was persuaded only by a cabinet majority to refrain from resigning. When a Government is defeated in a no-confidence vote, the president must proceed to consult with the Groups on the formation of a new Government, as he does in midterm also on resignation of the Government by choice, or of the prime minister, or on the death of the prime minister. If no Government can be formed enjoying the support of a majority of the Knesset, a dissolution law is enacted, usually on the initiative of members, which fixes the date for an election. In every case the retiring Government stays at the helm until replaced.

A no-confidence motion must, under the Rules, be taken as the first item on the agenda at the earliest regular Knesset sitting following the day on which it was submitted; the usual practice, however, is to allow forty-eight hours. A Group may also propose no-confidence at the close of any debate, and though the Rules prescribe that the vote is then to be taken at the next sitting, the convenience to the Knesset of expeditious disposal of such a question has usually persuaded the House Committee to advance the vote to the same sitting, when it is taken before any other vote on the item. Further, the Government may itself notify the Knesset chairman that it regards the vote on a particular matter as a question of confidence.

When a Government with a precarious majority in the house must strain to survive a no-confidence motion, it may have to depend on the coalition majority in the House Committee to defer the debate so as to allow time for all Government supporters, even ministers on missions abroad, to return in time for the vote. With the same purpose the House Committee may extend the debate, as it did for three no-confidence motions concerning a strategic cooperation agreement with the United States, proposed on 2 December 1981, when the coalition in the house had only a majority of one: instead of the usual single round of Group statements following the Government's reply to the movers, a ten-hour debate was fixed by the Committee.

More critical in votes on no-confidence motions than narrowly based Governments has been the uncertain cohesion of coalition partners. In 1955, after the General Zionist Group abstained in a vote on a motion of no-confidence in the Government over the Kastner case, which involved the charge of collaboration with the nazis by a *Mapai* leader (and both *Mapai* and the General Zionists were then in the coalition), Prime Minister Sharett resigned, bringing down the Government; he had no other way then to compel the two General Zionist ministers to resign from the cabinet. Again, after the Government had been given the constitutional means of ousting ministers from a dissident Group (by a measure described later), the National Religious (NRP) Group abstained on a no-confidence vote over an official late-Friday ceremony held on 10 December 1976, and deemed to have desecrated the Sabbath. Ejecting the NRP ministers and excluding their Group from the coalition, Prime Minister Rabin was, however, left with a minority Government that could not expect to survive another test of confidence, and it resigned to forestall defeat.

Because a no-confidence motion cannot be denied, it has been used by opposition Groups on occasion simply to raise a matter for which no other procedure is available, as they did on 11 July 1962, in connection with the Government's handling of an extradition, when budget debates ruled out consideration of members' motions, and an urgent motion on the matter had not been recognized. Further, since a no-confidence motion takes precedence over other business, it can be employed also as a dilatory device, as was done by the small Groups in 1973 to impede the first and second readings of the Knesset Elections (Amendment No. 4) Bill, whose purpose was to alter the system of computing vote remainders in a way that would diminish the prospects of small parties.

A Government defeat in a no-confidence vote occurred, in fact, only once, on 14 February 1951—and this when the Government announced that it regarded as an expression of no-confidence the rejection of the education minister's proposals for school registration (in a wider controversy over religious education). However, Government defeats when a question of confidence has not been involved have been many and more frequent during periods of a bare coalition majority, as under the Rabin Government in the first few months following its formation, and during periods under both Begin Governments. Such reverses have been dealt by the Knesset on every kind of proceeding: members' bills and motions have gone forward when the minister concerned sought to have them removed from the agenda; Government bills, even financial, have been defeated, and highly critical opposition summation motions have been adopted upon termination of general debates. The Knesset perhaps achieved a record when it voted contrary to the Government line four times on two successive days: on 29 December 1981, the house removed from the order paper two motions concerning compensation of the Sinai evacuees—though the defense minister was for a floor debate on both—and later that sitting adopted a resolution censuring the Government for failing to make the regulations necessary to administer the Assurance of Income Law which had been enacted over a year before; then, the very next day again, the house committed a member's motion on prices of dwellings in face of the justice minister's opposition.

As on the floor so in the committees where coalition members are even readier to register dissent, the Government has often been dealt defeats. A striking case was the revolt of the nine Alignment members of the Law Committee on 27 January 1971. Though their Group was then the coalition mainstay, they all voted against the Government's rent control proposals. The support given by most opposition committee members notwithstanding, the proposals were rejected. Even in the Finance Committee, whose every decision has implications for the public purse, setbacks to the Government are not uncommon; a characteristic instance was the Committee's refusal to approve rises in electricity and telephone rates on 13 April 1983, in a pointed protest against the finance minister's absence from the country.

THE EXECUTIVE UPPER HAND

While, as we have seen, the Government's ultimate responsibility to the Knesset is indubitable, it is in possession of manifold powers—political, legal, and practical—many granted intentionally by the Knesset, and some of which appear at times to eclipse the legislative arm. To begin with, the cabinet, sitting in the house and consisting of the coalition parties' leaders, in fact directs the Knesset, confident generally of the backing of its parliamentary majority. While common political affiliation facilitates harmony between a minister and his parliamentary Group, he can claim a certain independence from it as he generally owes his appointment largely to the party, who chooses its representatives in the Government (including the prime minister). At the same time, given the centralized party-list electoral system, the ministers, as senior party members, wield considerable influence in the nomination and ordering of candidates for election to the Knesset. Thus Knesset members of the coalition may be dependent on their ministers for continuation of parliamentary careers while obligated to them for past preferment.

The Government is free to act over wide fields without recourse to the Knesset, so long as it does not infringe any law or tamper with the constitutional system: for example, the Government on its own responsibility alters currency exchange rates, establishes and severs diplomatic relations, and may decide on questions of war and peace. This was the practice even before 1968 when the Basic Law on the Government confided sweeping residuary powers to the executive in its Section 29, which states: "The Government is competent to do in the name of the State, subject to any law, any act whose doing is not enjoined by law upon another authority."[1]

In the making of treaties and other international agreements the Government has virtually had a free hand. It may negotiate, sign, and ratify a treaty or convention without bringing it at all before the Knesset. While the Basic Law on the President of the State provides that the president "shall sign such conventions with foreign States as have been ratified by the Knesset,"[2] the Government does not read this to mean that the power to ratify treaties is vested in the Knesset, but rather that in those instances that the Government should choose to bring a treaty before the house, it is to be signed by the president. Since an identical clause was contained in the Transition Law of 1949 and construed by the Government in the same way from the beginning, its reenactment in the Basic Law, in 1964, is regarded as parliamentary endorsement of the Government's interpretation. Furthermore, the legality of the Government's practice of making treaties without resort to the Knesset was confirmed by the Supreme Court in an extradition case in 1967.

While Knesset participation in treaty-making is at the Government's discretion, agreements whose fulfillment requires changes in domestic law, will of necessity be brought before the house. In the first such instance, the Government brought in a bill in 1952 to give effect to the Prevention of Genocide Convention adopted by the United Nations. However, when some members demanded that the convention be first separately approved by the Knesset, the Government would not allow the creation of such a precedent and consented only to the adoption of a resolution "that approval be given." In another notable case the Knesset was made aware of Israel's accession in 1950 to the Madrid Agreement on the prohibition of improper geographic names for wines only in 1957, when the Government, having determined to implement the agreement, introduced an amendment to the Merchandise Marks Ordinance.

Members of the Knesset have urged that it must have a say in the approval of international undertakings, but their bills to this purpose have never got beyond preliminary consideration. The Government, on the other hand, has even initiated measures like the Extradition Law of 1954, which makes it possible to conclude new agreements without any further act of the Knesset, and like the Legal Assistance to Foreign States Law of 1977, which lays down that ministerial regulations for the implementation of provisions in international agreements with respect to the furnishing of documents and collection of evidence, "shall have force of law notwithstanding the provisions of this Law, or any other Law."[3] Though Justice Minister Dov Yosef stated in 1963 and again in 1964 that the Government agreed to lay on the Knesset table before ratification any treaty of more than routine significance, such a practice was adopted only in 1984, after Justice Minister Moshe Nissim had offered to lay all but the more urgent treaties at least two weeks before ratification. The attorney-general instructed legal advisers of ministries to submit copies of proposed treaties to the Knesset together with a schedule of the changes in Israel domestic law they would require. If the Knesset takes any stand on a proposed treaty, this is to be brought before the cabinet during its discussion of the issue. The instructions make an exception, however, for treaties requiring urgent or secret approval. Conventions of the International Labor Organization, whose constitution requires parliamentary tabling, have been regularly laid in the Knesset.

Though no Government has formally yielded any part of its treaty-making prerogatives to the Knesset, important instruments in recent years affecting Israel's relations with her neighbors in decisive ways have been submitted for parliamentary ratification: they include the disengagement of forces with Syria in 1974, the 1975 Sinai agreement with Egypt, the Camp David accords in 1978, the peace treaty with Egypt in 1979, and the agreement with Lebanon in 1983. In the last case the draft agreement was placed before the Knesset only after a member's motion on the subject had been put down. It can nevertheless be fairly said that the custom is already established that documents of such weight are brought before the house for approval; when the Government would not consent to debate of the Memorandum of Understanding for Strategic Cooperation with the United States in 1981, it was confronted by no-confidence motions of four opposition Groups.

Turning to the Knesset Rules of Procedure, we find that "right of way" has been conceded to the Government by diverse provisions (many described in earlier chapters), enabling it to control most of the Knesset's time, to put its views before the house with facility and to expedite its business there, while checking, as it finds need, members' initiatives. Government business takes precedence in the house on two of the three weekly sitting days, and through the entire week while the budget proposals are under debate. A Government statement will come before any other business, even a no-confidence motion. Such a statement will eliminate from the agenda members' motions on the same subject, or, if made early enough, keep them from being put down at all. The Government's prerogatives include also the right to ask that its motion be voted first or that a debate be discontinued. A minister speaking in the Government's name has right to the floor at any stage of a debate; and so has a deputy minister on matters assigned him by the minister. No time limit is imposed by the Rules on a minister's speech except when on replying to a member's motion he consents to plenary debate or proposes a committee remit; he then has up to fifteen minutes.

Government bills, as shown in Chapter 10, are favored by the Rules in numerous ways over those of members. Further, the preliminary debate of a member's bill is not taken before there is a nod from the Government, as is the case of a plenary debate due in consequence of a member's motion. The committee's reconsideration of any bill, or part of it, may be called for by the Government as well as by the committee chairman.

In the legislative sphere there are many instances—independent of the Rules— of accretion to the Government's powers through Knesset deference. Though the Knesset adopted a resolution in 1950 assigning the preparation of Basic Laws to the Law Committee (cited in Chapter 3), the presidium affirmed in 1963 that the resolution in no way detracts from the Government's right to propose such laws. Another notable case was that of the National Service Law of 1953 providing for substitute service of women exempted by the army on religious grounds; after the Government had found it impracticable to implement the measure through a period of twenty-six years, it was amended in 1979 (though under opposition protest) to state expressly that its implementation shall commence only when the Government so decides. A different instance yet was the enactment by the Knesset in 1981 of a dissolution law initiated by the Government though it had become established custom for such measures to be introduced by members; and this when five members' bills for dissolution had been introduced weeks before the Government's.

Resolutions of the Knesset, as distinct from its enactments of law, are not binding on the Government unless themselves adopted pursuant to a law. The Constituent Assembly, in the Transition Law of 1949 (with the same provisions included later in the Basic Law on the Government), decreed that the Government shall be responsible for its activities to the Knesset and shall hold office so long as it enjoys the confidence of the Knesset, this put an end, advisedly,[4] to the relationship prescribed in the Law and Administration Ordinance of 1948 that "The Provisional Government shall act in accordance with the policy laid down by the Provisional Council of State," and "shall carry out its decisions."[5] It was considered unnecessary to bind the Government to all resolutions of the Knesset, for as the ultimate sanction it could dismiss the Government—a step which could not be taken by the Council in the provisional period since both Council and Government had been appointed in the same manner (see Chapter 2).

When opposition members nevertheless sought from time to time to give binding effect to Knesset resolutions, pointing among other things to the minister's declaration of allegiance which pledges him to comply with the decisions of the Knesset, they were told by the Government that this would be direct interference in administration and would undermine the position of the Government as the executive arm. Consulted on the question in 1976, the attorney-general concurred with the Government and declared that the Knesset's decisions are binding only when pronounced through legislation, since its language is that of law. Similar rebuttals have been made by successive ministers of justice when members have attempted through legislation to compel Government postponement of an action while the Knesset is in the course of debating the matter concerned or has put it down for debate, either by house or committee. Replying on 23 November 1977, to a member's bill that would impose such a restraint, Justice Minister S. Tamir asserted that the Government must retain the authority to act at any time in any way it sees fit, and he adduced as a case in point the reception of Egypt's President Sadat earlier that week, which, under the proposed measure, would have been put off as the matter had been referred to a committee the week before, consequent on members' motions.

Neither resolutions of the house nor a committee's Conclusions on nonlegislative matters (both described in Chapter 9) obliged the Government to make any response whatsoever before 1976. That year, the problem of neglected committee Conclusions (such Conclusions are far more numerous than house resolutions because of the large number of members' motions whose subjects are committed, and far oftener call for some concrete action by the Government) was considered by the House Committee, and the Knesset adopted an amendment to the Rules requiring the minister concerned to inform the house within six months of any action taken. After Knesset Chairman Shamir drew attention in 1978 to the anomaly that while committee Conclusions entailed a report by the minister the resolutions of the house did not, the six-month rule was applied also to the latter.

In compliance with the foregoing changes in the Rules, ministers respond regularly with letters to the Knesset Chairman indicating what the ministry has done to meet the house resolution or committee Conclusions. Laid on the table of the house and published in the Knesset Record, the response, though respectfully worded, may be elegantly evasive or laconically noncommital. In any case, the Government is legally no more obliged to comport with such decisions than it was before the Rules were amended.

An important advantage of the Government is its possession and control of the great body of information concerning policy and administration—information vital to the Knesset's legislative and scrutinizing activities. This advantage is so much the more telling in view of the limited information resources available otherwise to members (see Chapter 5). While the Knesset Rules place an obligation on ministers to answer Questions, and to give information and explanations as required by a committee in its area of competence, both the Basic Law on the Government and the Rules themselves have set limitations in this regard. The Basic Law lays down that deliberations and decisions of the Government or of ministerial committees on matters whose secrecy the Government has proclaimed to be vital to the State are secret, and their publication is prohibited; only the Government, the prime minister, or a person authorized by them (generally the Government Secretary), may permit publication of certain things.

In the Rules there are further qualifications respecting a minister's duty to give information. In communication between Knesset committee and Government department, the provision that it shall be maintained exclusively through the minister (remarked upon in Chapter 7) of necessity trammels committee members in their attempts to secure full disclosure of facts. In the house a Question need not be answered by the minister if he states as his opinion that public answer may be damaging to state interests; in practice this hardly ever occurs as such questions are disallowed by the chairman. Not infrequently, however, an answer given is considered by the questioner incomplete or not pertinent; if his supplementary question fails to get a more satisfactory reply, he must resort to other parliamentary moves such as a Motion for the Agenda—which he is not always prepared to do, nor his Group ready to approve.

Members have complained that explanations with Government bills as laid on the Knesset table are deficient in that they do not include a full background review setting forth the proposal's budgetary aspects, as is done in the predraft memorandum circulated among the relevant ministries. With respect to delegated legislation, charges are made that regulations brought for committee approval at the last moment are often without any accompanying explanatory matter. In the joint committee on the defense budget (as noted in the preceding chapter) background documents, made available only during meetings because of their confidential nature, cannot be thoroughly studied by committee members.

Yet often the main problem of members is not insufficient data from Government sources; ministers will generally not deny them information they have asked for. Indeed, members are more likely to be swamped with official facts and figures, though these may be selective or biased. A member of the Knesset's Finance Committee has attested to the perplexity which may beset members when confronted by a welter of documents which they cannot possibly digest.[6] The difficulty of members then is to elicit the information which they need in order to fulfill their control and monitoring function. The house could ferret out the facts of a matter by appointing a committee of inquiry (described in Chapter 7), which can be equipped with special powers like those of summoning witnesses and papers and of taking testimony under oath; but this provision has remained effectively a dead letter, since the coalition will always regard its very application as a reflection on the Government. A member's motion in 1982 that the Knesset consider setting up a committee of inquiry to examine the Government's handling of the Sinai evacuation, which seemed to make exceptional progress with the subject appointed for floor debate, simply sat on the agenda for one and a half years and was struck off by the house as a stale item in 1983.

A Government that has resigned or is so deemed—whether because of defeat in a no-confidence vote or an election—is, paradoxically, least subject to parliamentary control. Though it can no longer be threatened with dismissal by the Knesset, it is not more limited in power to act than a duly invested Government; and while under the Basic Law on the Government it may no longer coopt ministers, neither may any of the incumbents resign. The problem would be marginal were it not for the long interval that may elapse between a resignation and the formation of a new Government. While the parliamentary Groups are authorized to take the initiative in proposing the prime minister designate if the president has failed to do so, there is no fixed time limit for the process; should this effort produce no positive result, there is nothing to compel the early enactment of a dissolution law that will fix the election date; and once enacted, the lapse of time until election day may come to four and a half months (see Chapter 4). After the caretaker Government that lasted nearly eight months in 1951, an attempt made in the Knesset to limit by definition the powers of such a Government proved abortive. In 1961 the country was without a properly confirmed Government from January until November. It has been recommended that to secure responsibility of caretaker Governments they be made subject to all Knesset decisions, as in the relationship described earlier that existed between the Provisional Council and Government, votes of confidence not being applicable.

COALITION GOVERNMENT

The manifest advantages of the executive branch of government, outlined above, are offset considerably by the constraints of coalition whose general effects on the Government are—as well as a drawn out process of formation—cumbersome structure, a tendency to indecision, and at times the aspect of a house divided against itself. The principles and ultimate goals of the several political forces allied in a coalition are various, their joint purpose being essentially to sustain the Government through a majority in the Knesset. Every Government since the birth of the state has rested on a coalition.

A coalition is formed upon agreement between the partners with respect to a program, and the distribution of ministerial portfolios and other offices. The signed coalition agreement consisting of any number of clauses usually sets out first the organizational and disciplinary provisions which are to bind the acceding Groups and their individual members. At the same time there may be stipulations in the document of a free vote on certain issues or of a general right to abstain on questions of conscience or religious matters. Freedom from coalition discipline with respect to a particular subject may be granted to one or certain partners, as occurred, for example, in 1977; the coalition agreement that year allowed *Agudat Yisrael* freedom of action in all religious matters. When the Democratic Movement for Change (DMC) joined the coalition some months later and a supplementary agreement was signed, DMC in turn was granted that freedom, as well as the rights of free expression and abstention on political questions concerning Judea and Samaria. More specifically, with respect to Government decisions on settlement in those areas, DMC members were given right of appeal to the Knesset's Foreign Affairs and Security Committee for debate and final decision.

While a coalition agreement is a formal contract, it is primarily an internal matter between the partners and not in a real sense an official document. Yet, so well is it recognized that the coalition agreement provides the practical political basis on which the Government is formed, that it has become customary to print it in the appendix to the Knesset Record, side by side with the Basic Lines of Government Policy, which is a distinctly official document containing the program that the prime minister designate must place before the Knesset in asking for its expression of confidence in his Government. And in practice while deviation by the Government from its Basic Lines of Policy, which is phrased in the most general terms, has been judged by the attorney-general to be of little consequence, any infraction of the coalition agreement is certain to bring sharp reaction and may lead to a Government crisis.

The allocation of portfolios, though an important element of the coalition understanding, does not usually appear in the signed agreement (except when a new partner joins an existing coalition, as occurred in the case of DMC just mentioned, where the signed supplementary agreement spelled out, among other things, the extent of its participation in the Government). The distribution of offices entering into coalition negotiations will in fact cover more than cabinet places; the unpublished part of the agreement may include also the appointment of deputy ministers and certain diplomatic and other posts, while figuring as well will be the disposition of Knesset vice-chairmanships and committee chairmanships. A notable coalition trade-off was made by the ultraorthodox *Agudat Yisrael* in 1977; with a parliamentary Group of four it was entitled to a minister, but since it was barred by its Council of Torah Sages from sharing directly in Government, it took instead two key committee chairmanships (see Chapter 7) and renewed the arrangement in successive coalitions.

In their composition all coalitions in the Knesset but that formed in 1984 to support a National Unity Government have conformed to one general pattern: the alliance of one large predominant Group (with a plurality in the house until 1981) from which come the prime minister and most of the cabinet, with a few smaller Groups. In strength coalitions have ranged from 61 to 87 members (the situation under Unity Governments being exceptional), with 120 the unvarying size of the house.

With regard to the leading Group in the coalition, three periods are to be distinguished. The earliest and longest period, until 1965, was that of ascendancy of the moderate labor party, *Mapai,* led by Ben-Gurion from the pre-state years through most of its career. With a plurality ranging from forty to forty-seven Knesset members, *Mapai*'s strength was always more than twice that of its nearest rival. The second period, extending through 1965–77 and marked by the emergence of enduring alliances between large parties and parliamentary Groups, was still one of labor leadership in the coalition, with *Mapai* aligned with other labor parties, and also merging its own identity in the new Labor party. But faced now by similarly combined opposition strength and with its reputation suffering in the Yom Kippur War setback, the Labor Alignment did not enjoy the same degree of hegemony as its precursor. The third period opened in 1977, when the *Likud* replaced the Labor Alignment as the central coalition element.

In the 1981 election the *Likud* won only forty-eight Knesset mandates to the Alignment's forty-seven, and in the course of the term a Group merger and two floor crossings reduced *Likud* strength further so that its ratio to the Alignment was forty-six to fifty. The *Likud* remained at the helm by virtue of the overall coalition majority of sixty-four. In sum, the trend has been toward a weaker central element in the coalition, with greater power shifted as a result to the several smaller partners. We shall look at the consequences shortly.

There was, however, one interval when a coalition could have been entirely dispensed with: when the newly formed Labor Alignment in 1969 had by itself an absolute Knesset majority (sixty-three members) for about nine months. However, as we saw (Chapter 1), both the existence then of a National Unity Government and a deeply rooted coalition habit deterred the Alignment from trying to form a Government independently; some simply did not consider sixty-three a realistic majority (which appears curious today, after the Rabin and Begin Governments took office in 1974, 1977, and 1981, with the support of only sixty-one members and governed for periods).

Broad coalitions to support National Unity Government have been formed only in times of emergency. In the first such period (1967–70) the two large adversary blocs, the Labor Alignment and *Gahal* (the forerunner of the *Likud*) both supported the Government but not always in full coalition. There were, strictly speaking, three National Unity governments. The first, established in the crisis of the Six Days War, in June 1967, and lasting until the death of Prime Minister Eshkol in February 1969, simply coopted three new ministers—two from *Gahal,* without portfolio, and Moshe Dayan of *Rafi* as defense minister. Since *Gahal* was never a party to the existing coalition agreement, it accepted discipline only in matters of foreign affairs, security, and budget. Golda Meir, who succeeded Eshkol, formed a Government with policy and personnel virtually unchanged, and it held office until the election of October 1969. The third National Unity Government, formed by Mrs. Meir after the election, was based on a coalition agreement including *Gahal* as a full partner; but the coalition was an uneasy one, the *Mapam* Section of the Alignment staying out because of *Gahal,* and, in turn accepting only limited discipline. The coalition came to an end after eight months in August 1970, when *Gahal* left the Government and the coalition over a question of foreign policy.

The keynote of the coalition agreement that, owing to a critical economic situation, gave rise after the 1984 election to National Unity Government, was parity between the closely matched Alignment and *Likud,* whose respective allies from the smaller parliamentary Groups only made for a finer balance. Among the provisions spelled out in detail were equal strength for both blocs in the Government and on the coalition executive, with the premiership to rotate between Mr. Shimon Peres of the Alignment and Mr. Yitzhak Shamir of the *Likud,* each to hold the office for half the Knesset term. While one served as prime minister, the other was to be vice-premier and foreign minister. The leadership of the coalition was to rotate similarly so that while the prime minister was from the Alignment there would be a *Likud* coalition head, and vice versa.

To take the unpopular measures needed to cure the economy, the two large blocs alone commanded a comfortable Knesset majority (eighty-one members), large enough to do without other coalition allies. Yet each bloc, looking ahead to the time when the Unity Government would come to an end, sought to satisfy the small Groups who would support it in a more narrowly based Government. There resulted a coalition of ninety-seven members and a Government of record size—twenty-five ministers. (The Meir Unity

Government of 1969–70 numbered twenty-four.) To counter this unwieldy size the coalition agreement provided for a "Cabinet" (interestingly, the first formal use of that word in Hebrew) of ten ministers, five from each large bloc, whose decisions in security and political matters, and any other matter brought before it by Mr. Peres or Mr. Shamir, would be final. Inner cabinets consisting of a restricted number of ministers from the leading political party in the Government had existed in fact also in the past. However, though wielding great influence, as did, for example, Prime Minister Meir's close circle of ministers, popularly referred to as "Golda's kitchen," those bodies had no official status.

A National Unity coalition, with a truncated opposition itself deeply divided, is by its very nature inimical to sound parliamentary government. The broad coalition of 1984, embracing ninety-seven members, placed a tight rein on individual initiatives in the Knesset so as to ensure that its disparate elements would hold together in support of the Government. At the same time the twenty-three opposition members comprising five small Groups at the two extremes of the political spectrum received not one committee chairmanship. Knesset Chairman Hillel, noting that parliamentary dissent might in these circumstances be stifled, declared that he would at all times abide by his duty of receiving motions of coalition members without regard to their having approval from the coalition executive.

Returning to our account of normal coalitions, the smaller parties who entered most coalitions numbered three or four (the number would be higher if one counted the two tiny Arab lists—sometimes three or four—who supported all Labor-led Governments but were not allocated portfolios). Joining nearly all coalitions, whether Labor- or *Likud*-led, was the National Religious party (NRP). Its Knesset Group, of ten to twelve members during most of its existence (though sometimes representing two separate, left and center, political entities), was of sufficient weight to shake Governments over issues such as religious education and Sabbath observance; its disaffections were the most frequent cause of short-lived Governments. Reduced by a breakaway to six Knesset members with the 1981 election, and then to five, after another defection, NRP was nevertheless a pivotal element in the strained coalition, providing two ministers (one holding two portfolios) and one deputy minister—more than it had often been awarded when twice as large.

Almost as constant a coalition partner as NRP—but only during the periods of Labor leadership—were the Independent Liberals (known earlier as the Progressive party). With four to six Knesset members they were influential in Government. Some coalition allies of shorter duration were the General Zionists, in the years 1952–55, and the more left-wing labor parties, *Mapam* and *Ahdut Ha'avodah,* who served on and off in Government.

The short period of alliance with the General Zionists was stormy; at one point they withdrew from the Government because they opposed the raising of the red flag in state schools on May Day, and later they caused the resignation of a Government by abstaining in a confidence vote. (But more than two decades later, as the Liberal Section of *Likud,* they were again in the Government.) Government crises were also occasioned from time to time by the left-wing coalition partners; though eventually they entered the Labor Alignment, intersectional differences, as we saw in Chapter 8, not infrequently rocked the coalition.

After the *Likud* replaced the Alignment as the leading bloc in Government in 1977, coalition stresses and strains were not less frequent. It is small exaggeration to say that the shrunken coalition and early dissolution of the Knesset in 1981 were caused mainly by the progressive splintering and ultimate disappearance of the *Likud*'s chief coalition partner, DMC, as detailed in Chapter 8. Further, in the coalitions of 1981 and 1983, the *Likud*—because its arch-rival, the Alignment, enjoyed numerical superiority—became ever so much more dependent on its coalition partners, who numbered eventually a half-dozen; taking account also of the three party Sections in *Likud,* the coalition effectively comprised ten political entities as shown in Table 9. The fragmentary character of these coalitions though different only in degree by comparison with earlier years, was more pronounced in the absence of any ''middle sized'' ally like NRP (whose twelve-strong Group was down to five), or like the defunct DMC (which had fifteen Knesset members in 1977).

The larger number of coalition allies was the cause of greater internal pressures on the Government, and even small Groups could exercise an influence held to be in excess of their Knesset strength. For example, the three-man *Tami* Group, intimating it might leave the coalition, delayed implementation of an urgent retrenchment program for weeks in 1983, until it was modified so its effects on low-income classes would be minimized; *Agudat Yisrael* with a Group of four, laid down, according to one coalition member, fifty-two of the eighty-two stipulations in the coalition agreement.[7]

The multiple pressures affecting the composition of the Government in any coalition are not often conducive to efficient structure. While every political component seeks, as far as it can, a large and influential representation in Government, there has to be a weighing and balancing that will leave all partners satisfied. In such circumstances it is difficult to avoid creating a redundant portfolio, tailor-made cabinet post, or a questionable deputy ministership. In the ratio of ministers to coalition members, which dropped from one to six in the First Knesset, to one to three in recent years (with the increase in cabinet size over the years from twelve ministers to some twenty), there has always been an attempt at even-handed allocation between coali-

Table 9

Coalition, Government, and Opposition
(October 1983)

Coalition Groups*				Opposition Groups*		
	Membership		Ministers		Membership	
Likud		46	15 (including prime minister)	Labor Alignment		50
Sections:				Sections:		
Herut	25			Labor party	40	
Liberals	17			*Mapam*	7	
La'am	4			Civil Rights and Peace Movement	1	
National Religious party (NRP)		5	2	Members at large	2	
Agudat Yisrael		4		Democratic Front for Peace and Equality		4
Tami		3	1	*Shinui*-Center party		2
Tehiya		3	1			
Movement for Zionist and Social Renewal		1	1			
State List		1				
Independent member		1				
		64	20			56

*For an explanation of Group names, see Glossary.

tion partners; yet, often, the smaller allies have come out advantaged. In the Shamir Government (formed in 1983), as is clear from Table 9, the ratio of members to ministers, which was 3:1 in the *Likud,* was exactly three for two small Groups, and two and a half for NRP, while for the one-man Zionist Renewal Group, the ratio was one to one.

In the allocation of portfolios in the Shamir Government (and in the preceding Government), the reward of the smaller coalition partners was even greater than is suggested by Table 9. One NRP minister was assigned two portfolios—interior and religious affairs (and these would have counted as three a little while earlier, before the police ministry was absorbed by interior); the minister for *Tami* received the portfolios of labor and welfare, and of immigrant absorption. On the other hand, in the *Likud* the only minister who could be said to hold more than one portfolio was the deputy prime minister, who was also minister of construction and housing; and, in fact, the office of deputy prime minister is by itself of little real content, a fact even more true after the creation in 1984 of a vice-premiership. While there may be two deputy prime ministers, there is only one vice-prime minister, and it is he who automatically acts for an absent premier.

Awarded additional portfolios, the NRP and *Tami* groups had each also a deputy minister appointed from their ranks, thus giving them two of the seven appointed from the entire coalition. Though a deputy minister is not a member of the Government, his appointment is considered a stepping stone to the cabinet. He acts for the minister in the Knesset as required—in debate, piloting of legislation, and reply to motions and questions—while carrying out assigned duties in the ministry. A minister with two portfolios is likely to assign effectively complete conduct and supervision of one ministry's affairs to a deputy minister, but he may equally manage without a deputy minister. The number and distribution of deputy ministers, though appointments are made by the relevant ministers, is a matter into which enter coalition considerations, and which must by law be approved by the Government. Their number has differed from one Government to another, ranging in practice from two to eleven.

While in no Government has there been a deputy minister for every minister, some have had two—again, to satisfy coalition requirements; for example, to look after the interests of religious schools, a second deputy minister of education was appointed in 1966, 1969, and 1970 from the *Poalei Agudat Yisrael* and NRP groups successively. Under the Unity Government of 1984, the coalition agreement specified that the Alignment defence minister appoint a *Likud* member as deputy minister, and the *Likud* finance minister an Alignment deputy minister. When the minister and deputy minister are not from the same parliamentary Group, their relations may not be easy. There may be friction even when the two are from different parties in the same Group, as occurred conspicuously in 1981 between Transport Minister Corfu of the *Herut* Section in *Likud* and Deputy Minister D. Shiffman of the Liberals.

The appointment of a relatively large number of deputy ministers by a Government with a slim majority arguably amounts to an extended interlacing of Knesset and Government which is largely to the advantage of the latter. As part of the executive arm (while, unlike ministers, who may also come from outside the Knesset, they must be members), deputy ministers do not enjoy the same freedom of action or speech as other coalition members, and have been dismissed on falling out with the minister or the Government. They do not as a rule take part in debates not related to their respective areas of official duties; though on Knesset committees, they will have little time for them. Thus, while they help secure the Government's loyal base in the Knesset, the potential forces of parliamentary scrutiny and criticism are thinned.

The above-mentioned case of the *Tami* Group of three, with two of its members coopted into the executive, and one left a rank-and-file Knesset member, is only one conspicuous illustration of the manner in which the structure of coalition Government will tend to go askew. Another notable example was that of the Democratic Group of seven, formed with the split in DMC, in 1978. The Democrats continued to provide three ministers (compared with the four of the fifteen-man DMC), and its overrepresentation by comparison with other coalition Groups caused resentment. The disproportion became much more glaring as successive defections from the Democrats reduced their Group to three by 1980; althought the Democrat justice minister, S. Tamir, resigned from the cabinet soon afterward, the three-man Group was left with two representatives in the Government, one a non-member. Members' bills seeking to set a maximum of thirteen or fourteen ministries, with the purpose of limiting the distortion possible in the composition of a Government as the result of coalition bargaining, have proved abortive.

Since program and allocation of portfolios are primarily the outcome of bargaining between the coalition partners, any later change that may affect the delicate balance becomes a source of intracoalition conflict. For example, before the *Tehiya* Group was coopted into the coalition in 1982, it was necessary to prevail over declared intentions to vote against the move, on one hand, from *Agudat Yisrael* because the new partner was to be given a free vote on religious issues,[8] and on the other hand, from the Liberals within *Likud,* who demanded at the same time award of a new, information portfolio;[9] even the appointment of Mrs. Sarah Doron to the cabinet in 1983, to make up the agreed complement of six Liberal ministers after an earlier resignation, could be effected only after prolonged negotiations with *Agudat Yisrael,* who suspected she might not support its legislation. Also intersectional rivalry within a Group may have a paralyzing effect, as occurred in 1975, when Prime Minister Rabin's proposed combination of the Labor and Social Welfare ministries into one Social Betterment Ministry was turned down by his own Labor party because the needed reshuffle would place the combined portfolio in the hands of a minister of *Mapam,* its Alignment partner, while one of its own ministers would be transferred to a more junior portfolio. Circumstances such as these have led one observer to describe the cabinet as "a federation of ministry heads rather than a Government."[10]

The drawbacks of coalition government are perhaps felt most by the prime minister. The intensive and drawn out negotiations which he must hold with potential partners bring him up against the trammels of coalition from the outset. Ben-Gurion when presenting his Government in the newly elected Second Knesset in October 1951, after the president had, in August, assigned him the task of its formation, told the house that he had in the interval met fifty-five times with seven parties before arriving at a coalition agreement with a few of them.[11] The bargaining needed to put together other Governments has been not much less arduous, except in cases where the new coalition and Government were both essentially continuations of their predecessors, as upon the resignation, in absence of any crisis, of the prime minister, or upon his death.

Respecting the choice of ministers by his partners to the coalition agreement, the prime minister has nothing to say. And though in his own party he may have a decisive voice in making the cabinet assignments, he may often have to bow to its will in that regard even if he is the undisputed party leader: for example, Ben-Gurion, whose authority was almost unlimited, had to defer at least twice to his party's wishes with respect to appointment of a minister;[12] and when Golda Meir, at the height of her popularity, chose H. Bar Lev as minister of commerce and industry, it did not pass unchallenged within the Labor Alignment. Illustrative generally of the coalition situation were the difficulties of Prime Minister Begin in replacing resigned ministers, notwithstanding the unprecedented authority conceded him at one point by his Liberal partners in *Likud,* to choose the ministers from their Section: it took from October 1979 to March 1980 for him to replace the resigned minister of foreign affairs; after the resignation of Defense Minister Weizman in May 1980, disagreement about a successor compelled Mr. Begin himself (pursuant to provisions in the Basic Law on the Government) to hold the defense portfolio for over a year, until the following election.

The zeal of each coalition ally to control the appointment of cabinet personnel accounts for the practice followed early on when a new minister was to be appointed: the Government would resign and another would be formed to include the addition. Only in 1952 were amendments passed to the Transition Law providing that additions to an incumbent Government, or a transfer of functions between ministers, could be made simply with Knesset approval.

To secure united support of its program and of the Government, a code of discipline has been an essential ingredient of every coalition. A typical example is the code which formed part of the agreement signed in 1974 between the Labor Alignment, Independent Liberals, and Civil Rights Movement. It laid down, among other things, detailed procedures for clearance of individual members' parliamentary initiatives with the coalition executive, relevant ministers, and member groups; for moving of amendments; and for voting on coalition lines. The signed coalition agreement may contain the outlines only of disciplinary provisions, as did that of the Likud-led coalition, drawn up in June 1977 and reconfirmed by successive coalitions, which provided for the composition of, and direction by, the coalition executive, and for adoption of a disciplinary code.

A Knesset member in the coalition is bound by two or three rings of discipline that are not always concentric: his party's Section (if he is in a federative Group); his Group; and the coalition. Conflict of loyalty is prevented in large measure by overlap of personnel on the executive committees of these bodies, and by attendance at their meetings, as occasion demands, of affiliated ministers; before the coalition executive, the Government is expected to bring every matter prior to its introduction in the Knesset. However, a coalition agreement is essentially one between the member Groups. And indeed, except when a coalition is so small that a nonconforming individual can jeopardize its majority in the Knesset, its troubles are generally due to the dissent of member Groups, or of their Sections (as noted in Chapter 8).

The extent to which a contentious question may set coalition allies against one another, drawing all ready lines of cleavage at once, was perhaps best illustrated by the civil marriage issue which came to the fore in the 1970s, while the coalition consisted of the Labor Alignment, NRP, and the Independent Liberals. In 1972, when a bill by the Independent Liberal G. Hausner to make civil marriage possible for persons refused marriage by the Rabbinate was about to come up in the house, the Government (who had also to take account of the NRP Group's stand) decided to apply coalition discipline against the bill and to determine whether it would not affect the status quo in religious matters and thus contravene the coalition agreement. The Independent Liberals, however, refused to back down from their advocacy of the bill and were supported by the *Mapam* Section of the Alignment—thus splitting the third coalition partner down the middle. A serious crisis was averted only by putting off the vote after the bill's preliminary consideration. When an identical bill in 1976 produced the same conflicting alignments, a warning by NRP that it would regard the bill's reference to a committee as a clear violation of the coalition agreement had the desired effect—its removal from the agenda. The coalition was saved, but not without a glaring display of disunity. While the Independent Liberals and *Mapam* were allowed freedom to vote according to their position, the entire Labor party Section of the Alignment, whose greater number would be decisive, was compelled to oppose the initiative despite protest from its ranks; the repressed dissenters were allowed only one abstention and a statement on the vote.

A code of discipline, as the above case shows, may be only of limited value when the partners differ in their interpretation of the coalition agreement. Moreover, up until 1962, ministers could not be dismissed if they or their parliamentary Groups voted contrary to Government policy, or for any other reason. If determined on a minister's ejection from the cabinet at any cost, the prime minister had to resign (unless the Government as a whole did so), bringing the Government down with him so that he might form a new Government of the desired composition. Prime Minister Sharett took this step to oust his General Zionist cabinet colleagues in 1955, as already noted, and Ben-Gurion acted similarly on two occasions, the first time in 1957, when he could not secure the resignation of the ministers from *Ahdut Ha'avodah* after they had leaked confidential information, and again in 1959, when that Group and *Mapam* voted against the Government's decision to sell arms to Germany. The only cases of a forced resignation were Ben-Gurion's effective ouster by slow degrees of Foreign Minister Sharett over policy differences in 1956, and Prime Minister Eshkol's elimination from the cabinet in 1965 of Housing Minister Y. Almogi, who had publicly taken sides with Ben-Gurion, who was then the premier's harshest critic; and in both instances the departing minister was from the prime minister's own party.

Prime Minister Ben-Gurion's inability to oust rebellious ministers without himself resigning motivated him to seek a legal sanction for their discharge. Consequently, in 1962 provisions were enacted (as an amendment to the Transition Law 1949) requiring a minister to support the Government by vote in the Knesset plenum, on pain of dismissal, and making him similarly responsible for the votes of his parliamentary Group. The amendment provides that a minister voting against or abstaining on a Government proposal is deemed to have resigned from the Government from the day on which it makes a statement in the house to that effect; and that he is likewise deemed to have resigned, upon a Government statement, in the event his Group has voted for or abstained on a motion of no-confidence in the Government, a question concerning budget, financial, or defense matters—or any other matter to which the Government chooses to apply the clause. It is stipulated, though that in a case of Group dissent the Government must first decide within a week that there has been an infraction under this provision; a Group may also receive the Government's prior consent to vote independently or abstain.

The 1962 coalition-discipline clauses were criticized by the opposition for turning the tables by reversing, as it were, the principle of Government responsibility to the Knesset in making the house, albeit through the coalition Groups only, accountable to the Government. On the practical side, the provisions are hedged by significant qualifications: the effective resignation of the minister hinges on a formal statement by the Government to be made at its discretion within the limit of two weeks from the date of the minister's transgressing vote, or of the Government's decision that a Group vote constituted an infringement of responsibility under the provisions.

The cautious formulation of the 1962 amendment took account of coalition facts which often make it expedient to overlook or forgive dissenting votes or abstentions of political allies so as to preserve the Government's parliamentary majority. And indeed, since the amendment's adoption, the coalition discipline provisions have been disregarded far more often than applied. For example, in 1969 the cabinet decided in advance to refrain from adopting a decision in connection with the NRP Group's declared intention of abstaining in a confidence vote over Sabbath television; after the Independent Liberals refused to withdraw their separate amendments to the definition of a Jew in the Law of the Return in 1970, the coalition executive merely recorded this as an infringement of discipline; and in 1978, when the *La'am* Section of *Likud* abstained on a vote of no-confidence, the coalition decided against applying the legal sanction.

Also the failure of ministers to support the Government on cardinal questions has been overlooked; both the abstention of Finance Minister Y. Hurvitz in 1980 on a no-confidence motion concerning the Government's policy on Golan, while seated at the Government table, and the refusal of Energy Minister Y. Berman to support the Government's Golan Bill in 1981, passed without invocation of the discipline clauses. The only time the clauses were applied was in 1976, when Mr. Rabin dismissed the NRP ministers, and as we saw above, the Government then lost its necessary coalition base and resigned.

The 1962 discipline clauses are moreover applicable only to the vote and do not provide for dismissal of a minister who is disloyal in other ways, who leaks confidential information or makes public statements conflicting with Government policy, or is simply inefficient. For years, legislative efforts of members to empower the prime minister to remove a cabinet colleague in the interest of good government met with a stock reply from the Government: that in coalition circumstances any move by the premier to discharge a minister would produce a Government crisis. However, in 1981, recognizing perhaps that the prime minister must be vested with such a power in order to overcome clashes also with his own party colleagues in the cabinet, the Knesset amended the Basic Law on the Government so as to state that a minister is responsible to the prime minister, and that the prime minister, may dismiss him after notifying the Government, having then only to inform the Knesset upon taking the step. Though coalition realities may in practice dissuade any prime minister from applying the 1981 dismissal amendment to a minister not from his party, it was found advisable to stipulate among the parity provisions in the National Unity coalition of 1984 that the prime minister would not exercise that right against a colleague from the vice-prime minister's camp except on the latter's request.

A closely related question, associated like the above with the problems of coalition government, has been the extent of individual ministerial responsibility to the Knesset. While a minister is clearly answerable for his department to the Knesset both on the floor and in the committees, no real parliamentary sanction can be brought against him. Members' attempts to make the individual minister subject by law to a vote of no-confidence have been resisted by every Government with the claim that this could only have a divisive effect on the coalition and undermine the Government. Another official argument curiously advanced was that a sanction against an individual minister is already available, only it is politico-public; but under the party-list electoral system, this could only mean penalization of the next candidates list of his entire party. However, with the aforementioned 1981 amendment, the Knesset rendered its verdict also on this question by juxtaposing in one section the disposition concerning the minister's responsibility to the premier with that fixing the Government's collective responsibility to the Knesset (Sec. 4 of the Basic Law as amended)—as much as to say: the prime minister being vested with the authority (albeit theoretical) to dismiss a minister, the only way for the Knesset to get at the minister is to move no-confidence in the Government.

The weaknesses of coalition Government have been succinctly described by two former ministers: Dov Yosef, who held various portfolios from 1949 to 1966, draws attention to the time-wasting hassles between ministers representing the different coalition partners, with some acting the part of an opposition within and diverting the Government from its main business, or compelling compromises repugnant to the majority;[13] Gad Yaacobi, a former transport minister (and, again, Minister of Economy and Planning in the 1984 Unity Government), voicing the same strictures and emphasizing the difficulty of such a Government in making decisions, compares it to a "co-ordinating committee of dissimilar interests and views."[14] However, as against such claims, some observers have noted a positive side to coalition Governments—that they provide a built-in system of checks and balances against arbitrary executive action.

THE OPPOSITION

While it is essentially through the coalition that Knesset and Government work in concert, the opposition is by nature the spearhead of critical parliamentary oversight. Though questions, members' motions and bills, and criticism of Government policies emanate from all quarters of the house, their proportion from the opposition is significantly greater; and a Government defeat is due more often to the absence of a sufficient number of coalition members than to their cross-voting (this is less true in committees, and within the coalition-Group forums, where disapproval of Government actions by coalition members is a commonplace). Though no single parliamentary Group is officially recognized as the opposition, rule and convention imply such recognition. Further, developments in recent years have effectively given the leading opposition Group a new important role—if we except only the intervals of National Unity Government, which from the parliamentary standpoint are an aberration, necessary as it may be.

The rights of opposition Groups on the floor, on committees, and in other Knesset activity are ensured by rule and practice. Providing for proportional division of speaking time between Groups in party-basis debates, the Knesset Rules lay down that the largest opposition Group shall be called to put up the first speaker; that much prized right, when contested by two Groups of equal strength in the house, has been awarded to the one whose list actually received the larger number of votes in the election. The Group quotas of members' motions and bills, introduced in 1966, have been consistently allocated by the House Committee so as to favor opposition Groups out of recognition that coalition views are in large measure presented by the ministers, whose time and opportunities for speaking in the house are, besides, unlimited. One of the tellers appointed by the chair to count a vote will always be from the opposition. On committees the opposition's participation is vouched by the rule that members shall be assigned to them on the principle of Group representation. Some committee chairmanships have always gone to the large opposition Groups, as have vice-chairmanships of the Knesset. Established custom also ensures the presence of opposition members on Knesset delegations abroad.

The most serious weakness of the opposition has been its many-striped composition. Ranging in number over the years from three to eight—with four or five the most usual—the opposition Groups have often included the opposite extremes of the Knesset's political spectrum. Even in their common desire to overturn the Government they would dissipate their strength, each, for example, usually presenting a separate summation motion after debate. The appearance of an integral opposition was retarded by the proportional party-list electoral system; and despite that system's generous endowment of the opposition Groups with leadership by the regular return of top names, they could not realistically present an alternative Government.

Two events in 1965 ushered in a change of status for the opposition—and effectively a new political pattern for the parliamentary system. That year saw on the one hand the combination into one bloc of the long-standing opposition forces, *Herut* and the Liberal party, into one electoral and parliamentary bloc (as *Gahal* at first, and later embracing additional Groups, as the *Likud*), and on the other hand, of the Labor parties, *Mapai* and *Ahdut Ha'avodah,* as the Labor Alignment. In truth, there had been earlier combinations of parties and Groups, as noted in Chapter 8; but those were short-lived, and while the Alignment in 1965 was only a reunion of forces that had earlier separated, it was lasting and grew further, like the *Likud,* in number of components. Though both consolidations were accompanied by concurrent fission (the Independent Liberals splitting from the Liberals, and *Rafi* from *Mapai*), each bloc went on to grow further, coopting fresh political elements; and the federative Group of each in the Knesset gained standing so that when not in the Government coalition it was far and away the leading opposition Group both in number and repute.

Thus the 1977 election merely reversed the positions of the *Likud* and Alignment Groups in the Knesset, the *Likud* moving from the principal role in opposition to the leadership of the coalition, the Alignment switching over in the opposite direction; but the opposition as such in fact gained new importance now, being led for the first time by men who had already been at the helm of Government (whereas the *Likud* opposition, previously, had behind it only the brief association with the National Unity Governments, in which it had not been the chief element).

The emerging Government-opposition relationship between *Likud* and Alignment has strengthened an important convention. Not only does the Prime Minister take the chief opposition's leaders into his confidence at critical moments, as he did, for example, on the eve of the 1956 Sinai campaign, of the Six Days War in 1967, and of the Entebbe hijack rescue in 1976; he also briefs them privately and consults with them from time to time on foreign policy and defense matters, whether prior to a state mission abroad or an important debate, or as occasion otherwise requires. The chairman of the Knesset's Foreign Affairs and Security Committee generally attends these meetings. Nevertheless, there are opposition complaints that such meetings are too few. Regular talks between the prime minister and the opposition leader have been proposed by a coalition floor leader.

A growing recognition of the special role of the largest opposition Group can be noted also inside the house. At extraordinary sittings, such as, for example, those addressed by visiting Presidents Sadat, Carter, and Mitterand, it has become accepted practice for the leader of the main opposition to appear as the only speaker after the prime minister, though this manner of proceeding on earlier occasions had given rise to protest from the smaller opposition Groups. Further, the Groups agreed between them that speeches of the prime minister and of the ''leader of the opposition'' would not be disturbed unduly by interjections, though the understanding is often honored in the breach. Significant too is the face-to-face seating of the *Likud* and Alignment in the chamber, an arrangement followed, with only a brief exception, since 1970, when the previous rank-order seating of Groups by size was abandoned.

Each of the two Groups when out of office sought also by its own organizational means to create a serious and responsible opposition, but was hampered at times by its federative character. *Gahal* set up a "shadow cabinet" in 1973; as the *Likud,* in 1974, it proposed an alternative budget. When the *Likud* Group sought in 1976 to establish teams for monitoring by subject area the whole range of ministries, there was friction between its *Herut* and Liberal sections over choice of personnel. In 1980, with the Labor Alignment in opposition, its chairman, Shimon Peres, attempted to set up a joint opposition executive committee to include also representatives of three smaller Groups; but the move was resisted by the Alignment's *Mapam* Section.

Members' bills that would grant official status of opposition leader to the head of the largest opposition Group, provided it numbers at least twenty or twenty-five members, and make him something of a counterpart to the prime minister, have been rejected both by Alignment and *Likud*-led governments. However, neither these parliamentary checks, not intersectional impediments like those just mentioned, are as significant as the unmistakable materialization which has occurred, of an opposition that is in fact a likely alternative Government. The 1981 election, by returning the two large adversary blocs in equal strength and eliminating or reducing at the same time any other sizeable Groups, has further reinforced the trend toward a virtual two-party system.

Nor was the process halted by the seemingly greater political fragmentation which occurred in the election of 1984. Of the thirteen small Groups a number committed themselves in advance and unconditionally to one of the two blocs as allies in any Government that might be formed, so that in the result the two-party pattern was in fact reinforced (see note after Table A11): and though both sides entered the National Unity Government, the coalition agreement deliberately set out explicit terms of parity between "the two camps." While the Labor Alignment at the same time underwent an important change of composition, losing the leftist *Mapam* and taking in the new centrist *Yahad,* its Group in the Knesset remained one of the two large federative bodies with undiminished potential as the chief support of a more narrowly based Government or as a cohesive opposition.

Perspective of a Strengthened Knesset

JEREMIADS about the present low estate of parliament and its loss of ground to the executive are no less common in Israel than elsewhere; and indeed, instances in which the Government has its will in the Knesset through the coalition majority are a commonplace, while on the other hand, as we have seen, it is capable of sustaining occasional parliamentary defeats, making sure that on no-confidence votes—which are in any case an ultimate weapon sparingly employed—all its supporters are on hand. Nonetheless, in a variety of ways the authority of the Knesset has been reinforced and, arguably, the tilt of power has been in favor of the legislative arm.

First, the resolution of particular questions has not infrequently secured the Knesset an accretion of power, whether upon its self-assertion or the Government's voluntary concession. An early instance was the Transition to the Second Knesset Bill of 1951. As proposed by the Government, the bill would have left a parliamentary interregnum between terms; the Law Committee changed this so that the term of an outgoing Knesset would end only with the convening of its successor. Further, an amendment moved by members on the second reading and adopted provided that this measure, and certain election legislation, would not be subject to alteration or suspension by a minister's Emergency Regulations. Since then, other enactments have been given the same immunity. A more recent and distinct example of the executive's subordination to parliament was the provision in 1968, in the Basic Law on the Government, making the transfer of functions between ministers subjects to Knesset approval, and thus to a debate before the vote; previously, only announcement in the house was required. That Basic Law also made parliamentary approval mandatory for the creation, unification, or division of ministries, which had earlier been solely the Government's prerogative.

Second, and of more general import for the augmentation of Knesset powers, was the cumulative weight of certain developments and events that have already been described. With respect to legislation, executive discretion has been narrowed in two ways: the laws tend to be more detailed, while ministerial regulations affecting matters of principle are made more consistently subject to approval by a Knesset committee. And the committees, each within its purview a watchdog for examining and cross-questioning ministers and officials, have sharply increased their activity; while in earlier years a permanent committee would on average meet less than fifty times in a session, since 1970 that number has been over eighty.[1] At the same time, the Knesset is alert to any inclination of the Government to use a committee in order to by-pass the house. Thus, for example, when the finance minister declared on 14 February 1984 that he would double the travel tax by an administrative order with the approval of the Finance Committee, after the house had earlier adopted amendments rendering nugatory his bill to that purpose, the Knesset quickly reacted: the next day the matter was raised in the house as a point of privilege by an opposition leader, and Chairman Savidor replied that he had already spoken that morning to the minister, and the latter had assured him that on second thought he would table a redrafted bill.

The appointment of the state comptroller as commissioner of public complaints in 1971, and the establishment in 1974 of a separate Committee on State Control, always chaired by an opposition member (except under the National Unity Government), have reinforced systematic Knesset supervision of Government activity. At the same time, the number of members' bills enacted into law has increased, so that in the 1977–81 Knesset they accounted for nearly a fifth of the legislative output (see Table 7). And with respect to important international agreements, as noted in Chapter 12, consultation of the Knesset has become virtually mandatory despite the Government's exclusive powers in that sphere.

Also, the very circumstances of coalition government, as we have seen, give the parliamentary Groups great powers while weakening the executive. And though this weakness was often offset by a divided opposition, the emergence of large federative Groups in the Knesset have tended to the formation of an opposition substantially united. Indeed, as Table 9 shows, not only was Mr. Shamir's Government (like its predecessor) faced by an opposition whose leading Group, the Labor Alignment, outnumbered the major coalition Group, *Likud;* his own *Herut* Section within *Likud* did not enjoy nearly the same predominance as the Labor party Section did within the Alignment.

Further, the switch to a *Likud*-centered Government in 1977, after nearly thirty years of Labor rule, went, in the nature of things, to redress somewhat the balance of power between Knesset and Government. While there had been many changes of Government during the decades of a *Mapai* or Alignment plurality, enjoyment by the same dominant political force of uninterrupted hegemony from the birth of the state (with smaller coalition partners varying according to ups and downs in the latest poll) enabled it to consolidate the position of the Government while controlling all main power foci in the Knesset as well as the most influential cabinet portfolios. In contrast, the first *Likud*-led Government had, among other things, to countenance the assignment of the chairmanships of two important Knesset committees—finance and labor—to its small coalition partner, *Agudat Yisrael;* and Mr. Begin, casting about for a foreign minister, had to draw Moshe Dayan away from the Labor Alignment; of the three successive finance ministers, two were from parties other than Begin's *Herut*—the Liberal, S. Ehrlich, and the State List's Y. Hurvitz. Under the second Begin Government in 1981, the leadership of the coalition was for the first time placed in the hands of a member not from the coalition's dominant group, Mr. Abraham Shapira of *Agudat Yisrael*. Further, *Likud*-led Governments had twice to accept election by the Knesset of the opposition's candidate as president of the state (Mr. Yitzhak Navon in 1978, and Mr. Chaim Herzog in 1983).

Finally, it is a mark of firmly founded parliamentary democracy that a minority Government was never considered—let alone, established—in Israel. In the political stalemate that resulted from the 1984 election, one of the important spurs to a National Unity Government was the fact that both Alignment and *Likud,* though each had smaller allies, flinched from the idea of taking the helm in a minority Government. And many were the occasions in earlier years, when on the one hand the difficulties of forming a viable coalition, and on the other hand an opposition divided between extremes and the parties unprepared for another election, might have well resulted in a minority Government capable of holding office for an indefinite time. Though, as noted in Chapter 1, historical reasons and the weight of habit did not favor such an outcome at any time, it is no exaggeration to assume that these were underpinned by the ground principle that Government may rest only on a Knesset majority.

Appendix

Knesset Election Results

The following data is from *Toldot Habehirot Laknesset* (Knesset Election History), ed. P. Yerman (Jerusalem: Ministry of Education and Culture, Central Office of Information, 1982); Gad Yaacobi, *The Government* (Tel Aviv: Zemora, Beitan, Modan, 1980), (in Hebrew); and Records of the Central Elections Committee.

Table A1

The First Knesset (elected 25 January 1949)

Total vote (86.9% of electorate): 434,684
Quota per mandate: 3,592

Group*	Percentage of Vote	Number of Mandates
Mapai†	35.7	46
Mapam	14.7	19
United Religious Front†	12.2	16
Herut	11.5	14
General Zionists	5.2	7
Progressive party†	4.1	5
Association of Sephardim and Eastern Communities†	3.5	4
Communist party	3.5	4
Nazareth Region Democratic List†	1.7	2
Fighters List	1.2	1
WIZO	1.2	1
Yemenite Association	1.0	1

*For explanation of names, see Glossary.
†Entered the coalition.

Coalition strength: 73. The Government's resignation in 1950 over the question of education in immigrant camps and the formation of a new Government did not alter the coalition's composition.

Table A2

The Second Knesset (elected 30 July 1951)

Total vote (75.1% of electorate): 924,885
Quota per mandate: 5,692

Group*	Percentage of Vote	Number of Mandates
Mapai †	37.3	45
General Zionists	16.2	20
Mapam	12.5	15
Hapoel Hamizrahi †	6.8	8
Herut	6.6	8
Communist party	4.0	5
Progressive party	3.2	4
Democratic Arab List †	2.4	3
Agudat Yisrael †	2.0	3
Sephardi and Eastern Communities List	1.8	2
Poalei Agudat Yisrael †	1.6	2
Mizrahi †	1.5	2
Progress and Labor †	1.2	1
Yemenite Association	1.2	1
Farm and Development List †	1.1	1

*For explanation of names, see Glossary.
† Entered the coalition.

Coalition strength: 65. During the term there were three changes of Government, two brought on by disagreements within the coalition, and one by Prime Minister Ben-Gurion's temporary retirement and replacement by Moshe Sharett. In the course of these changes the coalition numbered eighty-four between December 1952 and June 1955, by taking in also the General Zionists and Progressive party and excluding *Agudat Yisrael* and *Poalei Agudat Yisrael*.

Table A3

The Third Knesset (elected 26 July 1955)

Total vote (82.8% of electorate): 853,219
Quota per mandate: 6,938

Group*	Percentage of Vote	Number of Mandates
Mapai †	32.2	40
Herut	12.6	15
General Zionists	10.2	13
National Religious Front *(Mizrahi, Hapoel Hamizrahi)* †	9.1	11
Ahdut Ha'avodah †	8.2	10
Mapam †	7.3	9
Torah Front *(Agudat Yisrael, Poalei Agudat Yisrael)*	4.7	6
Communist party	4.5	6
Progressive party †	4.4	5
Democratic Arab List †	1.8	2
Progress and Labor †	1.5	2
Farm and Development List †	1.1	1

*For explanation of names, see Glossary.
†Entered the coalition.

Coalition strength: 80. Though leaks of information from Government meetings caused the prime minister to resign in mid-term and form a new Government, the coalition remained unchanged.

Table A4

The Fourth Knesset (elected 3 November 1959)

Total vote (81.6% of electorate): 969,337
Quota per mandate: 7,800

Group*	Percentage of Vote	Number of Mandates
Mapai†	38.2	47
Herut	13.5	17
National Religious Front (NRP)†	9.9	12
Mapam†	7.2	9
General Zionists	6.2	8
Ahdut Ha'avodah†	6.0	7
Religious Torah Front *(Agudat Yisrael, Poalei Agudat Yisrael)*	4.7	6
Progressive party†	4.6	6
Communist party	2.8	3
Progress and Development†	1.3	2
Cooperation and Fraternity†	1.1	2
Farm and Development List†	1.1	1

*For explanation of names, see Glossary.
†Entered the coalition.

Coalition strength: 86

Table A5

The Fifth Knesset (elected 15 August 1961)

Total vote (81.6% of electorate): 1,006,964
Quota per mandate: 8,332

Group*	Percentage of Vote	Number of Mandates
Mapai†	34.7	42
Herut	13.8	17
Liberal party	13.6	17
National Religious Front (NRP)†	9.8	12
Mapam	7.5	9
Ahdut Ha'avodah†	6.6	8
Communist party	4.2	5
Agudat Yisrael	3.7	4
Poalei Agudat Yisrael†	1.9	2
Cooperation and Fraternity†	1.9	2
Progress and Development†	1.6	2

*For explanation of names, see Glossary.
†Entered the coalition.

Coalition strength: 68. The coalition remained unchanged through two changes of Government, one involving the replacement of Prime Minister Ben-Gurion by Levi Eshkol, the other a dispute within *Mapai*.

Table A6

The Sixth Knesset (elected 2 November 1965)

Total vote (83.0% of electorate): 1,244,988
Quota per mandate: 9,881

Group*	Percentage of Vote	Number of Mandates
Alignment *(Mapai, Ahdut Ha'avodah)*†	36.7	45
Herut-Liberal Bloc *(Gahal)*	21.3	26
National Religious Front (NRP)†	8.9	11
Israel Workers List *(Rafi)*	7.9	10
United Workers party *(Mapam)*†	6.6	8
Independent Liberals†	3.8	5
Agudat Yisrael	3.3	4
New Communist List	2.3	3
Poalei Agudat Yisrael†	1.8	2
Progress and Development†	1.9	2
Cooperation and Fraternity†	1.3	2
Ha'olam Hazeh	1.2	1
Community party	1.1	1

*For explanation of names, see Glossary.
†Entered the coalition.

Coalition strength: 75. Though the National Unity Government formed in 1967 included also *Gahal* and *Rafi,* these two were not parties to the coalition agreement.

Table A7

The Seventh Knesset (elected 28 October 1969)

Total vote (81.7% of electorate): 1,247,981
Quota per mandate: 11,274

Group*	Percentage of Vote	Number of Mandates
Alignment (Labor party, *Mapam*)†	46.2	56
Herut-Liberal Bloc *(Gahal)*†	21.7	26
National Religious Front (NRP)†	9.7	12
Agudat Yisrael	3.2	4
Independent Liberals†	3.2	4
State List	3.1	4
New Communist List	2.8	3
Progress and Development†	1.9	2
Poalei Agudat Yisrael	1.8	2
Cooperation and Fraternity†	1.6	2
Ha'olam Hazeh	1.2	2
Free Center	1.2	2
Communist party	1.1	1

*For explanation of names, see Glossary.
†Entered the coalition.

Coalition strength: 102. With the departure of *Gahal* from the National Unity Government in 1970, the coalition numbered seventy-six.

Table A8

The Eighth Knesset (elected 31 December 1973)

Total vote (78.6% of electorate): 1,566,855
Quota per mandate: 12,424

Group*	Percentage of Vote	Number of Mandates
Alignment (Labor party, *Mapam*)†	39.6	51
Likud (*Herut*-Liberals, State List, Free Center, Land of Israel Activists)	30.2	39
National Religious Front (NRP)†	8.3	10
Religious Torah Front (*Agudat Yisrael, Poalei Agudat Yisrael*)	3.8	5
Independent Liberals†	3.6	4
New Communist List	3.4	4
Civil Rights Movement (CRM)	2.2	3
Progress and Development	1.4	2
Moked	1.4	1
Bedouin and Arab Village List	1.0	1

*For explanation of names, see Glossary.
†Entered the coalition.

Coalition strength: 65. With the formation of the Rabin Government in June 1974, following Mrs. Meir's resignation, the coalition numbered sixty-one, with NRP staying out, while CRM, Progress and Development, and the Bedouin and Village List were included. When in October 1974, NRP joined the coalition and CRM left, there was a coalition of sixty-eight.

Table A9

The Ninth Knesset (elected 17 May 1977)

Total vote (79.2% of electorate): 1,771,276
Quota per mandate: 14,173

Group*	Percentage of Vote	Number of Mandates
Likud (*Herut*-Liberals, *La'am*, State List)†	33.4	43
Alignment (Labor party, *Mapam*)	24.6	32
Democratic Movement for Change (DMC)	11.6	15
National Religious Front (NRP)†	9.2	12
Democratic Front for Peace and Equality (Communists, Black Panthers)	4.6	5
Agudat Yisrael†	3.3	4
Shlomzion†	1.9	2
Sheli	1.6	2
Flatto-Sharon‡	2.0	1
United Arab List	1.4	1
Poalei Agudat Yisrael	1.3	1
Civil Rights Movement (CRM)	1.2	1
Independent Liberals	1.2	1

*For explanation of names, see Glossary.
†Entered the coalition.
‡Mr. Flatto-Sharon was the only candidate on his list, so that its large surplus vote went unused.

Coalition strength: 61. With the entry of DMC in October 1977, the coalition rose in number to seventy-six, only to shrink back by degrees to less than a majority of the house. A dissolution law was therefore passed in February 1981.

Table A10

The Tenth Knesset (elected 30 June 1981)

Total vote (78.5% of electorate): 1,937,366
Quota per mandate: 15,312

Group*	Percentage of Vote	Number of Mandates
Likud (*Herut*-Liberals, *La-am*)†	37.1	48
Alignment (Labor party, *Mapam*)	36.6	47
National Religious Front (NRP)†	4.9	6
Agudat Yisrael†	3.7	4
Democratic Front for Peace and Equality (Communists, Black Panthers)	3.4	4
Tehiya	2.3	3
Tami†	2.3	3
Telem	1.6	2
Shinui-Center party	1.5	2
Civil Rights and Peace Movement (CRM)	1.4	1

*For explanation of names, see Glossary.
†Entered the coalition.

Coalition strength: 61. When in October 1983 Yitzhak Shamir formed a new Government following Mr. Begin's resignation, the coalition numbered sixty-four, after there had been a number of changes of affiliation.

Table A11

The Eleventh Knesset (elected 23 July 1984)

Total vote (78.1% of electorate): 2,073,321
Quota per mandate: 16,786

Group*	Percentage of Vote	Number of Mandates
Alignment (Labor party, *Mapam,* Independent Liberals)†	34.9	44
Likud (*Herut*-Liberals, *La'am*)†	31.9	41
Tehiya-Tsomet	4.0	5
National Religious Front (NRP)†	3.5	4
Democratic Front for Peace and Equality (Communists, Black Panthers)	3.4	4
Sephardi Torah Guardians†	3.1	4
Shinui-Center party†	2.6	3
Civil Rights and Peace Movement (CRM)	2.4	3
Yahad†	2.2	3
Progressive List for Peace	1.8	2
Agudat Yisrael†	1.7	2
Morasha†	1.7	2
Tami	1.5	1
Kach Movement	1.2	1
Ometz†	1.2	1

*For explanation of names, see Glossary.
†Entered the coalition.

Coalition strength: 97. This number resulted from changes that took place at the formation of the Unity Government: *Mapam* took its six-man Section out of the Alignment; Mr. Y. Sarid left the Alignment to join CRM; *Yahad* entered the Alignment.

The plethora of Groups listed above may appear more tractable if the two camps in the coalition are listed as follows:

Alignment and allies,	*Likud* and allies,
Shinui—Center party	Sephardi Torah Guardians
Ometz	*Agudat Yisrael*
	Morasha

NRP-neutral

The above two-camp array is even more inclusive than shown, for should the Unity Government fall apart, a narrowly based Alignment Government could be sure also of CRM's pledged support and could be equally confident that *Mapam* would be back in the coalition. On the other hand a *Likud*-led Government could count also on *Tehiya*'s support.

Notes

1—PRE-STATE INFLUENCES

1. Theodor Herzl (1860–1904), a Viennese journalist and playwright, was the founder of modern political Zionism and is regarded as the father of the state of Israel. The term "Zionism," in use for some years before the first Congress, is credited to another Viennese Jew, Nathan Birnbaum.

2. By 1936 there were Zionist Federations in forty-five countries while the total membership of the World Organization increased from 114 thousand in 1899 to well over two million in 1946. See N. M. Gelber, *Hacongressim Hazioniym* (The Zionist Congresses) (Jerusalem: Executive of the Zionist Organization, 1956).

3. Cf. *Standing Orders of the Congress,* Transl. from the German (Jerusalem: Executive of the Zionist Organization, 1947), Art. 26; *Takanon Haknesset* (Knesset Rules of Procedure) (Jerusalem: Government Printer), 1959 Rule 56, and 1965 Rule 56.

4. See, for example, remarks in the debates of the Provisional Council on its Standing Orders and on the nation's first election law. *Moetzet Hamedina Hazmanit, Protocol Hadiyunim* (Tel Aviv: Government Printer), June 17, 1948, p. 37; Oct. 28, 1948, pp. 16–17.

5. Zionist Organization, *Constitution,* transl. from the German (London, 1929), Art. 50.

6. For instance, in 1929 a delegate could be elected by two thousand votes, and in Palestine, by one thousand. *Ibid.,* Art. 25.

7. *Ibid.,* Art. 53.

8. I. Cohen, *the Zionist Movement* (London: Muller, 1945), p. 128.

9. See B. Akzin, "The Role of Parties in Israeli Democracy" *Journal of Politics* 17 (Nov. 1955), p. 509.

10. The most used election posters of the Alignment were simply large "you can depend on" pictures of Golda Meir, Moshe Dayan et al. See, for example, advertisement in *Jerusalem Post Magazine,* 17 October 1969, p. 9.

11. This attitude was well summed up by J. Marcus in "Avoda Zkuka Lemafdal" (Labor needs the National Religious party) *Ha'aretz* (Tel Aviv, daily), January 31, 1969.

12. See M. Duverger, *Political Parties; their Origin and Activity in the Modern State,* transl. Barbara and Robert North (London: Methuen, 1951), p. 325.

13. The practice of adjudging each community a religious group to be granted a large measure of autonomy had prevailed in the Middle East since ancient times; nor did it end in Palestine with the Ottoman regime. It was carried over by the mandatory and later into Israel's legal system. Even today personal status in Israel is within the jurisdiction of the courts of the repective religious communities.

14. The Executive Committee was officially recognized only years later with the passing of an amendment to the Regulations. Palestine, Gazette, March 15, 1934. p. 218.

15. For instance, in 1931 the Assembly, with a membership of seventy-one, appointed a National Council of twenty-three members and twenty deputy members. *Pratei-Kol Asefat Hanivharim* (Protocols of the Elected Assembly) (Jerusalem: Central Zionist Archives) 9–12 February 1931, Resolutions, p. 7.

16. *Ibid.,* 7–11 October, 1920, Resolutions, p. 3.

17. For lists of members by political group of all four Assemblies, see M. Attias, ed. *Sefer Hateudot shel Havaad Haleumi Leknesset Yisrael b'Erez Yisrael* (Documents of the National Council of the Jewish Community of Palestine), 2nd ed. (Jerusalem: Raphael Cohen, 1963), pp. 430–39.

18. M. Burstein, *Self Government of the Jews in Palestine since 1900* (Tel Aviv: Divan Book Shop, 1934), pp. 110–11.

19. *Ibid.,* p. 120.

20. For the pertinent lists of Congress delegates, assemblymen and Knesset members, see *Din Veheshbon Hacongress Hazioni Ha-22* (Stenographic Report of the 22nd Zionist Congress), Basle, 9–24 Dec., 1946, (Jerusalem: Executive of the Zionist Organization, 1947), pp. 26–32; Attias, Documents, pp. 438–39; *Divrei Haknesset* (The Knesset Record) (Jerusalem: Government Printer), 14 Feb. 1949, pp. 3–4; and *Israel Government Year Book* 5730 (1969–70) (Jerusalem: The Central Office of Information, 1970), pp. 38–39.

2—THE PROVISIONAL STATE COUNCIL AND GOVERNMENT

1. Z. Sharef, *Three Days* (Tel Aviv: Am Oved, 1959), (in Hebrew), pp. 103–104.

2. *Moetzet Hamedina Hazmanit* (Provisional State Council), Protocol, 8 July 1948, pp. 12–13.

3. *Ibid.*, 12 August 1948, pp. 23–24.

4. See *ibid.*, 30 December 1948, p. 38; 21 January 1949, p. 30.

5. *Ibid.*, 2 December 1948, p. 4.

6. *Divrei Haknesset* (The Knesset Record) (Jerusalem: Government Printer), 7 March 1962, pp. 1494–95.

7. *Moetzet Hamedina Hazmanit,* 23 June 1948, p. 10.

8. *Ibid.*, 20 January 1949, pp. 9–12.

9. Sharef, *Three Days,* p. 102.

10. *Minhelet Ha'am. Pkudat Yisud Hamedina. Hatza'ah Shishit* (Peoples Administration. Establishment of the State Ordinance. Sixth Draft) (Jerusalem: Israel State Archives) 7 May 1948 (File No. 466). Finally adopted as the Law and Administration Ordinance.

11. Sharef, *Three Days,* pp. 41–42.

12. *Ibid.*, pp. 220–21.

13. *Moetzet Hamedina Hazmanit,* 1 July 1948, p. 14.

14. *Ibid.*, 9 December 1948, p. 20.

15. *Ibid.*, 22 July 1948, p. 16.

16. *Ibid.*, 14 May 1948, p. 9.

3—IN QUEST OF A CONSTITUTION

1. *Moetzet Hamedina Hazmanit, Va'adat Hahuka* (Provisional State Council, Constitution Committee), Booklets Nos. 1–5, (Tel Aviv, 1948).

2. See *Moetzet Hamedina Hazmanit, Protocol Hadiyunim* (Debates), 13 January 1949, pp. 9–12, 20.

3. *Divrei Haknesset* (The Knesset Record) (Jerusalem: Government Printer), 13 June 1950, p. 1743.

4. *Ibid.*, 8 May 1950, p. 1329.

5. A. Rubinstein, *Hok Umishpat Beyisrael Bishnot Hashivim* (Israel's Legal System in the Seventies) (Van Leer Institute of Jerusalem), Publications, 1, 1972, p. 2.

6. *Divrei Haknesset,* 3 February 1964, p. 937.

7. Holders of Public Office (Benefits) Law, 1969, Section 6(a), 23 *Laws* 107.

8. For an English translation of the judgment, see *Israel Law Review* 4, no. 4 (October–December 1969), pp. 559–65.

9. See press communiqué of the Law Commitee, 11 February 1976. Justice Minister H. Zadok opened the first reading on 17 February.

10. See exchange between S. Ehrlich and Justice Minister Shapira, *Divrei Haknesset,* 6 February 1973, p. 1565; 27 February, p. 1837.

11. According to N. Nir, *ibid.*, 5 February 1963, p. 1039.

12. *Ibid.*, 9 February 1960, p. 586; 7 November 1962., p. 85; 15 January 1964, pp. 787–92.

13. *Ibid.*, 31 August 1966, p. 2530.

14. *Ibid., 6 August 1968, p. 3094.*

15. *Ibid.*, 17 September 1973, pp. 4438, 4440.

16. "Yom Hahuledet shel Haknesset" (The Knesset's Birthday), *Akadamot* (organ of the Labor party's university graduates), January 1973, p. 10 (author's translation).

17. See Defense (Emergency) Regulations 1945, *Palestine Gazette,* Suppl. 2, 27 September 1945, p. 1055. Some of these Regulations, which empower the administrative and military authorities—as successors to the high commissioner and the military commander of the mandatory power—to place persons under police supervision; to detain and even to deport them, were replaced only in March 1979 by the milder Emergency Powers (Detention) Law.

18. *Divrei Haknesset,* 4 June 1974, p. 1584.

19. Second Knesset (Transition) Law, 1951, Secs. 9–10, 5 *Laws* 95.

4—ELECTIONS AND PARTIES

1. See tables in *Jerusalem Post,* 7 January 1974.

2. See Yehoshua Bitsur in *Ma'ariv* (Tel Aviv, daily), 27 February, 1981.

3. Sarah Honig, in *Jerusalem Post Magazine,* 22 May 1981, p. 5.

4. See views of Justice Minister M. Nissim, cited by A. Wallfish in *Jerusalem Post,* 16 December 1983.

5. According to Professor A. Arian, as reported by Lea Levavi in *Jerusalem Post,* 10 July 1981.

6. These include B. Akzin, "The Knesset," *International Social Science Journal* 13, no. 4 (1961), pp. 567–82; Avraham Brichta, *The Social Political and Cultural Background of Knesset Members in Israel* (Hebrew University of Jerusalem: Ph. D. diss., 1972 (abstract in English); E. Gutmann and J. M. Landau, "The Political Elite and National Leadership in Israel," in G. Lenczowski, ed., *Political Elites in the Middle East,* (Washington: American Enterprise Institute for Public Policy Research, 1975); D. Caspi, "How Representative is the Knesset," *Jerusalem Quarterly* No. 14 (Winter 1980).

7. *Divrei Haknesset* (The Knesset Record) (Jerusalem: Government Printer), 3 February 1969, p. 1384.

8. Records of the Central Elections Committee.

9. See *Ha'aretz* (Tel Aviv, daily), 29 December 1974.

10. See Avraham Brichta, "Women in the Knesset: 1949–1969," *Parliamentary Affairs* 28, no. 1 (Winter 1974/75), pp. 31–50; Research paper by Giora Goldberg, reviewed by Y. Sussman in *Jerusalem Post,* 26 January 1984.

11. Shevah Weiss and Avraham Brichta, "Private Members' Bills in Israel's Parliament—the Knesset," *Parliamentary Affairs* 23, no. 1 (Winter 1969/70), pp. 31–32; Shevah Weiss, *Haknesset* (The Israeli Parliament) (Tel Aviv: Achiasaf, 1977), pp. 225–26, 242.

12. Records of the Central Elections Committee.

13. G. S. Mahler, *The Knesset: Parliament in the Israeli* Political System (London: Associated University Presses, 1981), p. 174.

14. Gad Yaacobi and Ehud Gera, *The Freedom to Choose* (Tel Aviv: Am Oved, 1975) (in Hebrew), p. 55.

15. See L. Boim, "The Financing of Elections," *Israel at the Polls; the Knesset Elections of 1977,* ed. H. R. Penniman (Washington, D.C.: 1979), p. 199; Aryeh Wolman, in *Jerusalem Post,* 5 July 1981.

16. Report of the state comptroller, Mr. Y. Tunik, to the chairman of the Knesset, 15 March 1982.

17. *Ibid.*

18. See Aryeh Rubinstein, *Jerusalem Post,* 11 September 1983.

5—KNESSET MEMBERS

1. M. Shahal, chairman of the Alignment Group, cited by Aryeh Rubinstein, *Jerusalem Post,* 20 June 1983.

2. *Divrei Haknesset* (The Knesset Record) (Jerusalem: Government Printer), p. 1414.

6—KNESSET ORGANIZATION

1. *Jerusalem Post Supplement,* 30 August 1966, p. 9.

2. "Parliament and the Audio-Visual Media," *rapporteur* N. Lorch, *Constitutional and Parliamentary Information,* 1st Quarter 1978, p. 20.

3. A. Zidon, *Beth Hanivcharim* (The Knesset—Israel's Parliament) (Jerusalem: Achiasaf, 1964), p. 151.

4. See *Jerusalem Post,* 24 January 1980.

5. Rule 22, *Knesset Rules of Procedure,* [transl. S. Sager] in *Constitutional and Parliamentary Information,* 1st Quarter 1982.

6. *Divrei Haknesset* (The Knesset Record) (Jerusalem: Government Printer), 15 July 1980, pp. 3876--78.

7. The two members were M. Virshubski of *Shinui* (six members) and G. Hausner of the Independent Liberals (one member). The sponsor of the bill was A. Rubinstein of *Shinui.*

8. Nahum Nir of the *Ahdut Ha'avodah* Group was elected chairman on 2 March 1959.

9. See *Divrei Haknesset,* 2 March 1982, pp. 1653–54; *Jerusalem Post,* 4 March 1982.

10. *Jerusalem Post,* 1 August 1979.

11. *Ibid.,* 3 June 1982.

12. M. Avidov-Cohen, elected vice-chairman in 1981.

7—COMMITTEES

1. See M. Brecher, *The Foreign Policy System of Israel, (London: Oxford University Press, 1972), pp. 131–32.*

2. *See Y. P. Flaxer, Haknesset Uvaadoteha* (The Knesset and its Committees) (Jerusalem: Ahiever, 1977), p. 171.

3. *Jerusalem Post,* 11 January 1974.

4. Brecher, *Foreign Policy System,* p. 130.

5. A. Wallfish, in *Jerusalem Post,* 20 April 1979.

6. *Ibid.,* 14 June 1981.

7. *Divrei Haknesset* (The Knesset Record), (Government Jerusalem: Printer), 3 April 1973, p. 2511.

8. Flaxer, *Haknesset Uvaadoteha,* p. 112.

9. *Jerusalem Post,* 16 November 1980.

8—PARLIAMENTARY GROUPS

1. Mark Segal, in *Jerusalem Post,* 5 January 1978.

2. See *Ma'ariv* (Tel Aviv, daily), 12 January 1982.

3. A. Zidon, *The Knesset—Israel's Parliament* (Jerusalem: Achiasaf, 1964) (in Hebrew), p. 124.

4. *Ibid.*

5. *Nohal La'avodat Hasiyah Baknesset* (Procedure for the [Labor Alignment] Group's Activity in the Knesset) (mimeo.), 3 November 1974, p. 3.

6. *Jerusalem Post,* 27 December 1979.

7. As quoted by Mark Segal, *ibid.,* 21 March 1975.

8. See *Jerusalem Post,* 15, 16, and 17 December 1981; *Ha'aretz,* 23 December 1981.

9. See A. Wallfish, in *Jerusalem Post,* 11 November 1981.

9—THE KNESSET AT WORK

1. *Nohal La'avodat Hasiyah Baknesset* (Procedure for the [Labor Alignment] Group's Activity in the Knesset) (mimeo.), 3 November 1974, p. 4.

2. *Divrei Haknesset* (The Knesset Record) (Jerusalem: Government Printer), 20 October 1980, pp. 95–96.

3. *Ibid.*, 1 December 1980, pp. 690–91.

4. See *Jerusalem Post,* 11 November 1981.

5. Shevah Weiss, *Hakneset* (The Israeli Parliament) (Tel Aviv: Achiasaf, 1977), p. 187.

6. Gad Yaacobi, *Hamemshalah* (The Government) (Tel Aviv: Am Oved, 1980), pp. 63–64.

7. *Divrei Haknesset,* 27 March 1973, p. 2272.

10—LEGISLATION

1. *Hatakanon La'avodat Hamemshalah* (The Cabinet Rules of Procedure) (mimeo.), Jerusalem, June 1977, pp. 14–15.

2. On 23 June and 7 July, 1980.

3. A. Zidon, *Beth Hanivcharim* (The Knesset—Israel's Parliament) (Jerusalem: Achiasaf, 1964), p. 201.

4. Rule 133, *Knesset Rules of Procedure,* [transl. S. Sager] in *Constitutional and Parliamentary Information,* 1st Quarter 1982.

5. According to Mr. S. Jacobson, deputy-secretary of the Knesset (December 1981).

6. See A. Barak, "Subordinate Legislation," in *Studies in Israel Legislative Problems,* ed. G. Tedeschi and U. Yadin (Jerusalem: Magnes Press, 1966), pp. 225–26.

7. The examples are from Y. H. Klinghoffer, *"Takanot Sha'at Herum Beyisrael"* ("Emergency Regulations in Israel"), in *Sefer Yovel LePinhas Rosen* (Pinhas Rosen Jubilee Book), ed. Haim Cohen (Hebrew University Students Press, 1962), pp. 86–121.

11—SCRUTINY AND CONTROL

1. Gad Yaacobi, *Otsmat Haeihut* (The Power of Quality) (Haifa: Shikomona, 1972), p. 49.

2. Interview with S. Ginosar, *Davar* (Tel Aviv, daily), 19 August 1983.

12—THE KNESSET AND THE GOVERNMENT

1. 22 *Laws of the State of Israel* 257 (Authorized Translation from the Hebrew) (Jerusalem: Government Printer).

2. Sec. 11(a)(5), 18 *Laws* 111.

3. Sec. 14, 31 *Laws* 102.

4. See *Divrei Haknesset* (The Knesset Record) (Jerusalem: Government Printer), 16 February 1949, pp. 42–43.

5. Sec. 2(b), 1 *Laws* 7.

6. Z. Shoval, as cited in Shevah Weiss, *Haknesset* (The Israeli Parliament) (Tel Aviv: Achiasaf, 1977), p. 147.

7. See interview with Mr. Yitzhak Berman in *Ha'aretz* (Tel Aviv, daily), 24 September 1982.

8. See *Jerusalem Post,* 27 July 1982.

9. See *ibid.,* 20 July 1982.

10. Avraham Tal, in *Ha'aretz,* 2 Janury 1979.

11. See *Divrei Hakneset,* 7 October 1951, p. 198.

12. P. Y. Medding, *Mapai in Israel; Political Organization and Government in a New Society* (Cambridge University Press, 1972), pp. 172–73.

13. Dove Joseph, *In Quest of Peace* (Givatayim-Ramat Gan: Massada, 1975) (in Hebrew), pp. 370–71.

14. Gad Yaacobi, *The Government* (Tel Aviv: Zemora, Beitan, Modan, 1980) (in Hebrew), p. 271.

PERSPECTIVE OF A STRENGTHENED KNESSET

1. *Statistical Abstract of Israel 1981* (Central Bureau of Statistics), p. 561.

Glossary

Hebrew terms used only once in the text and explained there, and other terms in effect self-explanatory, have not been entered here.

Agudat Yisrael (Association of Israel)—Orthodox religious political party, more traditional than the National Religious party.

Ahdut Ha'avodah (Unity of Labor)—Left-wing party which merged with *Mapai* and *Rafi* in 1968 to form the Israel Labor party.

Ahva (Fraternity)—Parliamentary Group formed in split from the Democratic Movement in 1980. Dissolved in 1981.

Alignment—A bloc formed in 1965, it consisted entirely of labor elements until 1983, when it took in the Independent Liberals. In 1984 *Yahad* joined it while *Mapam* left.

Aliyah Hadashah (New Immigration)—Centrist political group formed in 1944 by German-speaking refugees. It merged in the Progressive party which became ultimately the Independent Liberal party.

Ashkenazi (pl. Ashkenazim)—A Jew whose origin is Northern, Central, or Eastern Europe.

Balfour Declaration—Britain's expression of support in 1917 for the establishment of a Jewish national home in Palestine in a letter from Foreign Secretary A. J. Balfour to Lord Lionel Walter Rothschild.

Cooperation and Fraternity—An Arab list that supported Labor-led Governments.

Democratic Front for Peace and Equality—A bloc comprising the Communist party and a splinter of the Panther movement, a protest group of underprivileged persons.

Democratic Movement—Formed in 1978 as a split from DMC. In 1980 it underwent further fission and by 1981 disappeared.

Democratic Movement for Change (DMC)—Its platform internal party democracy, efficient government, and electoral reform, it won fifteen Knesset seats in 1977. In 1978 it broke up into three: the Democratic Movement, *Shinui*-Center party, and *Yaad*.

Development and Peace *(Petuah Veshalom)*—A one-man candidates list in 1977. S. Flatto-Sharon was elected.

Divrei Haknesset (The Knesset Record)—The verbatim record of Knesset proceedings.

DMC. *See* Democratic Movement for Change.

Farm and Development List—An Arab list in the 1950s, it always supported the coalition.

Fighters List *(Reshimat Halohamim)*—Submitted by members of the erstwhile *Lehi* (Hebrew acronym for "Fighters for Freedom of Israel") underground. Represented only in the First Knesset, by one member.

Free Center *(Hamerkaz Hahofshi)*—Formed in 1967 in split from *Herut* Movement. Existed until 1977, for a period within *Likud* bloc.

Gahal (Hebrew acronym for *Herut*-Liberal Bloc)—Formed in 1965. With other groups it later created the *Likud* bloc.

Ha'ihud (The Amalgamation)—A party formed in 1981 for advancement of the disadvantaged, with a parliamentary Group of two. Failed to return any members in the election that year.

Ha'olam Hazeh (This World)—A political group led by the editor of a weekly of the same name who was its sole representative in the Knesset during most of its existence (1965–73).

Hapoel Hamizrahi (The Mizrahi Worker)—a religious labor Zionist party that merged in the National Religious party (NRP) in 1956.

Herut (Freedom) Movement—The political successor of *Irgun Zevai Leumi*. Formed the *Gahal* bloc together with the Liberals in 1965.

Histadrut (Federation)—The General Federation of Labor Unions.

Independent Liberal Party—Earlier the Progressive party, it took its name when it separated from the Liberal party in 1965 after four years of amalgamation. In 1983 it entered the Alignment.

Irgun Zevai Leumi (National Military Organization)—An underground body during British Mandate, more militant than the larger underground, *Haganah* (Defense). Referred to briefly as the *Irgun*. It formed the *Herut* Movement in 1948.

Kach Movement—A militant anti-Arab group. Appeared in the Knesset with the 1984 election.

Kibbutz (pl. kibbutzim)—A collective settlement.

Knesset (Assembly)—Israel's unicameral parliament of 120 members.

Knesset record. *See Divrei Haknesset.*

Labor Alignment. *See* Alignment

La'am (To the People)—A grouping in the *Likud* bloc.

Liberal party—Up until 1961 the General Zionist party. It entered the *Gahal* bloc in 1965 and the *Likud* in 1973.

Likud (Unity)—A bloc formed in 1973. In 1984 it consisted of *Herut,* the Liberals, and *La'am.*

Mapai (Hebrew acronym for "Land of Israel Workers party")—The leading Labor party and dominant coalition element until 1968, when it reunited with two dissident parties as the Israel Labor party.

Mapam (Hebrew acronym for United Workers Party)—More left-wing than the Labor party. In the Labor Alignment from 1969 to 1984.

Mizrahi (Hebrew contraction for "Spiritual Center")—A religious-Zionist party that merged in 1956 with the affiliated *Hapoel Hamizrahi* into the National Religious party (NRP).

Moked (Focus)—A political group whose members came primarily from the Israel Communist party. In 1977 it merged in *Sheli.*

Morasha (Heritage)—a political alignment formed in 1984 between *Poalei Agudat Yisrael* and a new religious Zionist group, *M'tsad* (Fortress).

NRP—National Religious party.

Ometz (Courage)—A political group organized in 1984 around Yigael Hurvitz and pledged to support economic austerity; also a ginger group within the Alignment formed in 1981 to press for a more effective opposition.

One Israel *(Yisrael Ahat)*—A one-man parliamentary group, 1980–81.

Poalei Agudat Yisrael (Workers of the Association of Israel)—An Orthodox religious party affiliated at times with *Agudat Yisrael.* With another group it formed *Morasha* in 1984.

Progress and Development—An Arab list that gave support to Labor-led Governments.

Progress and Labor—An Arab list (1951–59). Supported the *Mapai*-led coalitions.

Progressive List for Peace—A Jewish-Arab Group advocating a Palestinian State on the west bank of the Jordan River.

Progressive party—A middle-of-the-road body that amalgamated with the General Zionists in 1961 to form the Liberal party. It separated in 1965 as the Independent Liberal party.

Rafi (Hebrew acronym for "Israel Workers List")—Formed by Ben Gurion and his followers in 1965, when they left *Mapai.* When most of *Rafi* merged in the Labor party in 1968, the rest formed the State List. Since then, both "*Rafi*" and "State List" were assumed from time to time as names by smaller parliamentary Groups.

Revisionists—Pre-state organization for establishment of Jewish state in full territory of mandate. Represented in the Provisional State Council, they later joined *Herut.*

Sephardi (pl. Sephardim)—A Jew descended from refugees of Spanish Inquisition. By extension, reference is to Jews from Eastern or Oriental origin generally, as well as from Mediterranean and Balkan countries.

Sheli (Hebrew acronym for "Peace and Equality for Israel")—A Left-wing grouping which won two Knesset seats in 1977, and none in 1981. In 1984 its followers dispersed to other parties.

Shinui-Center party—Meaning "change" in Hebrew, it originated in 1973, in the wake of the Yom Kippur War. A component of DMC (1977–78).

Shlomzion (Peace in Zion)—A political group which joined the *Likud* bloc after contesting the 1977 election. Its two Knesset members later went separate ways.

State List. *See Rafi.*

Tami (Hebrew acronym for "Israel Tradition Movement")—A party founded in 1981 to advance interests of the Sephardi communities, its membership is chiefly of North African origin.

Tehiya (Revival)—A party formed in 1979 by defectors from the *Likud* in opposition to withdrawal from Sinai. With a like-minded group *Tsomet* (Juncture), it formed *Tehiya-Tsomet* in 1984.

Telem (Hebrew acronym for "State Revival Movement")—Founded around Moshe Dayan, it won two Knesset seats in 1981. It fell apart the same year, after his death.

Torah (Doctrine)—The Law of Moses, comprising the full teaching of Orthodox Judaism.

Tsomet. See *Tehiya*.

WIZO—Women's International Zionist Organization.

Yaad (Goal)—A one-man parliamentary Group (1978–81).

Yahad (Together)—A centrist party organized by Ezer Weizmann in 1984. After the election it joined the Alignment.

Index

THE PARLIAMENTARY SYSTEM OF ISRAEL

was composed in 10-point Mergenthaler Linotron 202N Times Roman
and leaded 2 points, with display type in Lydian,
printed sheet-fed offset on 50-pound, acid-free Glatfelter Antique Cream,
Smyth sewn, and bound over binder's boards in Joanna Arrestox by
Maple-Vail Book Manufacturing Group, Inc.;
with dust jackets printed in 2 colors by Philips Offset Company, Inc.;
and published by

SYRACUSE UNIVERSITY PRESS

SYRACUSE, NEW YORK 13210